RUNAWAY FATHER

RUNAWAY *father*

One Man's Odyssey From Revenge to Love

Lee Coburn

Red Fox Publishing

Red Fox Publishing
677 120th Avenue. N.E., Suite 163
Bellevue, Washington 98005

Library of Congress Cataloging-in-Publication Data
Runaway Father
One Man's Odyssey from Revenge to Love
Lee Coburn, — 1st ed.
ISBN 0-9664596-4-4 (pbk)

Printed in the United States of America
First Paperback Edition
10 9 8 7 6 5 4 3 2

Cover and interior book design by Kathleen McAffrey, Starr Design
Cover photographs by Dan Schlatter
Interior photographs by Lee Coburn

If unavailable in local bookstores, additional books may be purchased by visiting the Runaway Father Website at: http://www.lcoburn.com You may contact the publisher, either by email: RedFox@lcoburn.com, or by fax 1-425-455-4629. To obtain additional copies of this book by mail, see order form at end of book.

For every child,
who deserves loving parents

The spiritual path is one of falling on your face,
brushing yourself off,
turning and looking sheepishly at God,
and then taking the next step.

— Sri Auibindo

ACKNOWLEDGEMENTS

As I traveled my journey of growth necessary for the completion of this book, many people contributed along the way.

I am grateful to Richard Gardner for organizing and cataloging hundreds of scenes from thirty-five of my personal journals spanning the eight years following my children's abduction. His superb structuring of the story and his many creative ideas have withstood years of rewrites and content editing. Richard's unflinching acceptance of me in my darkest hours, seen so vividly in my journals, began my healing and set me on my path to self-acceptance. He gave me the courage to pursue my vision for sharing this story.

Roberta Kehle's enthusiasm for my book, after critiquing the first completed manuscript, inspired me to continue when I most needed reassurance.

My deepest gratitude goes to Janet Gill, valued friend and writing mentor. Her meticulous editing and countless creative suggestions provided invaluable substance and clarity to the book. Her frequent penciled suggestions in the margins and her "go deeper or cut" directives led me to express my deeper truths. Her vigilant pursuit of excellence is apparent on every page. Thank you, Janet, for your unwavering dedication to the vision of this book and to me as a writer.

Many others inspired me in their unique way on my personal journey. Kellie Vaughan Jones, since our meeting that first Christmas in Seattle, has been a continuous source of support and encouragement; my friends and fellow spiritual travelers at the Center for Spiritual Living in Seattle have guided me towards a higher way of living and being. Kathleen Higgins, who offered valued insights into the importance of healing those parts of ourselves that prevent us from reaching our full potential. My treasured friend, Don Vitale offered valuable guidance and inspiration during my years of searching for myself to find something worthy to express.

Special thanks to Eleanor Rawson of Rawson Publishing. Her constructive critique of the manuscript encouraged me to rewrite certain sections to strengthen the book's focus.

I wish to thank my former wife and her husband for their unwavering love of Lori and Ryan. Accepting them back into their lives with open hearts strengthened my belief in the message presented here.

My greatest thanks go to the two most important and remarkable people I know, my son and daughter. They continually remind me how gratifying it is to be a parent. Their indomitable spirits have been the inspiration and the driving force behind this book.

From my heart, I wish to thank my mother and father for loving me unconditionally upon my return. You welcomed me home without question, and with open arms after being gone for nearly a decade.

And finally, there is not enough space to express my gratitude for the many people who have helped me along my journey. You have all been my teachers and by that you have touched my life profoundly. I thank you all.

A Message To My Readers

Following a divorce and bitter custody battle, I became a "Visiting Father" to the two people I loved most in the world — my ten-year-old daughter, Lori, and my eight-year-old son, Ryan. But by court decree, another man would raise my children. Unable to cope with my feelings of loss, anger, and betrayal, I responded by kidnapping my children.

In *Runaway Father*, you'll travel with me on my journey into a world of deceit, a world of hiding out and of coping with the constant fear of being discovered. A parallel inner journey reveals my growing awareness of the ultimate source of my anger that led to my destructive action. Throughout *Runaway Father*, scenes and vignettes of our life on the run show how insights and gradual shifts in my values came at unexpected moments along the way.

I came to understand that my anger had little to do with the actions of others, but everything to do with my own inner state of being. My unhealed childhood wounds kept me from loving myself and others. By taking personal responsibility for my actions, I opened the door to my inner self and gradually to greater self-acceptance. *Runaway Father* encourages each of you to look at how you too, can grow from the dark turns of your lives.

I know now we all live a spiritual life on a journey of awakening to love. Such is the journey shared with you here in the belief that as I offer my story, we will meet heart to heart.

"The secret of life is in the shadows
and not in the open sun;
to see anything at all,
you must look deeply into the shadow
of a living thing."

— Ute saying

ONE

LEAVING HOME

We need others to heal ourselves.
By such sharing and listening,
we begin to practice the principle
of unconditional love.

— Charles L. Whitfield, M.D.

"I hear you kidnapped your children."

All these years alone with it, and suddenly it was there in front of me, spoken directly and in public. The woman said it casually enough, but with a watchful, slightly mischievous glint in her eye. A stranger had at last hurled the long-expected poison spear, and I wasn't even sure of her name. Margaret — no, Marjory somebody.

Conversation ceased. The others looked at me, obviously shocked, waiting for confirmation. The fire crackled softly; ice clinked in somebody's glass.

I lifted one shoulder and let it drop, looked down at my drink.

Someone, probably Kellie, came to the rescue with a change of subject. I managed to join in, but I knew it wasn't over. Now that the secret was out, it wasn't going to be left alone. I could feel it in the awkward rhythm of the new discussion, in their sidelong glances. The men seemed more prone to let it pass, but the women were restless. Not threatening, just wanting to know for sure and hungry for details. What is it like? What did you feel? How did you change your identity? How did the children react? Are you ashamed, guilty? What about the mother?

Here in Kellie's living room, among these twelve, eight were friends of long standing. From them I could count on sympathy and trust. None of them were likely to rush to the phone and call the FBI.

But how could I be sure? Childnapping had been in the news, and reactions were usually extreme. The responses often had more to do with emotional war between the husband and wife than with the welfare of the children. During one recent exchange, a mother had declared only half-jokingly that she would rather see her children dead than in the custody of their father.

I watched this stranger, Marjory, out of the corner of my eye, trying to remember if she had mentioned having any children of her own. Was the man with her a friend or her husband? Did he work for anybody I was doing business with?

I was surprised at my excitement. We had lived for seven years with the threat of discovery and had learned to keep cool in far worse circumstances, but this was different. These people weren't the FBI or the police, and a kind of reckless eagerness had hold of me. I thought of the framed cartoon poster at home, a souvenir of my surprise fortieth birthday party: two caricatures of me, profile and frontal, and in antique lettering: "WANTED — LEE LANDEL — Attempt will be made to surprise and surround suspect."

Well, here I was, surrounded and surprised. The irony of it made me want to just let go and laugh out loud. I felt the hysterical urge for relief bubbling up, threatening to burst through. I wanted to start talking and not stop until it was all out in the open, everything from the plans for suicide and murder to the moments of sheer joy and freedom on my road to self-discovery. All of it coughed up, confessed, cleared away.

That scared me. This overwhelming impulse to just let go and let fate and a stranger take over.

But the truth was the story couldn't be told yet, because it wasn't all resolved. Lori and Ryan were not quite ready for reconciliation with their mother, and I was not finished with myself. Although the time for the last rite of passage was drawing near with its promise of release and deep change, we were still in jeopardy.

I was like a prisoner waiting for final word from the parole board and from my soul as well. The sunlight through the bars had never been so beautiful and the urge to claim it never more insistent.

But this was too soon, this gray Seattle winter of 1983. My new business wasn't doing badly, although national economic recovery had slowed. President Reagan was about to "perk up" American self-esteem with his invasion of Grenada. But more important to me, my daughter had just begun her first paying job and was looking forward to her first real date. Ryan, my son, had just started his freshman year at Shorewood High, and I had met a woman I thought I might be able to love.

The work wasn't yet done. Our great adventure wasn't over. What Lori, Ryan and I had managed against all odds — none of it was complete, all of it remained at high risk.

Everyone watched me as the conversation stumbled on. I tensed my jaw, braced myself, and waited for the question to come again.

I hear you kidnapped your children . . .?

One never really knows when something begins. But the day we departed for a new life, seven years prior to that party at Kellie's, will long remain a date to remember.

On that hot and humid Wednesday morning, July 28, 1976, I arose as Lee Coburn for the last time, prepared to vanish into permanent exile. The big, old oak trees along Ashford Dunwoody Road in north Atlanta had lost their accustomed brilliant green, and there were mutterings from the city council about water rationing. On the grounds of D'Youville Condominiums, two Chinese catalpa trees had died, and the magnolia behind our condo gave back black dust when you touched a palm to its trunk.

I had worked all morning in the hellish hot attic, packing the kids' old clothes and toys into the steamer trunk. At 10:00, I decided

I wouldn't be ready to pick them up by 10:30. I would have to phone and stall. With a last look around the attic, I started toward the stairs, but was pulled short by the sight of a framed photograph lying in a shadowed corner.

I went over to look down at it. Val's placid smile and soft eyes gazed warmly back at me through the dusty glass. My wife. My ex-wife, that is. The one I had begun to think of as "Whatzername."

Beautiful, damnit, still beautiful. I stared and the image smiled back. Val, always the quiet, thoughtful one. Demure. I tried to remember why the portrait had been exiled to the attic. She hadn't liked it; something about the hair. "It's not me," she had said. "It's somebody's fantasy."

Even in that dim light and under a patina of grime, she still had that untouchable glow. I tried to muster just one memory of the good times I knew we had enjoyed through the past twelve years of marriage and parenthood. Yes, we had had good times, but I couldn't think of a single one. They were all locked out by a wall of hurt and rage.

I smashed my heel on her face, then ground it down. I heard the glass crunch, then splinter. I didn't look at it. I headed down the stairs.

I dialed her apartment. I wondered what I would feel if the phone was answered by Doctor Edwin Reynolds, distinguished surgeon, "wife snatcher."

Val answered tersely. "Yes?"

"It's Lee. I'll be a little late. Eleven o'clock."

I could hear the kids in the background, Lori's voice excited. "Is it Dad?"

Val ignored her. "How long are you going to keep them?"

She knew the answer. The vacation had been arranged months before. We'd drive to Colorado, camp at state and national parks along the way, take it easy and plan one day at a time. I could feel her listening carefully at the other end and could visualize the glossed lips slightly apart, the blue eyes turned aside, the two incised lines of concentration between the brows. Oh, how she could concentrate. Surgical nurse Val Coburn holds the scalpel for the surgeon and eyes the patient.

"You know the plans," I said. Hearing her voice, imagining her with such painful clarity, I felt my anger expand toward explosion. I had to force my words out one by one, feeling locked and incapacitated, like a badly overheated engine. "I'll call you in eight days, once we know the return itinerary. When we get back, we can talk about the things in the attic and whatever else you want, okay?"

She didn't like that, the pushy lift of the last word. "Take care of them," she snapped, "and you call me in a week."

I slammed the receiver down. Bitch! My hands shook as I grabbed an envelope off the kitchen counter. In the upper left-hand corner, the name of her attorney's law firm glared at me. Addressed to me and stamped "registered," the envelope contained the final decree awarding custody of the children to her, plus half our possessions, plus child maintenance.

"The hell you say," I hissed at the envelope. "Now you're going to see."

I stripped off my sweat-soaked shirt and showered, changed to my traveling clothes: tie and shirt, light linen suit.

I carried the dirty shirt and envelope downstairs to my office. Once again, I went through my two briefcases, checking every document, legal and fake.

As I worked, I remembered Sid Silano as we had said good-bye, his voice frog-deep and thick with the rage we shared. "This is it, Lee, the real thing. From now on, you can't make a mistake, not a single mistake. The minute they know you're gone, they'll be on your ass like a pack of hounds. And they're the law, baby, which means they don't have to be legal."

I had already made two crucial errors. I was determined not to make another. I had organized my papers the night before, but to reassure myself, I quickly perused each document again. Also, checking my wallet, I found cash, Coburn ID, Landau ID, and credit cards. The Coburn credit cards I discarded. I would carry cash only. Traveler's checks were too risky. Too easy to spot my whereabouts if one were lost.

Everything looked in order. I hesitated a moment over the unopened envelope containing the divorce decree, then stuffed it into one of the cases. I snapped both briefcases shut and hurriedly carried them to my car.

After loading the rest of the suitcases, I returned to the house for a final tour of the rooms. At each room, I thought of Val's return. She had her own key. She was sure to enter the house. I wanted to leave the place faultlessly tidy and clean. Why? What difference did it make? Was it only habit and training? My father admonishing, "Either do it right or don't bother doing it." Or did I think Val would deem me a decent person because I had abandoned a clean house? Or was it a symbol of my rights, the purity of my intentions?

At one point, I found myself rubbing a chrome faucet over and over with a piece of paper towel. What rights? According to the courts, I didn't have any. What purity? I intended to steal my children from their mother.

Stop it, Lee. Snap to. Don't think. Keep moving. Make your last arrangements.

I ordered a taxi to be waiting in the parking lot at Century Center on lower Peachtree Street, at 11:15. Had I done everything? Had I come to the end of my endless lists of things to do?

I stood in the entryway, my feet glued to the parquet. Did I need permission to leave? The somber silence of the abandoned house engulfed me. I tried to leave but got stuck in my querencia. I had read the term in a book on bullfighting. It was that place in the bullring where the bull feels safest, but where it is the most dangerous. For me, it was that place on the living room rug where the wingback chair had stood for years. From this same spot nine months before, Val had announced she was leaving. But now, just for an instant, I went crazy again and saw something else, or thought I did as I stared down at the slightly worn spot on the carpet.

I saw a slender man, naked to the waist, on his knees with a rolled newspaper in his hand. He was beating the rug over and over and shouting, "I will not be a weekend father!" Night after night, he shouted his troth. Tears and sweat splattered from the apparition's hair and face. His mouth stretched open in virulent anger, released wordless howls — sounds of a dying, desperate animal.

After a second or two, I shook the memory, or thought I did. From the window sill I grabbed a crayon. I started for the twenty-foot-long wall covered with hand-printed foil. (Val and I had spent days selecting the foil design.) One last grand graffiti scrawled on her expensive print. "Here's to you, bitch." But I stopped. *I must be going mad,* I thought, and threw the crayon away. What was the point? In a few days, my absence would send its own message.

It was time to leave. When I reached the door, I discovered the wet shirt still in my hand. Without warning, I slumped against the wall and cried, a small boy kneading his sweaty shirt.

There were things we did as boys. Like run a needle through the skin on your inner arm after you pinch it first. All it takes is the need of boys to test themselves. Pinch yourself back to reality. Bite the bullet. Be a man.

I punched my fist through the wall plaster. "Bitch! You! You're making me do this!"

When I withdrew my hand, I saw my bleeding knuckles, then stuffed the soggy shirt into the hole.

I slipped outside and secured the door behind me. I'd torn free of my querencia, that place in the bullring to which the bull becomes attached and keeps returning. Where, when the bull is mortally wounded, it wants to die.

Some call their querencia Home Sweet Home.

Somehow, that childish gesture made things easier. I had the momentum now. Five hours, and our new life would begin. I squelched last minute doubts and went on automatic pilot.

As I maneuvered the 98 Regency out of north Atlanta, the city hummed through its morning rush, bustling with its twentieth century hustle.

Here in this lively, attractive city still clinging to its post-bellum style and elegance, I had put together a career, a respectable home, a family. But now I had to say good-bye forever.

I negotiated the narrow, looping curves up Ashford Dunwoody Road to Rollingwood Apartments and pulled in front of Val's place. I buzzed and Lori opened the door, her face beaming with excitement. She wore her favorite dress, the yellow frock her Grandma had made for her. My tow-headed, ten-year-old piece of the sun. "Hi, Dad!" With quick, light movements, her small fingers touched my sleeve and tugged me into the entryway.

Ryan's voice, brash with his eight years, piped huskily from upstairs. "I'll be right down, Dad. Did you bring my glove?"

"Got it. Let's go." His baseball glove and mine were nested together in one of the suitcases. We would play catch on the fields of our newfound freedom.

No sign of Val; she must have gone to work. Good. No ice sculpture woman peering out the upstairs window as I took my children away for a precious day, a grudgingly given weekend. No more of that.

Nor any sign of the good doctor. Probably at the hospital stitching up the morning's second craniotomy. That will be $3,500, madam. Next.

Bitch! Bastard!

Ryan came running. "I'm ready!"

Me too. I fitted their two identical, small zipper bags next to mine and closed the trunk. The kids clambered into the wide seat beside me, and we were off.

"Colorado or bust!" Ryan shouted.

I told them I had a surprise. "Guess what? We're not going to drive. We're flying to Colorado!"

They loved the prospect. They had flown once in a friend's single-engine plane and twice to Cincinnati to visit their grandparents.

"Yippee!" piped Lori. "We're going to travel in style. We'll get free juice and another deck of playing cards."

I added the clincher. "Later, we'll fly on a 747, Ryan. The big one."

"Wow, really, Dad?"

I pulled into the employee's lot beside Century Center. Here, the Olds wouldn't be noticed for a day or two. In a few days, the leasing company would receive my note advising them where to find the car. They would be receiving it back in excellent shape plus a half tank of gas. Never mind that the lease payments were three months in arrears. I emptied the ashtrays into the litter bag. Law-abiding lawyer-architect Lee Coburn, still trying to balance the books. I didn't like leaving all the bills, but survival's razor edge had made them unimportant.

I checked my watch as the taxi pulled in. The driver helped us transfer our bags. I shivered as we pulled out into traffic. On the toll meter in front of us, numbers flipped over as Atlanta flickered past. In the rear view mirror I could see the driver's quick eyes. His smile seemed watchful as he talked. "Nice day if you like ovens," he offered. "Vacation? Going west? Hey kids, you like cowboys? Your mom gonna meet you out there?"

His flood of questions was disturbing. Paranoia is like a fever that builds on anxiety. My nerves were taut. Was the man just a compulsive talker? Hadn't I read somewhere that taxi drivers dealt in blackmail sometimes, that many were police informants? I made myself answer casually, but carefully. I needed the practice, I told myself, for possibly worse encounters to come.

I was relieved when his babbling stopped.

He pulled alongside the Delta Airlines departing lane and unloaded our bags at the curb. As I paid him, he said, "Adios, friend. I hope their mother finds you in Colorado."

Inside, I was relieved to see a crowded check-in line. The harried agent had a quick smile accentuated by lipstick too red for her light brunette hair. Maybe she wouldn't notice me. Make small talk if necessary, I told myself, but nothing she will remember, nothing to make us stand out.

I had prepurchased our tickets under three phony names, all adult fares. I placed them on the counter. Deftly, the agent fluttered through each ticket. If she noticed there weren't two adults with me, she didn't say. I waited, ready to explain that my fellow passengers had gone on ahead to the gate, but it wasn't necessary.

"Flight 576, Gate Five, fifteen minutes. Thank you."

Now for our long walk through the crowd out to the connecting pod. People were everywhere. Eyes. I kept noticing their eyes.

During my six years practicing law in Atlanta, my contact with clients had been extensive. I frequently ran into people I knew. Would wearing dark glasses keep me incognito or make me look foolish? Or even worse, make me seem furtive. The crowd kept coming, and I kept wanting us to be invisible. I scanned the river of faces flowing toward us. Each step moved us toward a possible crisis.

Ryan wanted to know why there were so many televisions along the way. I explained about schedules, arrival and departures, all the while scanning the faces going past, dreading the moment of recognition. "Lee Coburn! How are you? Hi kids, where you off to?"

Ryan, chattering beside me, was still shy with strangers but full of questions for me. Lori was more self-possessed, observing, often more prone to keep her own counsel.

Both were well-dressed and vivacious — happy, attractive kids. They attracted attention.

"Hi there, where are you going, young lady?"

Lori smiled politely at the pleasant-looking, middle-aged woman. "Colorado. Isn't that right, Dad?"

"Well . . . I believe 576 goes to Houston. Do you have the wrong gate?"

"Houston first, then Denver," I said. "But maybe we had better check. Come along Lori, Ryan."

"Aren't we going to Denver, Dad?"

"I'll explain later, Lori. It's okay. Look, here's the plane."

Arrivals flooded the lounge, more possible acquaintances. I caught myself running my hand through my hair and peering from behind the screen of my fingers. At last, the announcement to board.

I wanted to grab Lori and Ryan and run down the ramp. *Easy, Lee. Go with the flow,* I told myself.

The stewardess greeted us with a wide smile and ruffled Ryan's hair as we slipped past. I eyed a gauntlet of upturned faces as we made our way up the aisle. Nobody familiar.

A squabble arose over who got to sit next to the window. Lori solved it. They would take turns, her first.

I sank into the aisle seat, leaning out just enough to scan the incoming faces. Nobody I knew. So far so good. Beside me, the kids examined the instruction cards, the Delta magazine. Ryan discovered the barf bag. "Let's practice!"

He buried his nose in the bag and sounds of comical disgorgement emerged along with giggles. Faces turned to look, amused smiles, but also eyes measuring us — single father with children. Divorced? Where's the mother?

"That's enough, Ryan."

Instant guilt at the sharp edge to my voice, a nervous glance at him. But he took it well, and the two of them begin giggling over something new. This reminded me of the stuff I'd been reading on child psychology and parenting. Children mirror parental anxiety; play is the catharsis for both parent and children. Would I be equal to the challenge?

How long would we have to sit there strapped to our seats? How long does it take to warm up a jet? What were they doing anyway, rebuilding the damn thing? I'd feel safer when we were off the ground.

At last, the screaming whine and wind up of the engines, then the long taxi out to the runway. Wheel, stop, blue skies, yellowed weeds leaning in the engine after-blast.

The vibrating wait, a quietness amongst the passengers, the kids whispering excitedly. *I'll send her a letter from Hawaii. Dear*

Whatzername, go to hell. You'll never see them again . . .

Finally the roar, the shuddering surge forward. Then the trundling hurtle down the runway with the kids squealing beside me, their faces pressed to the window.

The creaking resistance, the sudden lift, the stomach flutters against the diaphragm, and the great plane reluctantly rose.

Liftoff.

I sank back into the seat cushions, enjoying enormous relief. True, far greater difficulties no doubt awaited me, but at least we were on our way. Suddenly, I realized how far we had already traveled. Tears of sadness and fear filled my eyes as I fumbled for my dark glasses, stunned by the oceanic emotion that rolled over me. Aftershock, I told myself, the backwash of a delicious and vengeful triumph.

But a deeper pang screamed a greater truth. I had just violated the law I had always revered and in doing so had amputated a major portion of my life. No doubt my severed self would continue to torment, reminding me that in gaining I would also lose.

". . . the weather in Houston is clear and 82 degrees. Expected time of arrival, 1:32 Central Daylight Time. Please obey the no smoking signs when lit. . . ."

The kids had no trouble coaxing a deck of cards from the stewardess, which prompted Ryan to demonstrate to Lori his mechanical mastery of the fold-down table. Soon they were lost in their favorite card game, Spoon.

While they played, I strategized. Address the highest concerns first, I told my racing mind. Assuming we would need to walk the aisle to visit the restroom, I made a quick scan of all the passengers, up and back, as casually as I could. No familiar faces. Never mind first class; they had their own restrooms and would deplane ahead of us.

I regained my seat, reassured that at least I wouldn't have to explain about names yet. We had already effectively left behind our Atlanta identities. Lee Coburn and children were not listed on the Flight 576 manifest, only three adults whose three separate, bogus names I couldn't recall. Nor had I used Landau, the carefully documented name that I had been forced to abandon at the last minute due to one of my major blunders.

As long as no one on this flight or in Los Angeles recognized me or questioned the kids too closely, first names would get us through to Hawaii. But I would have to tell the kids about the drastic change in itinerary, and soon.

"Spoon!" crowed Ryan. "Flying to Colorado is more fun than driving, isn't it, Lori?"

Lori absently agreed, concentrating on her cards. But I saw the little tug at her brow, the two small lines deepening. I sensed her mulling over the uncertainty about our destination in the terminal before departing. Sooner or later, she would ask.

While they played, I began to worry about money. I had a little over five thousand in cash stowed in my wallet and moneybelt. Another fifteen hundred I had given to Sid Silano, to be sent for when we needed it. Until then, I planned on making every effort to conserve our resources.

My first savings I achieved by switching to half fares for Lori and Ryan for the remainder of our flight to Honolulu. The Coburn identity, I assumed, had been severed by our flight from Atlanta to Houston. But caution governed. Again I reserved and purchased our tickets under bogus names to avoid any possible tracing.

Two mistakes I had made in Atlanta haunted me. Both were potentially devastating to our exile. Except for those earlier blunders, for the moment, I believed we might be in the clear.

I must have slept. Dreaming about the mistakes, the consequences, a dreadful sinking feeling overcame me. I jerked awake to discover the plane in a slow descent, though the seat belt and no smoking signs remained off. Where were we? I saw Lori reading. Ryan peered out the window at the rising clouds as we descended.

"Lori. Ryan."

Two blonde heads turned in unison, their eager, bright eyes gleaming with trust.

"What do you think about going on to Hawaii and having our vacation there?"

I pulled two colorful travel brochures from my carry-on and handed them each one. Lori had studied Hawaii in school. Her glance checked out palm trees, white beaches, curling surf, dark-haired wahinis. She pointed. "Mukalua Volcano! Look, that stuff is lava, Ryan."

"What's lava?"

"Melted rock."

Ryan looked doubtful. "Oh."

"Well," I asked, "do you think we should go to Hawaii?"

Lori was immediately sure. "Oh yes, let's!"

But Ryan hesitated. He pouted with confusion. "Colorado is fun, too," he said tentatively.

"But we can go swimming in the ocean," Lori said as she pointed to a picture. "And they have whopping big surfs, Ryan."

He considered, eyeing the brochure. "Can we stay in a hotel with a swimming pool like this one, Dad?" He poked a stubby finger at a travel photo. "For sure?"

"For sure," I promised.

"We can swim in the pool or the ocean," Lori announced.

Still Ryan considered, fidgeting, his glance rolling toward the window, as if looking toward Atlanta, home, his mother. Maybe the umbilical cord had been stretched too far, too fast.

"We don't have to if you don't want to," I said.

Exactly how I would hold to that, I wasn't sure, but I meant it. I had vowed to myself that I would be straight and honest with them whenever I could.

Hastily scanning the brochure, Lori pointed out another photograph. "And you can learn to ride a surfboard, Ryan!"

That did it. Ryan's head came around and his eyes brightened. "Can I, Dad?"

"After you've had a few lessons."

He beamed, gave a judicious nod. "Okay." Then took the brochure from Lori. "Dad, how do rocks melt?"

❧

Leon Landers and two children, Linda and Ron, had no trouble picking up their ticket at the Delta desk, Houston airport.

But Lee Coburn, formerly of Atlanta, was having a little trouble with his biological clock. We had been in flight less than four hours, but I had been up since six that morning. More to the point, the past nine months had been the longest hell of my life, and now, it seemed, there was a chance, just a chance, that the worst might be over.

A dangerous presumption.

As the kids played happily through the two-hour layover, I fought the letdown preparing itself inside me and the urge to let up, relax, assume we were safe. I hadn't slept soundly in a long time, had managed to achieve semi-unconsciousness for only four hours the night before.

But I couldn't ease up now. Though it was highly unlikely we'd run into someone in Houston who knew me, the possibility still existed. My identity cut-off, I hoped, had been complete; but what about those stupid mistakes?

"You will not know when they start after you, Lee," Sid warned me, "so assume from the beginning that you're a fugitive."

I made myself scan every passing face, tightened at every glimpse of a uniform, and played Sid's warnings over in my mind. "Your new identity must have absolutely no resemblance to your former," he instructed. "Don't leave a footprint, a clue, a scrap of paper, anything that can be remembered or traced."

While watching the faces, I performed mundane, casual tasks — reading a newspaper, making notes, scanning flight schedules. All the time trying to fully grasp what I had done, what it meant to my future and the future of my children — that I was a fugitive and, in the eyes of the law, a criminal. Not to mention the emotional damage I might be inflicting.

What would my family think? I could see in my father's long sallow face, astonishment, then grim, narrow-eyed disapproval. In my mother's face, fright, worry, tears. My sister Randi, instant unsurprised censure. Lee always was willful, stubborn. A renegade of sorts.

I watched faces and fenced with the shadows. I struggled with all that I had been taught about obedience, the propriety of marriage, the dignity of law, the sanctified maternal role and rights of women.

Lori and Ryan sat beside me, too engrossed to care or understand. They giggled, bounced on their seats, chatted with a charmed elderly couple.

"What wonderful children," said the blue-haired woman, beaming. "I'll bet their mother is proud of them, too." She looked around as if expecting "their mother" to materialize, perhaps as Our Lady of the Wide-Bodied 747.

"She certainly is," I said, thinking, *Thank you, madam, I needed a nosy old bird like you.* "I've got an idea, kids, let's take a tour. Did you know the 747 has a stairway?"

At 3:45 p.m., Pacific Daylight Time, we landed in L.A. For those continuing on to Honolulu, there would be an hour layover. The kids wanted to say they had been on California soil. We deplaned, had a Coke, then found our way to the airport entrance, where they each solemnly planted a foot on a patch of yellowed California grass.

On the way back to the plane, the blue-haired lady spotted us across the lounge. "Yoo-hoo, we're going to Reno. Where are you going?"

"In the opposite direction from you, lady," I muttered, steering the kids toward the mouth of the on-ramp.

"She was a nice lady," Lori observed, waving.

One stewardess had made friends with Lori and Ryan during

our flight to L.A. When she saw them boarding, she asked if they wanted to see the cockpit.

"For sure," they chimed.

"Especially because it's a 747," Ryan added.

She escorted us upstairs to the forward-most door.

Stepping inside the cockpit, she introduced Lori and Ryan to Captain Brady. His gentle eyes twinkled as he lifted Ryan into his seat and Lori into the copilot's seat. Lost in the large cushions, surrounded by switches and buttons, they appeared dwarfed. The captain knelt next to Ryan and demonstrated how to move the control stick; Ryan made loud engine sounds as he pretended to be the pilot. Captain Brady showed them the altimeter and where to see how fast the plane traveled.

The kids chattered excitedly as we headed back to our seats. Ryan said when he grew up he was going to be like Captain Brady. If, that is, he didn't decide to become an astronaut.

Once we were in the air again, our eighth hour on the run, I made another aisle check. Not one familiar or threatening face in sight. And no sudden announcements on my earphones: "Is there a Mr. Lee Coburn on board? The FBI and your father would like a word with you." Only music on five channels.

The azure blue Pacific sank beneath billowing clouds as we ascended westward. We were now off the continent. A crucial step to freedom. Would I ever return? I couldn't. The kids soon quieted, tired but awake with anticipation.

I slept fitfully, reviewing every detail and haunted by Mrs. Wright's eyes.

One mistake could soon surface. I had used my first chosen alias, Landau, on the contract for the Pilgrim Mini-Storage space where I had stored our antiques. On the day I moved the grandfather clock, our neighbor, Mrs. Wright, had seen the clock sticking out the window of my Olds.

Of course, the Landau alias could be given up. In fact, it had been. But Lee Landau had applied for a Social Security card months before. I had received it at our D'Youville Condominium address and later used it on the mini- stòrage contract. Too many clear connections threatened my security.

My sloppiness had made me vulnerable to any well-trained investigator who would begin by interviewing the neighbors. Talk to Mrs. Wright. Connect clock, Pilgrim Storage, Landau rental contract, Social Security number, Atlanta address. Voila! Lee Landau is Lee Coburn, childnapper.

And hadn't I read that childnapping was soon to be made a federal offense? To say nothing of other infractions I may have committed. And I might lose the children — forever. How could I sleep?

I jerked awake in a harness of ice. It was my own cold sweat. Somebody was jeering. Or cheering? I checked Lori and Ryan. Squeezed shoulder to shoulder, they crowded close to the window.

"Wake up, Dad! It's Hawaii!"

Hawaii. My life dream come true.

I was about to set foot on my imagined paradise, not only for a vacation but to make it our permanent home.

We entered the terminal and joined the festive ambiance of the spirited crowd. I saw well-dressed travelers being festooned with flower leis by lusciously tanned, dark-eyed native women. I wished I had arranged for the children to have received the same greeting. Bright colors and flowers everywhere, on posters, shops, murals and the ubiquitous Hawaiian shirts and muumuus, created a living moving mural. Our imaginations painted images of a glorious vacation.

Our pace quickened as we moved hand-in-hand, delighted by the conviviality, myself gawking no less eagerly than the kids. But as we pushed through the crowd, I searched for a plan to follow after we claimed our baggage.

On the plane, I had decided our first move should be to rent a car, regardless of expense. With our own transportation, we could better reconnoiter the island. I also hoped that somehow it would make detection by authorities less likely. A man and two children on foot might attract attention and, perhaps, suspicion.

Considering the late hour, I decided it would be better to get the car in the morning. We carried our baggage to the airport Holiday Inn and checked in.

Half an hour later, I relaxed into a lounge chair at poolside while Ryan and Lori swam alone in the lighted pool. My watch, still on Atlanta time, showed 3:00 a.m.

I watched my two splashing penguins with wonder. Despite a complete change of transportation and itinerary, and being now twenty hours and 5,000 miles from home, they were unabashedly relishing this moment and this place. I admired and envied them. I wanted to be like that. So open, so adaptable, so ready to welcome life almost without doubt or question. But how could I, fearing the lasting change and loss I had now put into motion.

Psychiatrists suggest we care for our children only because they are "ego extensions," handy shields against mortality. But there is more to it than that. They are what we once were and once had, and often lose as we grow into the world. They are precious reminders of trust and joy in life, and if we let them, they can help us find our way back to life. That sense of joy and hope and even innocence was what I had lost back in Atlanta, along with the children.

A blonde head popped up at the pool's edge. "Too bad Mom isn't here," Ryan said. I nodded as he splashed away.

Now I had recovered purpose beyond myself and a chance to reclaim an openness to life for whatever it might bring. Yet beneath my hope, a deeper concern stirred. A new life yes, but at what price for us all?

Two

Growing Up

*Childhood is a time for play,
for experimentation, for fantasy,
for exploration. The mystery the
child is searching for is itself.*

— Leo Buscaglia, *Personhood*

When I was a boy, lawn sprinklers came on at summer's dusk, and the church bells called us in from our backyard adventures. We obeyed the bells and gave up our roles as pirates and dragons because darkness drew us home, and home was always safe, and home kept its promises.

Home promised to be dependable, watchful, and ruling. Home was where industry and obedience were rewarded and achievement was praised. Where indulgence and laziness had no place.

We hurried home or paid the price for being late: a finger snap on the forehead and a sore spot for a week. We returned because the calling was strong and always there, and family remained the same: mother and dad, my older sister Randi. Home was where we first learned love, and where I came to believe that marriage was forever.

And if not forever, then lasting, like the rusting but faithful John Deere tractor we used for small chores around the farm yard. On the farm, permanency was a way of life, consistency as certain as the rooster's morning pronouncement. Work went from sunup to the last light turned off in the barn. Survival came at every breath, and financial ruin was as near as the next hailstorm or summer drought. Couples had no time to harbor discontent.

Separation or divorce held no pondering in this small country town where hard work and commitment were the eleventh and twelfth commandments.

My home town, Fulda, Minnesota, population 1137, was so small every house sat on the outskirts of town and windows framed lustering wheat fields shimmering under the August sun. It even had a main street of sorts that ran two blocks long with a flagpole smack in the middle. The American flag flew on the Fourth of July and Memorial Day, important days, indeed, in my home town.

Between holidays, every Saturday night, local farmers came to town. Dressed in starched clean overalls, they gathered at the splintered benches in front of Brown's Cafe to prate mostly about the weather and then about the combine that broke down or occasionally about a new tractor or the birth of a calf. In bare feet and summer T-shirt, I played and listened to them talk. They spoke in low voices, serious talk it sounded to me. If there was humor, it was dry and sardonic, much like my father's. It must have passed over me, because I rarely heard them laugh. Then and there, I concluded life was too serious a matter to laugh out loud about some nonsense story.

Though we laughed little, we played with fervor. As dusk gave way to the mysteries of the night and crickets called us forth, secret passions raced in our hearts. We entered our dream time out in the orchards. For brief moments, we shed the tether of family to become pirates and outlaws. Here we dreamed of being different, of sailing free on our own to seize fame and fortune with audacity and courage, force and flair.

Every boy became a daring explorer, every girl an island to be inhabited. Within every law-abiding countryman there lurked a restless adventurer. Inside the faithful family man boiled the hot blood of a Viking marauder. And while the townsmen toiled with their conventionality, under moonlight, we whispered tall tales of future adventures.

Free spirits dreaming of setting sail on uncharted waters were not an uncommon picture, of course. But growing up proved more prosaic. If I could not chart my own destiny, I could at least record the present, hoping to find comfort in the certainty of my past. More than cathartic, journal writing became an attempt to comprehend the turns of my life.

Many years later, as a single father wondering how this could be, looking for clues, I jotted down a "table of contents" of my life while waiting for Lori to finish a ballet lesson. I was still struggling to understand why I had kidnapped my children. Had I been just another young husband who loses his marriage and decides to steal his children? I wanted to know.

Age 1 to 6	*Alone, needed affection, father absent.*
6 to 12	*Winged ears and a speech impediment*
12 to 16	*Ridiculed, sensitive, frightened. Shy, but adventurous and determined.*
16 to 20	*Ambitious, dreams of being an architect. Rural life nurtures free spirit. Shy in public and with girls.*
20 to 24	*Challenged, proudly pursues boyhood dream of becoming an architect.*
24 to 26	*Graduated. Confused. Married. Daughter Lori born. Unprepared to be a father. Just as unprepared to be a nurturing husband. Accepted to law school. Still preoccupied with composing an external façade.*
26 to 29	*School, family and finances a struggle. Son, Ryan born. Marriage falters. Growing panic.*
29 to 30	*Lost beneath veneer of confidence. Moved to Atlanta to seek "the good life." Idealistic but becoming aware of the moral pitfalls of the "jungle."*
30 to 35	*Ambitious and aggressive. Inwardly fragmented. Sense of impending loss. Loving*

kids, but too much the perfectionist. Identity all external. Fabrication begins to crack under glimpses of a fearful empty self. Afraid to express feelings. Walls everywhere. Successful, terrified, bewildered. Everything, yet nothing.

As Lori climbed into the van I closed my journal. A list alone couldn't give give me the answers. Somehow, I needed to go beyond.

❧

I met Val at a dance while at the University of Cincinnati studying architecture. She was a student nurse at a nearby hospital. She had soft, auburn hair to the middle of her back, full pouty lips, and clear, green eyes that gave way to a reserve and a mystery I found immediately appealing. A light scattering of freckles graced the bridge of her pert, cheerleader nose. I liked her friendly but contained politeness.

I soon learned we were kindred spirits. She, too, took herself seriously, too seriously. She also cared about her life and her work; she saw family as something to labor at quietly and stubbornly, something to perfect. After just a few dates, we wanted only to be with each other. I hoped she would become my wife and the mother of my children.

Often in our quiet moments, she would look up at me, eyes pensive, and urge, "Penny for your thoughts." Unfamiliar with expressing my feelings, I'd respond back with, "A penny for your thoughts." Her silence continued her mystery.

What did she think? What did she feel? I wondered if I really knew her. She talked readily about her work, plans for our family, anything functional or practical and immediate, but she spoke little about her feelings, preferring the safety of her own walls.

I was just as closed with my emotions. Looking back, I wonder if either of us knew what we really wanted or felt.

After we married and I graduated from the University of

Cincinnati, we moved to South Bend, Indiana, where I took a job with Armco Steel Corporation. Val worked as a floor duty nurse at Memorial Hospital. I wanted to move ahead as an architect and, after a year, applied and was accepted to Stetson College of Law in St. Petersburg, Florida.

We then began the hardest years of our marriage. Val worked the night shift at a local hospital and during the day took care of our one-year-old daughter, Lori. I worked part-time and once a week sold my blood to help pay tuition. It had taken nine years, but after passing three state bar exams and becoming a registered architect in Indiana, I became one of only two architect/attorneys in the United States, a specialist in architectural law and real estate development law. Unfortunately, without realizing it, I'd become a prisoner of my own accomplishments. The more I succeeded, the more I feared others seeing my empty self.

With three-year-old Lori and one-year-old Ryan, we moved to Atlanta, Georgia, selecting Rollingwood Apartments as our first step to better places. I was offered the contracts administration position with Zachary W. Henderson & Associates, Architects. We were an upwardly mobile family striving for some vague image of what we thought success and happiness were all about.

Our struggle continued, but steady progress followed. I passed the Georgia Bar and opened a law practice in a new office in downtown Atlanta. Our planned two years at Rollingwood Apartments stretched into four. Val returned to work at Northside Hospital. Finally, just before Christmas, we moved into our new condominium at D'Youville Trace, another triumphant step up, though we wondered how we'd keep up the mortgage payments. With Lori in the second grade and Ryan in kindergarten, they now attended the finest elementary school in prestigious north Atlanta.

Our years of single-minded determination and unceasing labor had paid off. But in a sense, nothing had changed. Inside, I was still the same insecure boy who had left Fulda to seek his fortune. Now that I had what I had always thought I wanted, doubt took hold. What "fortune" exactly had I been seeking so single-mindedly? I wasn't sure any more.

Loneliness and a growing sense of detachment began to creep into my consciousness. At my desk in the midst of work, I'd catch myself staring out the window at nothing, frozen over a thought, or feeling as though I had missed a turn somewhere. Why didn't I feel fulfilled? Where was the meaning to my life? Had I focused on creating an image just to keep from knowing myself? Had I been looking outward when I should have been seeking inward instead?

There were plenty of hints, of course. Val's shoulder cold to my touch in the hot Atlanta night, both of us pretending, neither asleep. Her increasing silences beyond household chatter at mealtimes. Even her meticulous attention to the children's needs sometimes faltering. Several times, I noticed her staring out the window at nothing, as if she had momentarily forgotten who and where she was.

I sensed her distance, but didn't understand it. Or was afraid to. I was Lee Coburn, 37, architect/lawyer, father, husband, also genial, cooperative, accomplished, confident. And what about rigid, scared, lonely, and uncertain? These traits weren't part of the image I'd created. The bells called me home to ambition and duty, while the inner pirate paced and muttered, yearning for open seas but afraid to face the incoming tide.

Val, unknown to me, harbored similar dreams of love and freedom. I longed for closeness with her again, yet was only vaguely aware of being terribly insensitive to her needs. We tried to talk, but instead the walls between us kept getting higher. For us both, I wanted to move beyond the walls that imprisoned me.

❧

Thursday, October 28, 1975. A day that would live in infamy. Not likely in the historical sense, but, as Jules Feiffer points out, it's the little murders that measure and mutilate the lives of common folk.

I had been working in my office at home all day, worried about the bills that had been piling up for months, and about the investment company my partners and I were liquidating. But those concerns, intense as they were, seemed artificial, an obsessional screen. There was something else, like a storm brewing.

The day was unusually warm for October, and a fly revived from some crack in the corner seemed out to get me. It was one of those big, glossy, bloated buzzers left over from summer. The creature swooped down on me at the desk, then lumbered away on heavy wings. Clumsy, yet it was somehow able to get away each time I got close with the swatter. I finally stunned the thing. With the swatter handle, I crushed it slowly, then suffered a quick twinge of shame, not because it was dead, but because I had indulged in such a trivial act of cruelty. Was torturing insects the only way I had to gain control over my life? Or was my inner turmoil and anger seeking outward expression?

I left my office to wander, as I had been doing a lot lately. I went from room to room, finally sitting for an hour outside, staring across the lazy creek in back of our condo to the gazebo in the rose garden. Our property had once been the grounds of a famous southern mansion. The lavish gardens to which I now fixed my glassy stare had been part of the grand herbary of this once proud and proper country estate. Giving way to the burden of its upkeep, the tired but stately mansion had been converted to a private children's school. In the days when D'Youville had held distance enough from the city for this to be a scenic place in the country, people had come out on Sundays for walks through the rose garden. I imagined young couples holding hands, strolling the grounds: She wearing her ruffled, looped dress and carrying a parasol to shade the afternoon sun; he in his Sunday best, looking proud to be courting his lady.

Snap to, Lee. Get busy. So much to do. Yet this sense of indifferent idling, killing time.

Until what?

The answer came at 6:30 that evening.

Val had been out of the house for four hours, unusual at that time of day, since as a surgical assistant she normally had surgery cases in the morning. I assumed she had gone shopping. The kids weren't home yet; Lori was at ballet class, Ryan at little league football practice. I was sitting on the couch with my feet on the ottoman, trying to read the Lawyer's Digest I had been unable to finish the past month. *Stop worrying, Lee. You can drown in floating anxiety. What was that expression the kids had brought home? Hang loose.*

I heard the front door whisper open, and I glanced across at the wall mirror and saw Val's reflection as she moved through the entryway. She looked spiffy, freshly made up. On second glance, a little tired, almost haggard under the makeup.

"Hi." I glanced aside and saw that she had no packages. Odd.

I expected her to say, "Hi, I'm back," and move on, heading upstairs or into the kitchen. Instead, she came over and sat in the wingback chair she loved but none of the rest of us ever sat in. The chrome and glass coffee table gleamed like ice between us. Knees together, back straight, her face like wood. Had she smashed up her car?

"What's up?" I asked, laying my magazine aside and feigning a flimsy smile.

"There's something I want to talk to you about."

Part of me felt it coming. What can a statement like that announce? Pregnancy, cancer, incoming ICBMs? I wanted to cringe, crawl away. Although I had no idea what she was going to say, I knew I didn't want to hear it. The kids. It had to be the kids. I started to get up. "The kids . . ."

"Not the children." A flick of her hand commanded me back down. She stared at the wall, unblinking. "I want a divorce, Lee."

A nerve in my ankle started to flutter; my foot twitched and twisted with a will of its own. Her expression didn't change.

"You're kidding," I said.

"I want a divorce." She continued her shielded stare.

I breathed deeply, trying to stay calm. Keep her talking. Work things out.

"Well look, let's talk about it," I stammered. "I mean, I'm glad it's out in the open, that's good, but now we should . . ."

"No, Lee. It's too late."

I hurried over her words, refusing to acknowledge them. "We need this, Val. Honesty. Open expression of our feelings, the bad along with the good, just say your piece. I know you've felt this damned distance, too. This could be the beginning of . . ."

"Lee, I'm moving into an apartment as soon as the lease is signed."

Finally it hit. A hammer blow to the side of the head. Worse. Like being disemboweled from the inside out. I could feel myself sinking, everything draining out, bleeding to death, the blood and substance of my life trickling away. I heard my own voice from a distance, quavering, struggling for calm. "Is there another man?"

"No," she said flatly. Too flatly and too quickly, I thought.

The clock struck seven. I got to my feet. "We can talk about this later. I have to pick up Lori and Ryan. His football practice is already over. . ." I had to get out of there, pull myself together, give her time to realize her mistake.

I was terrified, crushed, like a punished child. I wanted to weep and beg, lie, dodge, submit. But I was also instantly, monumentally angry. On the way to the car, I discovered the Digest in my hand. I threw it into the rose bush, spat out every foul word I could think of and slammed the car door so hard I thought the window would break. I was still trying to get control as I tore across the wood bridge to the street.

Bitch! Rotten, faithless, stinking, whore bitch . . .!

Did we eat dinner? I don't know. We must have gotten through supper with the kids somehow. I kept trying to assimilate the new data. When people win the lottery or a tornado takes their house away, they tell the TV cameras, "I can't believe it." They know it has happened, but they can't describe the way they feel. The heart lags behind the mind.

I kept at her. She didn't really want to do this. She couldn't mean it. Didn't she have any feeling for the children? No feeling for me, for any of us?

She said she did mean it and intended to take the children, the sooner, the better.

After they were in bed, Val sat cross-legged on the soft bedroom carpeting opposite me. Her hands played with one of those elastic hair barrettes, twisting it over and over.

"I'm going to do this, Lee. I don't know what else to say."

I pleaded. What about counseling? Couldn't we hang on until we got help? "You're throwing twelve years of marriage away without a qualm, without a fight . . ." We couldn't talk. An impenetrable wall separated us. I was free-falling into a bottomless crevasse.

"It's too late, Lee. I've made up my mind."

I pounded the floor. I wept. How could she do this? "Please, just for one minute, consider the cost to the kids. To me. Please?"

She sat motionless, except for her fingers pulling on the barrette. I wanted to rip it from her. Fear shuddered through my body. "How can you do this? I can't live without you."

She looked down, her eyes devoid of feeling. "This is something I have to do. For me, Lee, for me."

Later, I couldn't tell if I slept or died. Without Val and Lori and Ryan, I didn't want to live. Life had no purpose without them.

Unfortunately, I awoke to another day. Under the avalanche of grief, I dug for a ray of optimism. I managed to get up by pretending to be alive. Somehow this would work out. But without Val and the family, how could anything work out? Nothing I did alleviated the pain.

Val returned to the house the next afternoon to tell me she'd made a deposit on an apartment at Rollingwood Apartments, where we had lived before moving to D'Youville.

On the day she moved, I returned home around four o'clock, afraid she might still be there. She was gone. I took a tour of the house to see what she left. I didn't care. Furniture without my wife and children meant nothing. A few things remained. They would suffice. My office she had left intact. I sank into my leather chair, trying to piece together the rubble my life had become.

I was sitting there, still in a daze, when I heard her come in upstairs, surprised that she had returned. *Must be to get a few remaining things,* I thought. A short time later, I heard her yell downstairs to tell me she was leaving.

I walked outside to the parking lot to say good-bye but instead watched in silence as she packed her things into the station wagon. Numbness prevented me from attempting conversation.

Finished with her packing, she turned to me. "I guess I'm about moved," she said.

I tried to form words. Was there anything I could say that would undo what had happened? She stood with the car door open, her hand resting on the handle. I ached to be the husband she'd always wanted me to be. My face streamed with tears.

"Won't you come back?" I said.

"Lee, this is something I have to do."

We looked at each other, frozen in silence. Neither able to reach past our protective walls. She slid into the driver's seat and closed the door, then drove across the bridge, out of sight and out of my life.

I returned to the dark condominium. The light from our carefully chosen lamps, now gone, had been replaced by a somber density; the house had become a tomb. I felt my way through its chambers. I stumbled over an unused box. The shadowy silence intensified the nightmare which I longed to wake up and have over.

After that, each morning I awoke to rattle about the caverns of our once-busy home. The occasional pieces of furniture lay like abandoned rubble after a battle. I fumbled around, tripping over the shattered remains of my life, only to be reminded of the devastation I felt. How could I have been so blind? How could I have not seen our marriage deteriorating into cold indifference? What had kept me from expressing the love and passion I felt inside? I had lived so emotionally fearful, our marriage had become numb and lifeless. My futile searching only increased the agony.

❧

One afternoon, I received calls from both my partners in Professional Business Consultants, the real estate consulting company I owned.

Frank Tassano was the first to call. Five years my senior and a successful businessman, he had made a name for himself as a marketing genius. Initially, he had come to the United States from Uruguay to play first chair violinist with the National Symphony Orchestra in Washington, D.C. Fluent in five languages, he also had been Uruguay's Chess Master in world competition. It was his brilliance that had motivated me to become his personal attorney. Since we had become partners, interest rates had climbed to all time highs and the bottom had fallen out of the real estate market.

"Hey, Lee, it looks better. Our main investors, Ferguson and Baker, have seen the light and agreed to hold off another six months. They understand about interest rates. Hey, the economy's down, that's all. So cheer up, Lee. You all right?"

"Sure I am."

"Good. It'll be okay, Lee. Bye."

Sure, it'll be okay. The economy is collapsing, my wife has left with the kids. The condo payment is due. I'm without the second income to keep this expensive home afloat. I'm wandering around empty rooms, burning hamburgers in the kitchen, and my only friend in the world is a cat. Sure, it'll be okay.

An hour later, Stan Kramer called. Stan was a wealthy man with deep Atlanta connections. His father and grandfather had been judges. Stan's tone, always judicial, displayed a touch of patrician annoyance with this modern world of uncertain interest rates and interfering government agencies.

"It does seem the attorney general might be serious, Lee. Although, Lord knows, we have scrupulously kept to the course, while those rascals in the other syndicates have not. And now, the state seems determined to prove all syndications in violation of the securities laws. Our attorney assured us our limited partnerships were outside the definition of a security, but they're claiming otherwise. That out-of-state mailing we sent to Frank's violinist friend in D.C. may bring in the feds. I doubt they can make an indictment out of that. I only called to remind you, Lee, that perseverance and loyalty are bound to triumph in the end, as your namesake proved throughout his noble career. What do you say?"

"Well, Stan," I said, "Robert E. Lee did have to give up his sword in the end, but I guess you can lose the war and still win the battle."

"I don't think I get your drift."

"Nothing. Talk to you later."

"Yes, well, remember, Lee, loyalty's the thing."

The message was clear: don't make waves. That was all right with me. As far as I knew, there had been no intent to defraud. None of the investors were in for more than a few thousand. But the economy had taken its latest dive and construction had dropped with it. Property just wasn't turning over. The balls wouldn't stay in the air.

I had worried about the attorney general's inquiry for months, but now I found myself not caring. So what if the business went down the tubes? The destruction of my career, ruin of my reputation, fines, suits, even jail time, all seemed unimportant compared to what I faced in that empty house each morning when I crawled from bed.

I felt functionally dead, drowned in unbelievable shock and sorrow. I'd sit for hours behind my desk and stare out across the creek to the rose garden, then leave my office to walk through the hollow house and up to the third level to Lori and Ryan's rooms. They had been left undisturbed when Val moved. Lori's second-favorite rag doll lay on the pillow of her neatly made bed. In a corner of Ryan's room, his BB gun stood, retired from service, alongside a bag of marbles. Each time, seeing their empty rooms brought remembrances of bedtime stories, good-night hugs, soft words — "I love you, Daddy" — and now tears.

Even my contact with the kids seemed dreamlike, though we spent every weekend together. My first attempt at cooking brought jokes about paving highways with my macaroni and cheese. Lori and Ryan were better at having fun than I. Underneath their questions about divorce — "Why, Daddy?" and "Will you ever come home?" — I could feel their pain and confusion, as well as my own. We'd end up crying and holding each other; fighting the fear.

❧

Hang-up phone calls started occurring months before Val moved out. They came at different times of the day, usually in the late afternoon and evening. I had assumed the first few were misdials, but when I asked what number the caller wanted, the quiet click of a severed connection answered me. The calls came at irregular intervals. Three days could pass without one, but then I might get them two afternoons in a row.

At first, it only baffled and annoyed me. If it was some disgruntled PBC investor or a nosy neighbor or even Val trying to bug me for some reason, there was nothing I could do but ignore it. But gradually, the calls became a part of my ongoing fever, needling into my consciousness and adding to my rage.

Thanksgiving arrived two weeks after the ax had fallen. For twelve years, we had gathered for the holiday at Val's parents' house in Lawrenceburg, Indiana, driving a long eight hours to get there. This year, she was taking the children alone.

On Wednesday night, I called her parents' house, hoping I might talk to her mother. Claudia Bernett was a kind and caring woman, trim and small-boned, with fine facial features, like Val's. She and Val's father, Calvin, had a warm, easy relationship, and I had always gotten along well with both of them, almost as if I were their own son. Maybe somehow, Claudia would see my side of this and find a way to smooth it all out.

But Val answered.

"It's me," I said.

"What do you want?"

"How come you're already there?"

"I decided to fly instead."

"You should have told me," I said.

"Why?"

"Because I'm their father, damn it!"

Silence. I imagined her grim expression, that cold blue wall of ice. "What exactly is it you want?"

"To talk to my kids."

I heard the ruffle of the receiver being handed over, then Lori's cheerful greeting, "Hi, Dad!"

I told her about my plans for our next weekend together, emphasizing the fun we would have. She said it sounded great. Ryan acted subdued but livened up when I said I was buying him a new BB gun.

Then the good-byes, the heavy silence down the long-distance line, my hand slowly lowering the receiver into its cradle, and finally, my lonely struggle to cope with this new realization. Val had decided when and how to make the trip without consulting me, without even letting me know. She had denied my emotional and practical stake in the children's well-being and whereabouts.

She had acted as though they were entirely hers.

Thanksgiving passed in a haze of punishing nostalgia and boiling rage. Never in my life had I felt so abandoned and alone. In my clearer moments, I thought of friends and wondered why I didn't phone somebody and ask for help, seek some kind of sympathy.

What friends I had were really only acquaintances. It seemed safer that way; but you don't call on acquaintances in time of need. There were Nan and Jody Powell, neighbors at D'Youville. Their daughter, Emily, was Lori's best friend. We had come to know them during summer evenings around the pool. Nan had helped me organize a summer pig roast at the clubhouse. Jody and I had an occasional beer and visit at the pool.

There were others: Frank Tassano, Dell and Bob McClellan, the Bonners, Bakers, Harveys, and Wrights. Every summer, I crewed on Doc Makowski's Flying Dutchman; I had a deep respect for him. Of everyone, I felt the closest to Doc. He lived only two doors down. Yet I didn't go see him. Why?

Some were business acquaintances, of course, and I wasn't eager to have it be known I had personal problems along with the troubles at PBC. I couldn't risk jeopardizing the two consulting assignments I still had going. Money was important. But more than that, I'd noticed a reticence from couples about allowing intimate friendships to develop, especially across sexual lines. If Doc did already know, that would be because Val had told his wife Judy. At best, they would avoid us both.

As for letting anyone else know, I felt too ashamed to reveal the truth about what had happened to my marriage. I still nurtured the hope that I could somehow turn things back.

At the same time, something destructive was working in me, a plan brewed by growing anger. Raw instinct told me to wait, hold back, keep everything as secret as possible.

I did have one "friend" I considered calling. Shortly after our arrival in Atlanta six years before, Sid Silano had moved in next door with his then one-year-old daughter, Carrie. A neighborly friendship developed. Lori had watched the baby a few times; there'd been an occasional barbecue on Sid's back patio and some interesting conversations over beer. He was a solid-framed man under six feet with thick, dark hair and olive complexion. He spoke with a deep voice, affable and powerful. But he was incredibly gentle and loving with his daughter, almost unnaturally so, as though he was afraid somebody might come and take her away.

Although Sid never mentioned college, he was erudite and well-read. He'd quote classical verse to elucidate his stories, and his opinions were always well informed and reasoned. But then he'd shock his audience with some crude locker-room vulgarity or platitude like, "Women. Can't live with 'em, can't live without 'em."

He attracted and repulsed me at the same time. There were hints in his stories of paralegal activity, fraud, even felony. His eyes sometimes took on an animal ferocity, yet when they gazed at his daughter, they became soft as a doe's eyes. He could be talking about some abstract political matter, and his fleshy, dark-jawed face would flush and his voice thicken with emotion that seemed all out of proportion to the subject. And there were mysterious blanks in the narrative of his past life. He hinted at an abandoned career in Hollywood. His wife, he told us that first meeting five years before, had died suddenly, leaving him to raise Carrie. He never named the woman and never mentioned her again.

Something told me he would listen to my troubles; might even be able to help me if I decided to give in to the impulse growing stronger in me every day. I picked up the phone, then put it down.

Not yet. Too dangerous. There had to be some other way.

❧

Two days later, I came across a little scratchpad Val had left in a stack of papers beside the phone. On it, what appeared to be a Christmas list in her handwriting included a name which I didn't know:

Reynolds	*Braggi*	*jewelry box*
Playboy	*sweater*	*gloves*

I rarely read Playboy. British Sterling was my aftershave, not Braggi. And who the hell is Reynolds?

Grabbing the yellow pages, I scanned three pages of physicians, found nothing, then the second time through discovered a Dr. Edwin Reynolds, a surgeon at Northside Hospital where Val worked.

No. It can't be. I felt as if a knife had been thrust deep into me. Then came the nausea and desperate yearning to not believe. I looked for and found another doctor with a similar spelling, but he didn't work at Northside. Still, the list didn't prove anything. So what if it wasn't a shopping list for me? Val had other male friends associated with her work. I stuck the note in the spiral notebook I had begun to use as a journal.

Forget it, Lee, you're making yourself crazy.

Over Thanksgiving weekend, while Val and the kids were in Indiana, there were no hang-up calls. The following Wednesday afternoon, I picked up on another click. No calls clicked silent during the following weekend with Ryan and Lori, nothing through the entire week, then three during the first week in December.

Somebody was checking to see if I was home and doing it according to his or her schedule. The uncanny quiet at the other end, the slow, deliberate way the phone was hung up, convinced me it was Val. But my paranoia over her leaving me would make me think it was her, no matter how flimsy the evidence.

Two weeks before Christmas, while shopping at Perimeter Mall, I ran into an old friend, Dick Sherman. My greeting was wary; his, uncomfortable. When I asked about his wife, he didn't respond with the customary inquiry about Val and the children. He avoided my gaze, wanting to get on his way. He and his family lived next door to Val's Rollingwood apartment. I sensed he knew something, but I decided not to ask, and after a lame exchange of Christmas best wishes, turned to go.

He closed a hand on my arm. "Val seems to be getting along okay in her new place. I see you come and go with the kids. Stop in sometime and say hello."

I mumbled something about being pretty busy these days, but I would try.

His hand tightened. "There's something . . . it hurts like hell for me not to tell you, Lee, but Gail says I should keep out of it, and maybe she's right."

I studied his intense, obviously pained gaze. "Maybe she is right," I said. "Anyhow, I think I know what it is."

"Well, like I said, you're welcome to stop by for some Christmas cheer."

He dropped his hand and walked swiftly away.

THREE

GHOST OF CHRISTMAS LOST

Everything is Spirit in essence,
though hidden in manifestation.
If you had the perception, you
would see God in everything.
— Paramahansa Yogananda

Something about hiring a private detective three days before Christmas gave me a queasy feeling. Besides that, the vibrations from this little man made it seem all that much more ominous. Dressed in a gray business suit too large for his small frame, he acted professional but a bit too friendly, as if to hide the real furtive and unsavory character I suspected he might be. Maybe it was his steel weasel eyes hugging the narrow bridge of his nose that affected me. Nonetheless, I methodically told him the situation, gave him names and addresses, uttered a suspicion I didn't want to believe. The basic instructions were simple: find out if my wife was sleeping with someone else, in particular a doctor at Northside Hospital. He took notes, outlined his procedure and fees. We shook hands and he left cheerfully, whistling Dixie.

Christmas arrived like a steamroller of dread, grinding us down as we decked the halls with boughs of folly. With the pertinacity of two people grunting last words before a duel, Val and I agreed on Christmas arrangements: the kids and I at D'Youville Christmas Eve, all of us at her apartment Christmas morning.

A hollow hell all the way. Lori and Ryan adjusted as best they could, trying to cope with their jumbled home and the puzzle of their Christmas holiday chopped into pieces. How could they understand what had happened when their mother and father couldn't? As children do, they took the best and suffered in silence on the rest. Myself, I continued to feel imprisoned with no escape readily at hand. I hoped making dinner at D'Youville would offer a mild reprieve.

It seemed strange to grocery shop for a Christmas dinner I dreaded fixing. I arranged the dinner out of an obsessive desire to show my wife that I could cook an entire meal for her parents and the kids. *This is crazy,* I told myself, and yet I pushed on with it. We hope habit will save us from feeling the pain of change.

At least preparing for my dinner debut provided me a momentary escape from my distress. I worked furiously to have the dinner be a success, compelled to prove to myself and to "the enemy" that I could take care of the kids as well as "Whatzername." Her parents, Claudia and Cal, arrived for dinner with Lori and Ryan. Presents were placed under the fresh-cut tree we'd decorated the previous weekend.

Dinner consisted of stuffed, glazed Cornish hens, scalloped corn, sweet potatoes, molded salad, hot rolls, and dessert. All were complimented vociferously, but nobody ate much. Out of all the forced good cheer, Ryan spoke the most honestly when he blurted his judgment on the lemon meringue pie: "It droops too much to be a winner."

To myself I thought, *still not bad for a first try.* At least I had proved to Lori and Ryan I could cook and to "Whatzername" that I was not an incompetent parent.

After dinner, we sat around the tree and exchanged gifts, trying to act as if nothing were different. A cold and empty ceremony ensued as we tried, in Val's absence, to reenact the conviviality of holiday tradition.

Lori and Claudia stalwartly fought the threatening gloom. Claudia led us in carols, and we tried lamely to follow her. The evening eroded into long, awkward silences. Finally, good-byes and Merry Christmases were said almost in relief.

Morning came all too swiftly. I awoke from a near sleepless night dreading the hollow clang of Christmas pretenses ahead at "Whatzername's" apartment.

Claudia let me in with a sympathetic smile and led me to the kitchen, where Cal sat at coffee with Val's brother, Eddie, and his wife, Karen. Val was still upstairs, they said. Otherwise, here we all were, as we had gathered for the past twelve Christmases. Yet I found myself standing back away from the others, shifting my feet, reluctant to sit down. Claudia urged a cup of coffee on me, hoping to include me in the chatter, which seemed contrived.

I caught Lori's anxious glance and Ryan's worried frown and realized I had become odd man out. Perhaps, they would all have a better chance at a cheerful Christmas morning if I were not there. On this day of all days, the children didn't need to be reminded of the rift in their lives.

Claudia kept a friendly eye on me. Eventually, we moved to the living room, sitting around the tree, which held our favorite family ornaments. Finally, Val shuffled in, wearing a bathrobe, her hair a mess, no make-up, and looking spent. She said she had the flu. Could she be hung over instead? Or had she too had a sleepless night? Uncharitable, but I couldn't stop imagining the worst.

Christmas carols played on the stereo, candles burned, and ribboned presents waited to be opened. I heard Lori and Ryan's ecstatic cries when Val rolled in their new bicycles. We feigned surprise and delight as we exchanged presents. Nothing shut out the despair. Once I noticed Val was not wearing her wedding ring, any Christmas spirit I might have had disappeared. I couldn't stay any longer. I mumbled my good-byes, hugged the kids, paused before Val. She sat on a stool, her knees together under the chenille robe, her face lifted briefly to show me weary, pain-filled eyes. She whispered, "All I wanted was a simple, loving life."

I wanted to bend down, to take her in my arms, but I could not move. Her silent, heavy shrug confirmed that it wouldn't matter, that it was too late anyway.

Outside, a bleak overcast day added to my somber mood as I drove to the empty condo. I lay on the bed wishing I were dead. Second to that, I wished she were dead. But if I lacked the motivation to get up off the bed, how would I muster the energy to kill either her or me? Besides, the kids needed me. I'd promised to pick them up at three to take them to the park to try out their bicycles.

I tried doing some work, at least sat at my desk. At three, I called to tell them I would be over soon. Hearing the sounds of people laughing and talking in the background intensified my aloneness.

My trembling hand returned the phone to the receiver. I wandered into the living room and sat staring at the tree. A half dozen opened presents sat at its base. I remembered the sounds of other Christmases here: the children's laughter, the door bell ringing, Val's quiet murmur, and now and then her outright laughter, that animated release the children and I cherished because it happened so rarely.

Today, the room stood silent, the only suggestion of life the haggard face staring back at me in the wall mirror: Lee Coburn, the ghost of Christmas lost.

Wrenching pain cramped my insides, doubled me over and drove me to my knees. The knife again, that pain that never lets up.

Four

The Prophet

Beware of false prophets,
which come to you in sheep's
clothing, but inwardly they are
ravening wolves.

— Matthew 7;15

In mid-January, the investigator reported back. He had been unable to come up with any concrete evidence that Val was seeing a Dr. Reynolds or anyone else, aside from old friends. A detailed record of her activities covering three weeks showed when she had been home, at work, shopping, at the movies, or visiting friends. I cross-checked the addresses, and most were familiar, with half a dozen exceptions. None of the addresses matched that of Dr. Reynolds.

Could the detective have missed any late-night trips to his home? Might Val have gone out without being seen, visited her lover, then slipped back into the apartment unnoticed?

The investigator insisted that was highly unlikely, assuring me he had maintained a twenty-hour watch on her through the entire first week. He had planned to renew around-the-clock surveillance during the following two weeks if Val appeared to deviate from the pattern of the first. There had been no variation. My wife, he told me, lived an unusually conservative and regulated life: work, shopping, evenings alone at home with the kids, except for an occasional movie or dinner out with them.

No bars or nightclubs, no midnight visitors, no rich doctor/lover — apparently no lover at all.

I didn't believe it.

I paid him and sent him away to pore over his report. The next week, I visited the unfamiliar addresses. Two were apartment houses. Checking the downstairs mailboxes of one, I found no Reynolds listed. The other had a locked front security door and no doorman. I was unable to determine the names of its occupants. That apartment house was roughly halfway between Val's apartment and Reynolds' home.

What about telephone calls? The investigator had balked at a phone tap or other listening device; besides, it was too expensive. The hospital? Val was a surgical nurse; Reynolds, a surgeon. Who could tell what opportunities they had for intimacy?

I received two more of the mysterious hang-up calls in early January, so on the tenth of the month I wrote "Whatzername" a note:

Dear Val,
I know what's going on with these telephone calls.
Please discontinue them.
Lee.

❧

The calls stopped. My belief deepened that she had been checking on my whereabouts to make sure I did not catch her and her lover together. Despite the detective's report, I was sure she was having an affair and probably had been having one for months before she left. The conviction, however fevered and unconfirmed, was like a scab I could not stop picking at. Just the thought of her with another man made my blood boil.

Was I parting company with reality? There were, of course, alternatives for coping. I considered them all.

Suicide would get rid of my pain, but I wasn't that brave, and besides, Lori and Ryan needed me. I did think through the various methods, tried to imagine carrying them out. In the end, they all seemed selfish, even absurd. No, killing myself was not a good choice.

Killing Val was. She was the one responsible for all my misery. Eliminating her might help release the reservoir of anger trapped within me. I would arrange it to claim self-defense if I were caught.

Thinking more about it, I decided neither her nor my death solved anything. Seeing no other solution, I did the next best thing and imagined she disappeared. Meanwhile, I continued to refuse to accept the unacceptable — becoming a weekend dad.

I continued chanting, "I will not be a visiting father." Sometimes driving the car with no one near, I would shout the declaration as loud as my lungs could muster. My determination turned into fanaticism.

❧

Late in January, I had just finished slamming tennis balls against a backwall when a psychiatrist friend and tennis partner took me aside. Knowing about my anger, he suggested a better way to let off steam. "It works, Lee. You'll be amazed," he said.

That night, I tried his suggestion, selecting the spot where her wingback chair had stood. I rolled a newspaper tight and secured it with rubber bands, then knelt on the rug. On each upswing, I took a deep breath. As I brought the paper club down, slamming it hard to the floor, I wailed as loud as my lungs could scream.

"Eeeeeeeeaaaayah!"

Again and again, I let out explosive howls and beat the rug until the knot loosened inside me and I collapsed, face down, heaving with uncontrollable sobbing.

The psychiatrist suggested doing the exercise several times a week or whenever necessary. After the first week, six or eight howling slams would turn me into a limp noodle sprawled on the floor. Each session required a fresh newspaper, and the rug began to show the effects.

Finding a release for my anger must have helped me grieve for my loss, because I began to concentrate on what might happen legally. After researching everything I could find on family law in Georgia, I met with two attorneys, whose law practices consisted primarily of divorce cases.

Georgia law, like most of the thirteen colonies, was based on English common law. The fundamental moral and biological presumption behind divorce provisions was:

"Custody abides, by God's design, in the mother. She, before the father, owns the children." The only possible exception would be if she were proven insane or an unfit parent, and case law showed this to be a rare judgment. Case law in Georgia had determined adultery as insufficient grounds to rule the mother unfit. She could cohabit with whomever she wanted, leave the family unit when she wished and still be awarded custody of the children.

Shared rights and responsibility for the children ceased at the mother's discretion. Not the father's, not the court's — hers. So long as she was competent and sane, she decided who got the children, regardless of the causes or conditions of separation or divorce.

Had I, on the other hand, chosen to leave home and take the children, I could be charged with either interference with custody or abduction. Had I requested a custody hearing beforehand, custody was certain to be denied. Whether the mother requested a custody hearing before abandoning the marriage or after, custody was still hers simply by virtue of the fact that she was the mother.

In Europe, prior to the seventeenth century, custody had been commonly awarded to the father as breadwinner and, therefore, most able to help the children survive in those grim times. In the 1600s, attitudes on parenting began to swing in favor of the mother. The new reasoning grew from the unproven concept that the mother was more capable of nurturing (that is, loving, feeding, protecting, and educating the children) than the father.

I found a few decisions in which the courts were beginning to adopt the view that fathers could nurture as well as mothers. But my attorney friends, whom I had turned to for advice, were adamant in telling me I had virtually no chance of obtaining custody in the state of Georgia.

They showed me case after case where the mother had won custody, but none where the father had won. Joint custody, new in other states, remained untried in Georgia. The best I could hope for would be token rights to be with my children every other weekend.

"Resign yourself to being an absentee father, Lee," said my lawyer.

"Absentee father? No way, goddamn it!" I wanted to punch him, but realized it wasn't him I was angry at. I left his office nearly running. That wasn't the first time I had felt like assaulting some innocent bystander over my misery.

Now, at last, I had the right target. Just wait!

❧

Early February, the trees stood stark and patient along Chamblee Dunwoody Road. Three months had passed since Val had sunk the knife into me, and I was still bleeding. I phoned Sid Silano at his office, listened to his greeting, and decided my instincts were right — there was an unspoken understanding here and potential help. I told him Val had left me and taken the children. It was like spitting rocks to force the words out.

Silence. Then his wary, muted response. "It's hell, Lee, I know. I mean, I guess it must be hell. Who knows about it so far?"

"You're the first one I've told. My parents don't even know. I can't bring myself to tell them."

"It's hell," he muttered again to himself. "Cut to the guts, betrayed, blown away." I could feel him carefully considering. "But why me?"

"I'm not sure," I said. "Only I've got this feeling. I've had it all along, that you'd know about this sort of thing. I need to talk to somebody, Sid. I need advice."

"Yeah." Another silence. "Okay."

We arranged to meet at D'Youville late Friday evening. That gave me time to be with Lori and Ryan before their bedtime.

I had been seeing the kids every weekend and during the week on Wednesday evening. The three mile drive between the condo and Rollingwood Apartments had become my gauntlet. As often as twelve times a week I drove it, like a caged dog running the fence line. In between seeing them on Wednesdays and weekends, I attended baseball practice with Ryan three nights a week as assistant coach. Two afternoons a week, I drove Lori to her ballet class. With each of them, I attended monthly YMCA Indian Princess and Indian Guide meetings. No one knew my wife had left me.

The children must have been experiencing emotional curves as erratic as mine. Ryan was still wetting the bed, as he had been for the past couple years. And their last report cards had not been good. One minute, they were just kids having fun; the next, they were silent and pensive, staring out the car window, tears inching down their cheeks. They asked questions: What did divorce mean? Could Mommy take them away forever? And worst of all, in their glances, their sudden fears: Why? Why are you doing this to us? Why?

I gave them the best explanations I could, struggling to be honest but failing, in my confusion and pain, to satisfy their questioning hearts. Their mother and I just didn't get along anymore, I told them. But we had gotten married, Lori said. Hadn't we loved each other? Yes, very much, but people change, they grow apart. When we had children; had we still been in love then? Yes. We had wanted a family; everybody wants a family. If we wanted a family, why were we breaking it up now? Couldn't we try to come back together? Why divorce? Because these things just happen.

"Your mother loves you. And I love you very much. I want to stand by you always, watch you grow up, be there when you marry. You'll have kids of your own someday. Then you'll understand. Then. . ."

Lori turned away, her knuckles to her brimming eyes. "I won't get married. I don't want to have babies and not love my husband anymore. I'm never going to get married!"

Ryan stared straight ahead, his lower lip jutting below bewildered, sullen eyes. "Me neither, Dad. I'm going to play for the Falcons. Pro football players don't have to be married if they get touchdowns."

One Friday afternoon, I met Lori and Ryan for the weekend. Val watched us from the upstairs window, a slim figure, white as frost through the curtains, stood staring down. Her silence sent chills to our reunion. Returning along the gauntlet to our condo through Murphy Candler Park, the kids had little to say. One minute they were down, the other up.

To lift their mood, we decided to go shopping for tennis shoes. Their mother didn't allow them to wear the new sneakers she had bought for them while they were with me, because they were purchased with her money, she'd told Lori.

The kids loved getting another pair of tennis shoes. They pranced through the store, watching their racing-striped heels flash red, white, and blue. Once home, we started a game of Monopoly, then they decided to play along the creek instead. I watched them as they sat on the bank throwing stones at passing leaves.

After a while, I called them in for dinner. Macaroni and cheese again. Ryan granted that my cooking was improving. Lori assured me her ballet was getting better also. "I can stand for hours on my toes now, Dad." She beamed. After dinner, we had time to finish our Monopoly game before bedtime. At first, after Val moved out, the three of us slept in my bedroom, the children on the carpet in sleeping bags. We felt safer that way. Lately, they were content to be in their own rooms.

In the glow of light from their rooms, we sat on the soft carpet of the open balcony while I told them a "boy story." They loved hearing stories of when I was a boy, maybe because they knew they were true.

Sometimes, we would make a game of it. I'd tell them to name a subject, and I would remember a "boy story" about that subject. They liked starting the story, and I enjoyed a rich recall of my years growing up as small town boy in Fulda. Their eager faces quieted as they listened to tonight's story about pigs. In a while, they were ready to crawl into bed.

As always, when I tucked them in, I could feel my emotions surface. When I said, "Good night, Sassafras. . . good night, Melon Kid," my heart cried for their fragile spirits.

Lori didn't need a night-light anymore, but I always left her door slightly ajar so I could hear her if she needed me. Ryan's door I left open for the downstairs light to shine into his room. And Ryan had his Pooh Bear and his floppy donkey.

"Goodnight . . . I love you."

I could hear the tick-tock, tick-tock of the grandfather clock as I walked downstairs. I pushed the door to my office closed and walked over to the desk. For a moment I stood there, my hands resting on the back of the big leather chair, just looking at my life.

The grass-cloth walls were covered with degrees and professional certificates that once defined my existence. That world no longer mattered. None of it. What did matter lay asleep upstairs, on loan and conditional upon Val's approval.

"Dear God," I whispered, "I've lost claim to my life."

Shaken, I sank into the chair. I was spending more and more time here in my office. This was the one room in our empty house where it was possible for me to come and survive for a little while.

The glow from the desk lamp highlighted the gold lettering of the leather-bound books on the shelf, part of a small legal library brought home from the law office. As much as I was able to, I had focused on work. From the time Val had left, taking the children with her, I had tried to keep my mind too busy to dwell on my loss. But it was of little avail. They were gone, and I was empty.

There was a light tap on the sliding glass door, and Sid slipped in, his smile of greeting wide, as usual, but his glance flicked nervously around the room. "How you doin'?"

I shivered in the draft from the garden. "It's been hell."

"I believe that." He closed the door and headed for the sideboard. "Mind if I make a drink?"

"Sure, go ahead. None for me."

"You'll need one." He poured two glasses of sherry, placed one in front of me, and settled into a chair with his heavy legs stretched out, the glass resting on his belly. "You do not look well."

"I'm tired of the facade," I said. "Of hanging on, telling myself it will all work out somehow, keeping up the front."

He nodded, watching me over the rim of his glass as he drank. "There's another guy?"

"I think there is and has been for some time . . . a doctor or an intern. She probably met him at the hospital and it went from there. I think he's a particular doctor, older . . ."

"And he's got money, right?"

I nodded, miserable.

"Tell me," said Sid, "what did she say? Did you confront her about the other guy?"

"She. . ." The memory came rushing back with all the pain and anger redoubled. "I asked her when she said she wanted a divorce. She looked me straight in the eye and said, 'No, there's no one else.'" I slammed my fist on the desk. "She lied, and I'm going to prove it. There is another man, I know it!" I shoved the chair out of my way and paced across the room. "I'm going to find the bastard. And when I do, I'm going to make sure she doesn't get the kids. She'll be lucky to even see them again."

I collapsed back into my chair, shaking like a leaf.

"Women!" Sid said after a minute.

Even in my state of rage, I was startled by the tone of his voice — not merely anger, but real loathing. I glanced at him and caught the murderous glitter of his stare before he looked away, as if reluctant to let me see too much at once.

"Okay, I know how you feel," he said. "Exactly how you feel. Give me all the details, and then I'll tell you my story."

I'm not sure how long it took. Hours. I told him everything that had happened with me and Val and the children. When I finished, he told me he was living under a false identity and that he had childnapped Carrie and fled with her to Atlanta. He, too, had been threatened with loss of custody, so had planned and carried out a successful abduction. He was a fugitive, still threatened daily by arrest and the loss of Carrie.

He paused, his eyes wary. "I'm not going to tell you any more details right now. The first rule is: Don't trust anybody. I've already broken it. But I'll tell you this: I'm not sorry. I may be a fugitive, but at least I'm a father. I'm selling furniture, okay, but I've got Carrie. I lost, all right, but I'm not a loser. I've done it all, Lee. I can tell you how. Everything, every detail, every step. If you want me to."

We were drunk, yet sober, two very different men fused by bitter experience and mutual emotion. I was glad not to be alone, scared but eager to learn.

"Women," Sid muttered, his lip curled with contempt. "Love — they sell it. And if something better comes along — more money, a better lay, whatever, you're history. As for the law, the courts, forget it, Papa. Sacred in the eyes of the law is mother. And you can add another word to that one, pal. . ."

The crudity — it wasn't my style, but the bald truth was it echoed my deepest feelings. The heat of emotion in the room sickened me with its virulence, but also excited me with its promise of release. I had been holding on for so long.

"Hang on to that anger, Lee," Sid said. He leaned at me, his face wreathed in a strange radiance that was pain and pleasure all in one. "You're going to need it, all of it. It's a war, Lee. It's hate, or die."

"You're right," I muttered. "I need it."

"Okay." He stood up, finished his wine. "Next time, we'll go into detail. Just let me ask you one more time, are you serious about this?"

"I'm serious," I said. "I know this: I will not be a visiting father. She will not get those kids. I won't let that happen, no matter what I have to do."

"Good," he said, and the glass door hissed shut behind him.

FIVE

ENTER THE DRAGONS

Anger: "You mean one could be 'just angry,' with nothing extra — like a thunderstorm that comes and goes? Gosh, I wish I could do that!"

— Zen Master Suzuki Roshi

In early February, I phoned Sid and told him I wanted to hear the rest of those details he had mentioned.

He sounded wary and doubtful. Again, he checked on my resolve. "Are you sure you're going to do it?"

"Pretty sure."

"You're not going to like everything you hear."

"That's okay. I want to know it all."

"All right. I'm trusting you, Lee. It better not be a mistake."

He had a second-floor, two-bedroom apartment in an old brick building in south Atlanta. Nothing fancy, but comfortable.

His daughter, Carrie, came in from playing soon after I arrived. She was seven now, plump, cheerful, and sure of herself.

As Sid banged about in the kitchen, he informed me, "Dinner is casual around here. We're having scrambled eggs and toast."

While we ate, we shared lively conversation, including a brisk debate about whether girls should go out for Little League. Carrie won, but I had the impression Sid really wanted it that way.

She went off to her room, and over coffee, Sid told me his story. He said he had told no one his true identity for six years, except his brother.

His real name was Joe Diamichi. His yarns about the merchant marines and his earlier life were true. More recently, he had been in television and film production in Hollywood, gaining recognition for his specialized skills. He entered his forties with a new home, a beautiful wife, and a one-year-old daughter. About then, he became aware of his wife's discontent and began spying on her.

His voice thickened as he described how he'd stood in the shadow of his garage one night, watching an unfamiliar car pull into his driveway. The man, a business acquaintance, got out. Sid remembered the screen door swinging open, then his wife silhouetted against the kitchen light, the figures embracing.

At one point, he had made plans to kill her. Since they were both experienced aerobatic pilots, he planned a freak accident. He would make a concealed cut in her leather seat belt, take her for a ride in his open cockpit Pitts biplane, execute a double barrel roll over the LeBrea tarpits, and dump her out.

"Bury the bitch with the other dinosaurs, teeth a foot long and a brain the size of a goat turd. Your Honor, I don't know how it happened, but she never was bright; maybe she just forgot to buckle up . . . Oh, Christ." Sid covered his face with his hands, shook his head. "Well, you know how you boil, how it feels." He looked up. "But there are better ways to even the score."

He had worked his revenge by kidnapping Carrie, fleeing to Canada, then Atlanta, where he had lived for six years under a false identity as a furniture salesman.

He poured us each a glass of wine. We talked more. I was amazed at how his experience paralleled mine. At first, the shock and disbelief, the furtive campaign to prove infidelity, then the rage building toward this overwhelming compulsion to act.

"Do something about it, Lee. Don't just sit there in your misery and take it. Pay the bitch back by taking what is rightfully yours!"

Eventually, we settled down to a discussion of how he had accomplished his own disappearance.

He paused to add a little more sherry to our glasses. "First things first, Lee. Your change of identity. The most important and the toughest to do right. And the most dangerous. We're talking felonies here, Lee, ten to twenty in the slammer. Are you ready for that risk?"

"I think so."

He sighed, studied me, muttered, "You'd better know so."

"I have to know what I'm getting into first," I reasoned. "I can do it, if and when I decide to do it."

"I must be crazy," he said after a moment's more pondering, "but here goes. Come with me."

We walked down the hall into his bedroom. He pulled a thick envelope from a small safe in the closet. On the bed, he laid out a row of documents, originals in his real name and amazingly convincing counterfeits in his false name: Social Security cards, driver's licenses, military discharge, credit cards, all accompanied by original art, paste-ups, camera-ready photostats, and printed proofs. The whole package had been done by a "professional" and had cost him $2,000.

"Lee, you have to change your name. Lee Coburn has to disappear totally and forever. Change your birthdate, too, make yourself a different age. I made myself a few years younger. Why not? Keep in mind that from launch day on, they'll be on your ass like a pack of hounds, and these guys are the law, which means they don't have to be legal. Any trained investigator knows most people are inclined to choose names they can remember. Even professional criminals usually go for ones that sounds like their real names. Don't do it. No Colfax or Claburn. Use a name that starts with a different letter and has a completely different sound to it. The first thing you need is a new Social Security number; you can't get a job without one. Then there's the FBI. The first thing they'll do is scan the SS records, checking the millions of names beginning with "C" and a vowel or diphthong. They can cross-reference every way you can imagine and a few you can't, including pronunciation similarities. And then, there's money. Cash. You won't be able to establish credit at first. Money will be your life's blood . . ."

I concentrated, but three little letters kept sawing at my mind like the stinger music in a suspense film: FBI.

Sid left me to say goodnight to Carrie. When he returned, he told me in detail how to put together a new birth certificate and how to apply for a new Social Security number.

"When you have the birth certificate together, I'll drive you to the motor vehicles department. You're getting your first license, so you can't drive yourself. We'll use my car. And since the only ID you'll have will be the certificate, you might need me to do a little back-up bullshitting for you."

He grinned, looking a little tired, but with that metallic glint of defiance in his eyes. "You get good at it after a while, Lee. You have to. The first lie is the toughest, the first time you look them in the eye and take the leap. Just keep saying to yourself, 'Screw it, it's all a snakepit out there, anyway.' "

He took me to the door, his big hand on my shoulder. "Still want to do it?"

"I think so. I want to feel it out, at least be ready." I turned to face him. "So you decided not to . . . kill her?"

The glint again, the clenched teeth of the grin. "I decided I didn't care if she was alive or dead. What I cared about was to have Carrie with me, that's all."

"But you've got Carrie now."

His grin tightened and he started to remove his hand but did not. "You're smart Lee. I always figured you were. You want to know why I'm taking the risk of helping you? Well, let's just say vengeance is sweet. You get a taste for it."

I looked away. "Yes, I'm beginning to see that."

He chuckled and squeezed my shoulder. "Remember, when it begins to look difficult in the next few months, say to yourself, 'Just wait, just you wait.'" I could almost hear his teeth grinding out the words. He laughed and ushered me out the door. "We'll talk again."

The session with Sid left me shaken for days. It wasn't just the smoldering anger or the talk of murder. What really gave me pause were the consequences of what I was considering. In trying to have the children for my own, I could end up losing contact with them forever, along with my identity and everything I'd strived to become.

My desire to be a real dad to my children drove me to take action, even if it did mean self destructing from my vengeful rage. I wanted a part in shaping my children's values and who they would become as future parents. Once I connected with the truth of my deepest feelings, I became blinded to seeing any other solution but to kidnap Lori and Ryan.

Meanwhile, I had to go on living, trying to make money, seeing the kids on weekends, and keeping up the pretense of acceptance as the discarded father. Part of me clung to the hope that Val might somehow be persuaded to change her mind.

During the months ahead, I became four separate individuals: loving father, submissive cuckold, money-hungry professional, and secretly scheming kidnapper.

The future looked murky for PBC. The attorney general's office continued their investigations into our old real estate syndication activities. Neither Frank nor Stan phoned again; I didn't call them either. I was more concerned about my two consulting jobs, one that had to be completed by June 1 and another for which I hadn't been paid yet. I had no savings, and the bills were piling up. I had stock I could sell, but I needed thousands and all of it in cash. I put the bills aside, resolving not to pay any unless forced to. To stay organized, I began working from an ongoing list of things to do.

Make birth certificates, get Social Security card.
New personal and professional documents.
Get the kids' immunization and school records.
Make list of what to take, what to leave.
Rent storage space to store antique mirror, etc.
Decide where to go. When. Discuss with kids.

My experience in architectural drafting helped in creating new birth certificates. To cover my tracks in the production process, I had the type set in segments by different shops, using a different story at each place. The heading, *Record of Birth,* I set in gothic letters to match my old certificate. To match the ornate border on the original, I used stick-down graphic designs found at the art store.

The paste-up took hours and required meticulous care, but the final artwork looked acceptable. I made a copy before taking it to the printer, rather than use my amateur artwork.

I applied for a new Social Security card in the name of the alias I had decided on: Leland Landau. As a first-time applicant, I wasn't required to supply a birth certificate.

Time didn't permit setting up a blind mail drop before applying for my Landau driver's license. I used my D'Youville address, assuming the risk would be the same or worse with my box number. I further reasoned that it was the last name, not the first, they would try to trace. Thirty-seven years reacting to my first name had to be measured against Sid's warning about the risk.

I remember staring for a long time at the name, Lee Landau, trying to comprehend all that it meant to me and my future, to Lori and Ryan, to their mother. But I couldn't handle it, not all of it at once. All I could do for the moment was just keep going.

In mid-February, nearly four months after Val had dropped her bombshell, Sid drove me to the Motor Vehicle Licensing Department. My stomach churned. This was not just fibbing to some typesetter who couldn't care less, it was lying to a state official and violating the law, a law which I had sworn to uphold and protect.

I waited in line trying to muster an appearance of nonchalance.

The bulging uniformed clerk's brass buckle kept scraping against the high counter as he snapped at each applicant. His putty cheeks and gimlet eyes were those of a man who obviously believed that all the world should be as terrified of small errors as he.

As I filled out the form, I mentioned that I had been in the Middle East for several years and was glad to be home where the trains ran on time.

He liked that. "Those Arabs didn't know how to run things, and they're hopelessly corrupt. Identification?"

An appreciative glint in Sid's eye at my Middle East ploy buoyed me, but my nerves tightened again as I presented my artwork.

The clerk glanced at the birth certificate, scribbling away and muttering about what could you expect of people who were still riding camels and wore gowns in the sun. He seemed more concerned I not walk off with his ball-point, than with the information on the certificate.

"We check them in at the end of every shift," he explained. "Part of the annual attempt to reduce pen pilferage to below a million a year."

Next came the driving test, under the hard eye of a bulldog-faced examiner, his wide belt stretched by his bulging belly. His grim silence added to my jitters. Would I say something wrong? Would my driving be good enough? If I made too many mistakes, would he become curious and check out my application and birth certificate more closely? After the test, we pulled into the Department of Motor Vehicles lot. Mr. Bulldog perused his clipboard, glowered fiercely at me, and announced my grades were more than good enough.

I passed. My first test.

"You did okay," Sid allowed at our next planning session. "Now, let's continue the lessons."

We discussed registration at hotels, documents needed to register the kids in new schools, and how to parlay basic documentation like the birth certificates and driver's license into more impressive identity such as credit cards and bank accounts. Many of his lessons were less savory and closer to skullduggery: how to jump out on a restaurant bill by having a confederate call you to the phone, how to escape a week or more of bills at a resort by leaving behind throwaway luggage.

"So you lose a couple of bags and a second-hand set of golf clubs. You're beating a $500 bill."

He even had methods for stealing clothes from department stores, along with an assortment of what he called long and short cons designed to separate widows and other innocents from their savings.

I paid close attention to his instructions, for the more I learned what lay ahead, the more I feared I might have to fall that low in order to keep my children.

❧

In my spare moments, I read books on child rearing and child psychology. More than one book advised parents to occasionally relinquish the rigid postures of parenthood and play with their children. By letting our children see our playful nature, psychologists wrote, playing becomes a way to building intimacy.

And so we played. Each time, I experienced an open, easy, free self I didn't know existed. Perhaps we keep ourselves securely hidden for fear of looking silly or being ridiculed.

One blustery March weekend, the children and I traveled to Panama City, Florida. The gray skies and chilly weather couldn't dampen the pleasure of our being together. We toured the coast, strolled the beaches hand in hand, and built sand castles, free of the misery that awaited me in Atlanta.

The trips away gave me confidence in my ability to create peaceful, healthy experiences, apart from Val.

Driving back from the coast, I asked Lori and Ryan, "How would you both like to go to Colorado this summer? We could camp in the Rockies."

They loved the idea and began talking about all the things we could do on a longer trip. But they seemed depressed as I delivered them to Rollingwood. I bent to hug Ryan. He held me close, fighting the tears that always occurred at the end of a weekend together. Lori let me take her in my arms, then suddenly she clung to me.

"Why! Why do you always have to go away?"

"You know why," I said.

"No, I don't," she wept. "I just don't."

Val's silhouette appeared briefly in the upstairs window as I shuffled back to the car, trying to keep my shoulders straight and muttering to myself my bitter litany: "Wait. Just you wait . . ."

My telephone conversations with Val had become shorter and more constrained, quibbles over who got what of our common property and nearly telegraphic exchanges about the children. She had always been a guarded conversationalist, polite and with a ready smile, but passive. Now our words of exchange had become forced, laced with razor edges of disdain.

In early March, during one of our rare attempts at talking about the divorce, she offered to let me have the condo. "That's nice," was the only reply I could manage.

I couldn't deny my excitement as I hung up. Our equity was potentially worth $25,000, the maximum I needed to get away successfully with the children. It was a bone, of course, a tempting morsel, her bargaining ploy against the real issue of custody. I contacted a real estate broker and listed the condo for sale. To encourage an early close, I put together a sales brochure, aware that there were other units for sale in the complex that were not moving.

Until now, part of me still longed for reconciliation. But at the same time, the lawyer in me became more and more calculating, less willing to concede on anything. During our next conversation, as we quibbled over who got the blender (although it had been a Christmas present to both of us, it had come from her parents), I begged her again to try counseling. This time, in the midst of my pleading, I mentioned the word custody.

"The question of intent bears on the custody question, you know," I extemporized (it wasn't true). "I mean, it's to your best interest that the court believes you at least tried to save the marriage."

I went on to recommend a psychologist friend, who had offered to conduct the counseling. As I talked, I could sense the wheels of her mind turning. With Val, the quality of the silence was often more eloquent than her words. When I finished, she said she thought it was a waste of time, but she would talk to her lawyer.

A few days later, I received a letter from her attorney. His letter proposed certain conditions for counseling. The six weekly sessions would be conducted separately. Because I had insisted we use the same counselor, he would have to confirm in writing his professional credentials and that his discussions with Val were privileged and could not be used in a court of law.

War or not, I still hoped that counseling might make a difference. Maybe she would become disenchanted with the doctor's charm and money, or she might reconsider the right of the children to live with their father, or decide she needed further therapy to sort out her feelings before coming back to me.

On the other hand, I needed to delay initiation of divorce proceedings for as long as possible. The six weeks would do that. The time between my own sessions and visits with the kids I used to work my way down my latest list.

Prepare resume & professional materials.
Write Indiana Bar and Architect Registration Boards.
Purchase and license car in another state (?).
Sell stock.
Prepare power of attorney.

I hadn't yet decided whether the abduction should be by car or plane. Using a car would be more flexible and comfortable, but with greater risk.

The counseling took us into mid-April. The counselor spoke nothing of his sessions with Val, except to say that she had attended all six. Within hours of her last session, she came to the condominium dressed in her favorite color, blue, her soft auburn hair falling halfway to her waist and accented with dangling earrings. As usual, she wore a discreet powdering of makeup to hide the scatter of freckles across her nose.

She had never looked more beautiful. Watching her seat herself and turn a stony face to me, I wondered why she never seemed to have understood the joshing from men about her freckles was a form of compliment. Maybe she had understood but refused to accept it as friendly. In a way, for all her concern with her attractiveness, something in her resented the attention.

"I still want the divorce," she said, always the woman of few words.

"I see." I had been saying that a lot lately. Your marriage is over. I see. You are going to lose your children. I see.

There was no longer any hope, therefore, no point in hesitation.

"I want custody of Lori and Ryan," I said coldly.

"You do?"

She acted surprised. She was so used to having her way with me; accustomed to my passivity.

"You know how I feel about the children," I said. "What do you think? That I don't care about being a father to my kids?"

She grew paler still, "Well, yes, but since that's not possible . . ." Her eyes narrowed. "I didn't think you . . . I wasn't sure . . ."

"You can be sure now. And consider this: I know how you're saving on your doctor bills." I could taste my anger, bitter and painful, but at the same time sweet.

"What does that mean?"

"A bad joke," I admitted. "But to the point. A point I'm sure the judge will consider." In fact, I wasn't at all sure.

Now she got it. Hatred to match mine flashed briefly in her eyes, then she was on her feet. "You can't have custody."

"I have to go now," she announced, primly and firmly as a prom queen informing her date that the evening had come to an end.

"Then go!" I screamed. She strode to the door, slamming it behind her.

SIX

BLIND ESCAPE

Power will not overcome one's inferiority, ease an inner feeling of humiliation . . . Power serves only to deny these feelings.

— Alexander Lowen, M.D., *Narcissism*

Lori reported the next week that Val had taken her and Ryan to visit Dr. Edwin Reynolds at his big house on Viewcrest Place. That much now made sense — the Christmas list had been for Reynolds. Yet there was no proof they had been seeing one another before Val left me, nor was there any proof of an affair now. Apparently for certain, they were close friends. Her attorney must have advised Val there was little risk of her losing a custody battle on the grounds of adultery.

The details of their relationship no longer concerned me. I had made up my mind what I was going to do, and neither of them, together or separately, could stop me.

I still picked Lori and Ryan up on Wednesday evenings, still looked into their bewildered eyes as I left them, still drove the three-mile gauntlet home, dying inside at every thought of not being a dad to my kids.

Early signs of spring had arrived, and the trees hinted green along Ashford Dunwoody Road. Blooming dogwoods and flowers proclaimed a lush abundance of hope. I scarcely noticed.

When I drove, I pounded the steering wheel and repeated my litany: "I will not be a visiting father!" Sometimes, I screamed obscenities; at other times, I had to pull over and stop. Crumpled over the wheel sobbing, I'd become overwhelmed with remorse, as if facing certain death.

After the final confrontation with Val, I pondered every consequence of taking Lori and Ryan: the advantages, the risks, the moral dilemma, the guilt, not to mention the personal loss. Taking them meant paying a price for the rest of my life. It meant not seeing my family for many years; it meant losing all my professional credentials, which had taken me half a lifetime to acquire. My career, my life in Atlanta would end. I ran the risk of losing my equilibrium by going into a world reduced to nothing. Worst of all, if I failed, I could go to jail and lose the children forever. Worse still, the guilt and loss of my self-esteem.

The remorse and guilt, bad enough now, were sure to deepen once my anger dissipated. Even now, I wasn't able to avoid imagining Val's pain and how others would suffer as well.

But in the end, I rationalized it was Val who made me this vengeful. It was she who had decided to leave, causing all of us to suffer. Thanks to her, the children stood to suffer either way. I pushed to convince myself. The only difference now lay in who should bear the greater pain of parental loss, her or me.

As their mother, she is given custody automatically. Certainly, as their father, I deserved them just as equally. Yet the courts persist in holding me and all fathers as less capable of nurturing and caring for our children. I felt compelled to assert my right to be a dad, even at the risk of losing my freedom.

Until then, I would stop playing these different roles, father, dejected husband, Landau (whoever he was), and just be the dad I always wanted to be. That week, I received the new Lee Landau Social Security card.

But where would we go? At first, I had thought the easiest thing to do would be to load a trailer and drive north to Montreal or west to Denver. Colorado had milder winters than my home state of Minnesota, shorter, cooler summers than Florida. Sid reminded me going by car and trailer exposed me to too many contacts along the way. Better to fly and get off the continent. Tracing us to a foreign country would be more difficult. An English-speaking country would be best for the kids' schooling and my job hunting. I researched Australia and decided on Melbourne as having the most agreeable climate, preferring to be in a climate with four distinct seasons. I wrote the superintendent of schools inquiring about enrollment.

During the month of March, I concluded July would be our best time to leave. This would allow time to get settled before Lori and Ryan started school. When I looked at my lists and the dozens of uncompleted tasks, I didn't see how I could possibly be ready in time.

Soon after that final confrontation with Val at D'Youville, a letter arrived from Val's attorney requesting my signature on the Consent to Service Order, which would begin the formal divorce proceedings. I knew nothing would stop her now from filing or getting a final judgment, so I signed.

Early in April, I looked for storage space and settled on Pilgrim Mini-Storage in north Atlanta. While registering, I wore horn-rimmed glasses, my first anxious experiment with disguise. The manager asked for identification to verify my signature on the lease agreement. I gave her my Lee Landau driver's license. If she had asked for more, I would have shown my Landau Social Security card.

I had made a list of items I wanted to store and send for once we were settled: photo albums, my grandfather's framed antique mirror, grandfather's tools and tool chest. I moved the articles one by one, hiding them in the back seat or trunk of my car. Assorted heirlooms and favorite possessions I packed in two wood crates made for shipping. I moved the clock last.

Choosing an early morning hour, I maneuvered the crated clock into the back seat of the Regency. One end thrust precariously out the rear window. The shape still seemed recognizable: too shallow for a coffin, not rounded enough for a bass fiddle. As I backed into the street, I saw the curtains move in Mrs. Wright's front window two doors away. Crouching behind the wheel, I watched the withered fingers with their crimson nails pull back the yellowed lace, saw the glint of her bifocals. I would have to live in one of the town's fanciest condos, which also happened to have one of the nosiest neighbors around.

It didn't occur to me until I was returning home that I still had on the outdated horn-rimmed frames.

An imaginary scene rose like a horror film. The minute it became clear I had taken the children, the neighbors would be questioned, including Mrs. Wright. Yes, Mr. Coburn had been moving things at an odd hour, looking rather different wearing horn-rimmed spectacles. Investigators would canvas the storage companies, looking for a new tenant who wore horn-rimmed glasses and stored large unusually shaped objects. Why, yes, let's see here. It was Mr. Lee Landau.

"Luck won't always be with you. Sooner or later, you will make a mistake."

Later was all of a sudden sooner, and the panic was a throbbing kind of electric nausea.

I phoned Sid.

He was not amused, said he didn't have time to meet with me. "Take it easy, Lee," he said. "Like I said, it will happen, and you can't do anything but adjust. Dump the stuff and dump the name."

"But you don't know what that mirror means to me."

"You've got my advice. The only alternative is to move it to another storage place under another name. Personally, I wouldn't touch it. Whatever you do next, think it through, take your time."

Feeling vulnerable after the mix-up at Pilgrim, I decided to find a new last name. I chose Landel because it was different but close to my original alias, Landau. It could happen that, at some point, I would be forced to risk mixing documents showing both names.

But my time was rapidly melting away. Another Social Security card would not get back to me by launch day. Plus, I still had to get the children's school documents and create new facsimiles.

That same week, I stopped in at the administration office at Nancy Creek Elementary, where both Lori and Ryan were enrolled. The woman listened to my request for the kids' grade transcripts, excused herself, and returned to tell me the records weren't available for my use. Why? "Because custody of your children is presumed with the mother until the final divorce." she said.

My temper flared, but I hung on, pointing out that since there had not yet been a decree, we both still shared custody. The woman left again, this time to presumably consult the principal. She returned to say they would take my request under further consideration. Did that mean they would phone Val?

The children's immunization records became my next project. The doctor who had given them their shots was more cooperative. In a few days, I had the documents, complete with four associate doctors listed at the top. Now I could make new immunization records.

The next week, Lori and Ryan's transcripts arrived from Nancy Creek Elementary, showing their grades from the first grade on. I duplicated the form, inventing a fictitious school named Fair Oaks. I added a false address, county, and telephone number, along with a different name for the district superintendent. I had the series printed, using a different colored stock for each school year. Typing in the information, I hesitated over the children's last name, then decided I had to go with Landel to stay consistent. Finally, I entered the correct grades, resisting the temptation to improve them, then used different pens to sign the signatures.

There was risk in all of this. Worse of all, the risk to my own self-respect. At least the finished product matched the originals. Beyond that, all I could do was hope they would be accepted without cross-checking phone numbers or the existence of a Fair Oaks Elementary in Steward County, Georgia.

❧

Only two potential buyers had inspected the condo and neither had made an offer. I was still on a two-thousand-dollar monthly retainer for my consulting job for Rubert/Jenson and Associates and being paid every two weeks. No word from former business partners on investigations into our PBC syndications. The stock I had sold brought in a thousand. I continued putting off paying bills that could be avoided and hoarded every cent I could.

Still, I couldn't cancel the four-day camping trip to the Florida Panhandle I had promised Lori and Ryan. The time alone with them would be much needed sustenance before the final push.

We headed south across Georgia under crisp blue skies. The farther we drove from Atlanta, away from the divorce proceedings, Pilgrim Storage, and Mrs. Wright, the more I relaxed. West of Panama City, we found miles of deserted white beaches and sand dunes wind-shaped into serene sculptured forms; best of all, we saw no one but each other. Sitting high on a dune, gulf winds pressing me to the sand amidst the wild gray vastness, brought new hope. I felt free to be myself as a father and as a man.

The kids climbed to the crest of the highest sand dune. Leaping toward the ocean in front of them, they logrolled down the dune, bubbling with pleasure. Lori shouted she'd just found the perfect dune. Tiptoeing, as if not to waken the sleeping dune, she approached the virgin slope. She threw her arms wide, looked skyward, and flopped back into the sand. Sprawled butterfly-style and giggling, she fanned her arms and legs into the sand. Carefully getting up, she stepped aside to present her artwork.

"See, Dad, an angel."

So it was, an angel in the sand. Ryan practiced it, and so did I. We found another untouched slope nearby and each made our mark and stepped back.

Three angels side by side on the sun-drenched slope, touching wings, paper-doll style.

We three. A new beginning.

If we made it.

On the drive back, I discussed the vacation their mother had previously consented to through her attorney. Would they still like to go camping in Colorado? The decision quickly became unanimous, with much cheering and speculation from Ryan on the incidence of grizzly bears in the Rockies. We set the date for the Great Colorado Expedition: July 28.

I did not tell them that the date would be known to me as Launch Day.

Early in May, I looked for another mini-storage place and found one in a less affluent section of south Atlanta. They didn't ask for identification; just store whatever you want, come and go as you wish as long as you pay the rent in advance. Great. I began moving the heirlooms again and other treasures, making sure this time to drive around the D'Youville neighborhood and the sharp-eyed Mrs. Wright.

Sid's advice to leave well enough alone at Pilgrim haunted me. But the real damage — Mrs. Wright spotting me in my horn-rimmed glasses — had already been done. At least moving the heirlooms, important reminders of our heritage, along with the other treasured belongings meant they were safe until we sent for them later.

The south Atlanta storage space would be vacated after transporting the two crates to an air freight forwarder. For the things at Pilgrim Storage I would have to figure out a way to pay the rent through a mail drop.

Meanwhile, the divorce was inexorably proceeding. I had turned my end of it over to an older attorney friend, Rick Henning, but I maintained behind-the-scene involvement, making sure that I still appeared to be the reluctant husband, quibbling over petty details in hopes she wouldn't get her decree until after we were out of the state. If I left with the divorce final, I would be in contempt of court as well as in violation of the Georgia Interference With Custody law.

I continued to fight for custody, child support, life insurance equity, and equitable division of property, playing the role of angry jilted husband and difficult SOB, all of which came easy, considering the rage I felt. Custody was the issue I pretended to care most about. But delaying tactics finally ran out, and on May 28, the preliminary decree arrived in the mail. With it came formal notice that the final hearing would be held in the judge's chambers on June 3.

I didn't go to the hearing. What was the point? From earlier drafts, I knew what it declared as binding. Besides, I didn't care to be that close to Val or to see the pain in my children's faces after the dry, legal amputation.

In fact, at about the time that my marriage of twelve years was being legally declared dead, I was presenting our Siamese cat, Georgie Girl, to a neighbor, along with the cat's sleeping basket, food dish, and ten pounds of fresh kitty litter.

During the first desperate weeks after Val left, the cat had been my only companion, sleeping at the foot of my bed as I tossed and dreamed, always there with affection and ready for aimless play. As my resolve had deepened, I had taken less and less notice of her, several times forgetting to feed her. Just as it was time to accept the end of the marriage, I knew I must also put aside this symbol of the family now gone.

When I handed the cat to the woman, she said, "It must be difficult for you, Lee, losing Val, your kids, and now even your pet. Will you be seeing your kids on weekends?"

Nodding, I ruffled Georgie Girl's ears one last time, then left. I didn't look back. I couldn't.

❧

In my office, I took out the temporary decree, which was virtually certain to be the same as the final decree, and did some arithmetic.

The order granted custody of the minor children to Val, of course. I, "as father to his only children," was granted visitation rights consisting of every other weekend, commencing at 5:00 p.m. on Friday and ending at 7:00 p.m. on Sunday. In addition to those twenty-four weekends per year, the children would be with me for exactly one month each summer.

Val's time with them would be continuous, involved time. Mine would be sporadic and catch-as-catch-can. The numbers told the story: Mother 287 days. Father 78 days.

Lori and Ryan reported later that, on the afternoon of the final hearing, Val had complained of a splitting headache and had retired to her room. That evening, she took them to the Steak and Ale Restaurant for a "celebration" dinner. She told them I hadn't showed up for the final proceedings.

"Obviously, your daddy doesn't care."

As she paid the check, she said, "Your dad wouldn't do this for you."

Oh, yes, he would. We'd have many more and better "celebration" dinners, and none of them would include her on the guest list.

When the final decree arrived in the mail a week later, I didn't open the envelope. Choosing not to open it served as a symbolic refusal to acknowledge the validity of the thing. I wandered upstairs and placed it among the papers beside the bedroom phone. Again, I hadn't a clear idea why I put it there, except it seemed appropriate — next to our bed, where I had also discovered her Christmas list for the good doctor.

By now, I was in a trance, obsessed and distracted, thinking on five levels at once, frightened and awe-struck by my decision, yet determined to carry it through.

Through June, I worked on further documentation, new professional certificates, résumé, and letterhead for Leland Landel and Associates, Architects. Some I got only as far as the paste-up, others only the typesetting.

I had decided we would go on from Denver to the Hawaiian Islands. We'd be off the continent, but the schools would be American. I researched Hawaii, reading books and sending for a

Honolulu telephone book with its list of real estate development firms that might employ me. Against the possibility we might have to flee to a foreign country from Hawaii, I applied for a passport using Coburn, rather than the incomplete Landel documentation. The now inactive Landau name would be resorted to only in a dire emergency.

As for Hawaii, I thought the promise of sunshine, white beaches, and a real vacation would make my eventual announcement of our not returning more acceptable to the kids. Besides, I had always dreamed of living in Hawaii. If and when we got through this, we would all need a rest.

Sid appeared to be avoiding me since my fumbling of the storage situation. Maybe he thought I might blow it, and he would be implicated. I called him. He still sounded encouraging but said he didn't have time to meet with me. Something about a sales conference out of town. "But be sure to get in touch before you leave, pal."

The sense of being utterly alone returned, along with a feverish spurt of paranoia. Sid was the only one who knew my plans. Never mind could he trust me, could I trust him?

July, and Launch Day was now only weeks away. I closed out my bank accounts and squirreled away my cash in the office and in a moneybelt. In June, I had been obliged to pay a portion of the electric bill to keep the lights on and the water heater and refrigerator working, but I continued to stall on the other bills, the largest being the $550 monthly mortgage payment. I listed the financial liabilities I did not expect to pay off for some time to come:

$1,200 Mastercharge	*$5,000 Father*
$1,300 Bank Americard	*$1,500 Government loan*
$250 Penney's	*$1,000 Divorce legal fees*
$2,500 NBG loan	*$4,000 Keith*
$450 Back lease on Oldsmobile payments	*$1,650 Unpaid Mortgage*

Plus: Monthly child support payments (particularized in the unopened decree).

I didn't like the thought of running out on my debts, but by now, it was obvious the condo wasn't going to sell in time, and I needed every dollar. What with hoarding from weekly consultation checks and sale of the stock, I was up to only $3,500. I had hoped to have a total of $25,000. A $2,000 consulting fee was not due to be paid until August. I phoned the broker in charge, and to my surprise, he agreed to let me have it now. That brought my traveling fund up to $5,000.

Meantime, I ran an ad, offering the furniture and appliances for sale. I didn't like the idea of buyers trooping past Mrs. Wright's scrutiny and hauling furniture out, but she probably had already decided I was up to something.

The first day of the ad, a woman made an offer on the new washer and dryer. It had been listed in the settlement as belonging to Val, but I sold it anyway. My misdemeanors were already adding up, but as Sid said repeatedly, money was the life-blood of a successful escape.

The next day, in the midst of my hell-bent struggle with packing and last minute details, a man came and said he wanted all of the remaining furniture. One problem. He was leaving on vacation and wouldn't be home until the day before Launch Day. We negotiated a price of fifteen hundred dollars. He had credentials and looked trustworthy; his was an offer I couldn't refuse.

Launch Day minus two weeks. The passport arrived in the mail. I ran excited fingers over the photo: Lee Coburn and two children, Lori and Ryan.

If we make it. Dear God, let us succeed.

July 20, 1976. Launch day minus one week. I had signed and notarized a document giving power of attorney to my former business partners and timed the mailing with Sid's help to arrive after my departure. I also signed over power of attorney to the real estate woman handling the sale of the house, with instructions to mail net proceeds to my parents in Escondido, California. A portion of it would help repay my father's loan.

I planned not to tell my parents or my sister, Randi, until we were resettled, if then. Sid Silano: Trust no one, Lee, no one. The fewer people you tell, the less people you put under pressure and in personal jeopardy, and the safer you are, yourself. Tell no one. There is no such thing as a kept secret.

The final weekend I spent working on last minute packing and checking my lists, getting the documents in order, putting them in separate packets. There were three identities now: Coburn, Landau, Landel — the last and most important one the least effectively documented. It wouldn't do to get them mixed up. I also had to remember the bogus adult names under which I had purchased plane tickets for the first leg to Houston.

At times I had to pause, sit down, have some juice, and stop the names and numbers from whirling in my head.

By Monday evening, I had things more or less under control and fell into bed around nine, hoping to get a full night's sleep. The phone woke me around eleven. The buyer for the furniture was back in town. We arranged for him to bring a truck the next day. Tuesday morning, we spent loading his truck. Mrs. Wright's old Dodge was gone from her parking space, thank heaven. I took that as a good sign. At the last minute, the buyer asked for a couple of large plants as a bonus and got them. He wrote me a check for fifteen hundred dollars.

I wandered through the empty house, restlessly checking my bags and camping gear a second time. I no longer had an active bank account and the furniture buyer's check was written on a small bank on the west edge of the city. I would endorse it and give it to Sid for safekeeping at our farewell dinner that night.

We ate alone, toast and eggs again, poached this time. Carrie was at Girl Scouts. Sid grew reminiscent.

"Times are changing, Lee. My wife was known as a tomboy when I married her, your Katherine Hepburn type. Hell, I taught her to fly. In the end, she was better than me. Carrie, too, she's going to be something else. It's the women who are throwing the marriages away now. That's okay, I guess, but how come equality's still unequal? You tell me."

I gave him the check, and he promised to hold the money for me until I sent for it. We agreed I should call him at home, not at his workplace and I would use a code name: Jack Taylor of Chicago. He repeated his warnings about always covering my tracks, trusting nobody, bracing for mistakes, being prepared to take desperate measures whenever necessary.

At the door, we shook hands. Then, in final farewell, a strange intense look of mingled pain and relish came into his eyes. It was no surprise that his final words should concern women.

"You'll run into them along the way, of course. Chat 'em up, get them to bed when you can. Use them, or they'll use you. I think you know that by now."

"I guess I do," I said. In leaving, I felt more deeply than ever that contrary blend of fellowship and distaste I had always felt around Sid.

Alone in the dark parking lot beside my Olds, my emotion was more rudimentary. I had just said good-bye to the only confidant I had. I was on my own now, and scared.

The clock struck midnight as I walked in the door. The phone rang at 12:30. Val.

"I've made sure the kids have new parkas, since you'll be camping."

"That's nice."

"While you're gone, I'd like to come into the house and check for some things in the attic."

Panic. If she saw the old toys gone from the attic, she would know something was up. We had saved them over the years as keepsakes to give to the kids when they were grown.

"What things?" I stalled.

"Oh, Lori's teddy bear, Ryan's Bullwinkle."

"They'll be okay here."

"And the box of baby clothes in the attic, also. I just want to look around."

She would also see that the washer, dryer, and furniture were gone. I hadn't had time to change the locks; she still had a front door key. Besides, I knew she'd get into the house one way or another.

"Okay," I said.

"Good," she said. "They'll be ready at eight tomorrow morning. Call me in a week."

"You'll hear from us before the eighth day."

"I'd better."

Click.

Now I would have to move the toys and baby clothes back into the house from the south-end storage place. I tried to sleep, but didn't drop off until around three. The alarm jerked me awake at six. I crawled into the car, holding my coffee as I drove, spilling it twice. Inside the storage locker I sorted cartons, crammed them into the trunk and back seat, then drove back to the house through the humid dawn.

I would let her figure I had sold the furniture because I was leaving town on my own. But if the kids' toys and mementos were gone, too, she would quickly assume I was taking the children.

Teddy and Bullwinkle stared up at me as I stowed the cartons in the attic. There I found the framed portrait of Val and stood for long seconds staring down at it. The placid beautiful face stared up at me.

"It doesn't look like me," she had complained.

"I loved you," I muttered back, and put my foot on the dusty glass and the face beneath. The glass resisted a little, then crunched under my grinding heel.

I thought of removing it, but when I imagined her finding the picture, I couldn't resist leaving it there, even if it meant tipping her off to what I had done.

Realizing I wasn't going to be ready by eight, I rushed downstairs to call her. That was when I picked up the sealed envelope containing the divorce decree. I carried my sweat-soaked silk shirt downstairs, went through all my false documents twice, packed my two briefcases.

After loading the car, I made a last restless tour of the house, stuck for long minutes in my querencia, that place where the wing-back chair had stood, where she had announced she was leaving, where I had pounded the rug with the rolled newspaper night after night.

Still, I was unable to separate myself from this house of pain, staring at the foil-covered wall where I had planned to scrawl an obscene farewell. I threw the crayon aside. The smashed photograph was message enough.

Then struggling to get free of the house, weeping in the hall, putting my fist through the wall, stuffing the wet shirt into the hole.

Wait, just you wait . . .

Closing the door behind me for the last time, moving now toward freedom. The bright, excited faces of the kids. Our driving to Century Center to leave the leased car and switch to the taxi. The cabby's questions, his inquisitive face in the rearview mirror. The beginnings of paranoia.

Delta flight 576, the dry weeds leaning in the engine backwash, the plane lumbering down the runway.

Liftoff.

Exhilaration and fear through the three long legs of travel: Houston, Los Angeles, the continent slipping away beneath us, sleep and the nightmare of Mrs. Wright and the Mistake.

"Wake up, Dad. Hawaii! Hawaii!"

We checked into the airport Holiday Inn, and half an hour later I stood beside the lighted pool, watching the kids splash and play as if they had not just traveled 5,000 miles. Back in Atlanta, it was 3:00 a.m. Val was sleeping. Tomorrow or the day after, she would let herself into the D'Youville condo, would see the hole my fist had smashed in the wall, find the wadded shirt, then go up to the attic and discover the brutalized photograph.

I relished the thought. Sweet vengeance.

A sudden weariness set in. When the kids finally tired of the pool, we went to our room. They fell asleep the minute they hit their beds. I did the same.

Dreams filled my sleep: memories of boyhood in Fulda, playing in the alleys, waiting for the church bells to call me home, then Val at the Deaconess Hospital dance, placid and perfect, a dream goddess.

All I wanted was a quiet, loving life . . .

As I write, I see that man asleep from the distance of time. I feel a certain removed affection for him. He didn't know it, but he had only begun his desperate journey.

Seven

A New Beginning

Willfulness is characterized
by grandiosity and unbridled
attempts to control . . .
Willfulness is playing god.

— John Bradshaw

When we awoke, morning had grown up bright and sassy. Around the swimming pool, burnt flakes of sunlight sprinkled through the lazy palm trees, splashing shadows across the still water. Outside, the ocean air was a sweet liquid that enveloped me and made me feel like whistling or singing before doing another thing. Clearly, we had come to paradise where anything was possible.

After a leisurely breakfast, we walked to the rent-a-car desk, and paradise gave me my first nudging jolt. The lady attendant told me cars were rented only to major credit card holders. Worse still, I realized that if I used my Coburn or Landau Georgia driver's licenses and happened to get a speeding ticket or have an accident, the report could end up on computer records in Georgia within hours, thanks to the microchip.

"I don't use credit cards," I told her. "There are still a few traveling dinosaurs left like me who prefer to carry cash." I let her see the wad in my wallet.

"Well then," she cheerily suggested, "one week's cash deposit should do it. May I see your driver's license?"

I had no choice. The Landel identity was not yet supported by a driver's license, so I handed her my Landau license and promised myself to drive very carefully.

Perfect, a perky, red Subaru. Let's go, kids. We stowed the bags and piled in, Lori riding shotgun in the bucket seat beside me, Ryan leaning eagerly forward with his head between us.

"A pineapple field! Can we go watch them pick pineapples, Dad?" he asked.

The ocean, a sparkling sheet of crimson blue, stretched out to meet the sun-paled sky at the horizon.

"Let's go swimming!" cried Lori.

"And surfing!" Ryan added.

"Whoa! We'll do all of it," I promised them. "But first, let's get the lay of the land."

We drove with the windows rolled down, letting the ocean breeze-cool the car and blow our hair wild. Nimitz Highway turned into Ala Moana Boulevard. We passed the palm-studded lawns of Ala Moana Park, past Ward Warehouse and Fisherman's Wharf, then across AlaWai Canal. We gaped our way into Waikiki, passing the twenty-story mosaic on the side of the Hawaiian Village Hilton Hotel. As I turned right onto Kalakaua Avenue, we rolled by grand old hotels I knew only from my reading: the Royal Hawaiian, the Moana, the Ilikai. Everywhere were beaming faces and pineapple shirts, bare, sun-tanned arms and legs, shuffling thongs or bare feet. Thinking budget, I selected the Holiday Surf Hotel two blocks back from the beach.

For $32.00 a night, Lee Landel and two children registered and were elevatored to a newly furnished corner room on the seventh floor. Lori declared, "Plush! Now let's go swim!"

As we strolled the beach, I felt fish-belly pale, not having been near the D'Youville pool during the past miserable months.

I squinted and blinked in the sun, like a prisoner fresh from solitary. Quietly triumphant and thoroughly pleasured, I watched my nut-brown, blond Georgia aborigines venture into a surf the likes of which neither they nor I had ever seen. The surf rose up, broke, and foamed in. The kids shrieked with glee, retreated, then joined hands and charged back at the waves. Within minutes, they were swimming about as casually as they had at home in the pool.

I watched, concerned they might swim out too far. Seeing no lifeguard, I didn't want to leave their safety to chance. At this level of enthusiasm, I could tell they were going to be content, but maybe forgetful about the dangers.

Spreading a towel, I lay on the warm sand to relax. As I leaned on one elbow to watch them swim in the surf, I thought about the significance of our being here.

To my left, rising above the tree covered Kapiolani Park, rested Diamond Head Crater, her great eminence providing strength and peace to those who paused long enough to feel her power. The permanence of the majestic landmark, as ancient as Hawaii itself, made me feel fragile by comparison.

How had I come this far?

I tried to fathom the meaning of the past twenty-four hours. Had I come six thousand miles to lie on this beach at the foot of Diamond Head, to become nonexistent? Our lives would never be the same. But I didn't want them to be. How could I return to what my life had been — outside a decorative wrapper, inside a wasteland of despair and disappointment? I felt burning anger at Val for making me look at myself so closely. Would this anger lead me to an inner journey I had long avoided?

I relished the comfort of my body's snug fit in the loose, warm sand. How much better that we were six thousand miles away from "Whatzername." She had put me down in front of Lori and Ryan for the last time. She could have her Dr. Reynolds; she could live her life: and she could belittle me; but I lay here, relieved to be here even if I was full of worry over the future. Month after month I'd told myself to "just wait . . . just wait." Now she can wait.

Looking out onto the shimmering Pacific I felt scared yet satisfied, immensely satisfied. No longer would I be snuffed out, stepped on and relegated to being a weekend father by Val. Now, the pendulum had swung. Steaming inside, I thought, *You got what you deserved, Val. Now we can make a new life without your menacing, controlling presence. You bitch.*

But I also felt diminished and small. My life stood at a cold stop, empty. Could I build a life without a history or profession and do it with two children at my side? Had my vengeful rage set me on a course which would be destructive to everyone? Had I foolishly attempted the impossible? Worse yet, was I on a path of self-destruction?

I sat up to keep a better watch on the kids, at the same time furtively studying nearby faces. We were off the continent, far from Atlanta, but how could I be sure we were safe on this world-famous and popular beach? I could name a dozen professional and business acquaintances who vacationed on the islands.

Even more dreadful, sooner or later, I would have to tell the kids we were not going back. If they demanded we return, what could I say? What would I do?

I had told Val I would phone her in a week, by the eighth day of our "vacation." I promised myself I would tell the children before then.

Having a deadline helped. I propped my neck on a rolled towel to keep an eye on them. *Take it easy, Lee. This is the beginning of a new life. Enjoy it if you can. Take one day at a time.*

❧

After three days on the beach at Waikiki, we were still enjoying every minute and getting browner by the hour. While the children swam, I planned the next phase of our vacation, realizing the time had come for us to begin our camping tour of the island.

Looking at a map of Oahu, I noticed the coastline was dotted with beach parks. I hoped these were parks we could camp at along the way.

We checked out of the hotel and drove east to Koko Head Crater, past Hanauma Bay, and then north up the windward coast, exhilarated by the dramatic beauty of the lava coastline and new vistas at every bend in the road. By mid-afternoon, we had pulled into the parking lot at Makapuu Beach. Its famous surf rose ten feet high, breaking just offshore with such force you could feel the impact under the soles of your feet. We danced across the hot, white sand and laid out our towels.

Lori and Ryan were eager to go nearer to the pounding roar of the big waves. They promised me they would stay in the shallow after-wash. Once they were content, I swam out to try my hand at body surfing. The locals made it look easy. It wasn't. After half an hour of barely surviving, I headed back, struggling to walk in against the strong undercurrent.

Squinting through foaming salt water, I saw Lori sitting on a sand dune. She watched as the thundering surf broke over the swimmers, all dwarfed by the huge waves cascading over them after each new breaker crested.

Ryan played in the shallow backwash of the bigger waves that rolled far up onto the beach. The after-tow pulled him out to sea like hands that caress, yet threaten. Oblivious to any danger, he made his own fun, his eyes glimmering with delight.

He waited for the surf's foamy remains to spill over his legs, then pull him toward the water in the receding backwash. Left stranded on the glazed beach, he'd wait for another wave and another ride.

From her secure perch on the beach, Lori kept shouting to him, "Ryan, don't go out so far. Stay in the shallow water."

He couldn't hear her.

I walked over to him, "Come on, Ryan, let's get closer to the waves." We waded out deeper, while I kept a firm hold on his hand. I leaned down to speak, shouting over the deafening rumble, and for a crucial second I ceased to watch the ten-foot-high breakers.

One hit us. It crushed us to the ocean floor. Thrashed us out of control. We gulped sand and salt water. Stunned and confused, clutching Ryan, I fought for the surface. We popped up, lungs bursting for air. Ryan coughed and cried, spitting sand from his mouth. We stumbled to our feet.

Another wave slammed over us. Down again. Hard. Another grinding slide across the bottom. Our bodies pounded the ocean floor.

Close to blanking out, I gripped Ryan's wrist as if it were life itself, knowing if I let go he would be swept out to sea.

The frothing water subsided. We surfaced for air, choking, gasping. Still holding Ryan's wrist, we staggered to the dry beach. Ryan's face looked as if it had been scraped across a food grater.

Lori screamed, "Dad! Ryan! You nearly died!"

Maybe it hadn't been that serious, maybe it had. But for a few minutes, we sat huddled under the blanket of the afternoon sun, feeling what it was like to be together again. We clasped hands, reunited, thankful we were all alive. After a while, we loaded into the car and continued our tour of the island.

❧

Our days drifted one into another as we explored every beach we could find. If we were intrigued by something, we explored further to satisfy our curiosity. Time seemed to have washed out to sea. What mattered was our being together. Every minute was precious, as if any moment might be our last. Beneath the tranquillity and exaltation of our exile lay my deepest concern. Each campsite and every day of swimming moved me closer to the inevitable, telling Lori and Ryan we were not returning to Atlanta.

How could I tell them to lessen their anguish? I didn't want to hurt them. And yet I knew that not returning to Atlanta and their mother would be painful. What frightened me most was not knowing how much pain I might cause and what the emotional consequences might be. I was especially afraid for Ryan, whom I loved, but who had always been his mother's favorite.

I no longer questioned my decision to remain in Hawaii. For

months, I had thought through this moment of crossing over into a new future when I told Lori and Ryan we were not going home. Now I knew, with each passing day, I had to do it soon. I hadn't wanted to put off telling them beyond the eighth day. We were now into our tenth day of vacation. So far, our adventures had kept them content, but the time neared when they would ask, "Dad, when are we going home?" Better I tell them before they asked.

Ten days in Hawaii and we were as content to be together as on the first. We had yet to tire of the solitude, the beaches, the ocean, the pleasures of people at crowded parks, and especially the harmony and peacefulness of being together. Our temporary escape from worldly responsibilities was exhilarating. Yet in my heart, I carried a bundle of grave concerns for our immediate safety and our future existence. Only the sheer pleasure of living wild and free on a tropical island with the two people I loved and trusted most lightened my load.

Each day on these deserted beaches, walking and running and laughing and talking with Lori and Ryan, encouraged me to change my life. I had never felt so vulnerable, so open to understanding the inner self of me that had brought us to this island. My actions would be called selfish, even abusive, certainly illegal, yet for now I was driven to keep us together.

We camped at Kualoa Beach Park, moved north and visited Sacred Falls, climbing through bamboo groves to the fifty-foot waterfall, swimming in the ice-cold waters of the pool while the lacy falls misted us in fine spray. We continued north to the Mormon Temple and farther to the Kahuku Sugar Mill. Lori loved the mellow colors of the ancient wooden machinery, and Ryan gasped as he watched the caged mongoose kill a cobra.

Early afternoon of the eleventh day, we strolled the lavish grounds of Del Webb Resort, beautifully perched on the northernmost tip of the island. We milled about, absorbed in the natural splendor of ocean and ancient rocky shores, now graced with luscious lawns and occasional white sandy beaches. At the pool, we rested on chaise lounge chairs. Wearing our swimsuits, tanned and relaxed, we blended with the poolside crowd.

A boy Lori's age invited her and Ryan to play Marco Polo with the other kids. They dove in and were soon whooping and tossing the ball as if they were with old friends.

I marveled at how adaptable they were, how ready to take things as they came. Lori showed off her trim diving form. Ryan, knees and elbows to the sky, cannonballed from poolside. Lori followed from the three-meter board, making a higher splash.

I dodged the fallout and settled back into my deck chair. If only it could go on like this. I closed my eyes, clinging to the fantasy. Lori came over to dry herself and stretched out on the chair beside mine. I opened my eyes and just for an instant caught that sad, faraway look in her eyes, the two fine lines between her brows reminding me of Val. No, it wasn't going to be all that easy for me. They had worries, too. Now I would add to the pain their parents had brought them.

I ordered Cokes for each of us. When we'd been served, I took a deep drink, then a deep breath. "Lori, it's been on my mind to tell you something."

"What's that, Dad?"

"Well, I don't know how you'll feel about this, but I've decided we're not going back to Georgia. We are going to stay here in Hawaii. Maybe later we can return, but for now, this is where we're going to live."

The delicate frown returned to her brow. My heart sank. I had spoken it as firmly as I could, as fait accompli, established policy. What if she said she absolutely didn't want to stay? What if the pain of this was too much for her?

"You mean Ryan and I are going to go to school here?" she asked.

"Yes. We'll find a place in Honolulu and register the two of you for this fall. We'll make it our home."

"Does this mean we'll live here from now on?"

"As long as we can and as long as we like it. You see, if we go back, we won't be able to be together. In Atlanta, you would have a stepfather, and I'd only see you a couple of times a month."

The two lines deepened. "I'll miss Emily. She's the best friend I ever had."

She meant her D'Youville friend, daughter of Nan and Jody Powell. "I know she'll always stay special to you, but you'll make new friends here. Maybe someday you can see her again."

I waited, wondering if she saw in that the possibility that she might also see her mother again some day. Would she reveal her sadness over missing her mother?

"I'll miss my musical jewelry box and canopy bed," she said. "What will happen to them?"

We both knew they had been left in Val's apartment. "Your mother will keep them," I said. "Someday you'll be able to see her and your canopy bed again."

There, it was said. Like pulling my own tooth, but in her way, she had requested it, and it was, of course, her right.

"At least, I have my bracelet." She turned it thoughtfully on her slender wrist. A simple, twisted design of copper and silver, given to her by "Whatzername." Or had it been from Dr. Reynolds? I was beginning to hate the thing. But then, it was all the jewelry she had now.

"Yes, you have that," I said. "And we'll get you other nice things. We're only starting. We'll have a new and good life. I promise that."

Silence. She pondered. I stayed quiet, giving her space. The two little lines fluttered, then her brow smoothed, and she looked me solemnly in the eye. "Daddy, I think it would be fine with me, as long as we're together."

Holding her look at me, her face still serious, she said, "Daddy?"

"Yes?"

"What about Ryan? He's going to miss Mommy."

"I know."

"When do you think you'll tell him?" she asked.

I watched Ryan preparing to jump again from the diving board. He looked so slight and vulnerable, like a skinny, wet monkey.

"I don't know," I murmured. "Later. Don't say anything about this now, Lori. He's having too much fun. Maybe it would be best to tell him tomorrow morning. In the meantime, young lady, let's see you get up on that high board and do a straight dive, not just a cannonball."

She hesitated. "Do you think I can do it?"

"Just like you do from the low board, except push out a little farther, that's all. You can do it."

And she did, to a scattering of applause from the poolside crowd.

Lori had assimilated the news of not returning to Georgia as thoughtfully as if I'd said we were staying in Hawaii another month. She had struggled with her immediate feelings of loss, which had not included her mother, since she was still angry at her for breaking up the family. She must have concluded she could handle not going back as long as we were together.

She climbed the high board to prepare for another dive. Now Lori knew she wasn't going back. Nothing had changed. In her heart, she knew she would be without her mother, her best friend, Emily, and her canopy bed. I watched her spring from the board, arch, then dive like an arrow penetrating the water. *Lori will be all right,* convincing myself.

I worried now about telling Ryan. He was younger and had a greater attachment to his mother. Though he felt safe with me, I knew it would be difficult for him to accept not seeing his mommy again.

Shadows lengthened as the ocean breezes lost their warmth, reminding us that our rite of indulgence at the Del Webb Resort had come to a close. We didn't want to leave.

We drove west along the coastline. As evening light shimmered across the rolling surf, we passed Sunset Beach and the world-famous Banzai Pipeline. We continued around Waimea Bay through Haleiuea to Highway 93 at Awialua, heading due west to

Kaena Point. Earlier, I had decided we would camp the night at Moluleia Beach Park, hoping to add another adventure to our travels at Dillingham Field, the small airstrip nearby.

The entrance to the park lay just past the airstrip. Wind whipped off the ocean as if a storm were in the making. We found shelter for a camp site behind one of the high dunes that separated the park from the beaches.

Twilight and the distant sounds of campers quieted my nerves as I thought about telling Ryan. I built a fire and grilled porkchops while the children explored the dunes. As I crawled from the tent after unrolling the sleeping bags, a dog ran by with a porkchop in his mouth. Three remained for us. I stayed close to the grill until Lori and Ryan returned, by then famished.

After dinner, I sat watching the dune grass bend in the wind; the moon painted a silvery shine on every blade. A few brief spears of clouds moved across the face of the moon. I listened to the wind make its way southward across sugar cane fields. Tonight, I had to tell Ryan. But after the excitement of the dog and settling down around the fire, I decided to wait.

The early morning sun rose rich to illuminate our tent with pinkish light. Another perfect day in paradise; but I awoke with a headache, reminding myself, *for God's sake, tell Ryan.* Lori stayed near the tent, while I walked with him to the restroom. Finishing first, I seated myself in one of the playground swings to catch the cool breeze off the dunes.

Ryan emerged after completing what he called the day's "major job." He saw me and came over. In Honolulu, he had noticed some motorcycle types and had picked up the trick of rolling the sleeves of his pineapple shirt, ostensibly to display his biceps. My skinny little eight-year-old didn't have much to show yet.

"Sit a minute, Ryan."

"Sure. Great day, huh, Dad?"

"Yes. You know, I've been thinking about what it was like in Georgia."

His eyes lost their early morning luster. He looked perplexed and worried.

"I mean, we weren't happy there," I said. "It wasn't good, with you and Lori away all the time and the doctor and all. It was going to get worse, you know, once the divorce went into effect. I wouldn't be able to see you for more than a weekend at a time."

He stopped swinging, sat motionless staring away from me.

"We're going to stay in Hawaii, Ryan. Maybe later we'll return. Right now, we give up too much to go back."

I stood in front of him, watching bewilderment and then comprehension draw his face into a haggard mask. Tears rolled down his cheeks.

"Ryan . . ." I fell to my knees and wrapped my arms around him. His body shuddered, helplessly lurched against mine. My tears mingled with his. I felt pain and sorrow I didn't know existed. The two of us, alone in the middle of nowhere, hugged as if our lives depended on each other.

I had hurt my son, taking from him what I knew I could never give back. I would never forget the pain in his eyes that flowed from his heart onto my shoulder. Would there be a void forever haunting him, a sadness tingeing every corner of his future? Was this a wound he might never heal?

My body shuddered with fear.

I'm not sure how long I crouched there, holding him and trying to absorb his pain. If only I could draw it out of his small, shaking body, soak it up, and bear it myself.

I had tried to brace myself for this guilt. But no preparation would have eased what I was feeling: fear and shame all wrapped into one. I promised myself I would give back to him all that my life could offer, though I feared I would fail and his loss might never heal; that he might hold this against me for the rest of our lives.

Slowly, our crying stopped. He knuckled the tears from his eyes and drew away from me. I held his hand as we walked across the lawn to meet Lori. She immediately took charge of packing up, handing Ryan two sleeping bags to put in the car.

He straightened his narrow shoulders and managed a crisp, "Sure, no problem."

While they finished packing, I reviewed my situation. Val would be panicking now, telephoning mutual friends, prying for clues. Would she call Sid? Would he hold firm in our secret brotherhood of revenge? Had I tipped my hand to anyone in any way? By now, Frank and Stan would have puzzled over the power of attorney I had sent them. If complications arose with the business, would they consider my defection an opportunity to deflect the heat toward me? My mind raced with questions and concerns as we placed the last items of gear in the car.

In a sudden burst of exuberance, Lori and Ryan begged to drive the Subaru. Relenting, I gave them each a turn driving around the park, while I sat in the passenger seat, trying to appear relaxed. I was poised to turn off the ignition and pull on the emergency brake if things went wrong.

"My turn," I said.

I drove while they filled the car with talk about driving. We pulled into the parking area at Dillingham Field to watch the gliders soar the heat thermals along the coast, then return to swoosh in for their silent landings. Of course, the children wanted to go up in one but accepted taking turns in the seat of a grounded glider. Ryan cranked the controls and made machine gun sounds. Lori said she hoped someday she could sky-dive.

Driving away from the airfield, I felt Ryan again in my arms, braced against the pain neither of us understood. For us both, a permanent notch had been carved on our hearts. Would the scars made today ever heal? How deeply and how long would our lives be affected by this morning? How much damage had I caused?

We turned onto Kaukonahua Road through the town of Waialua, and headed south to Honolulu. Our vacation had come to an end. We'd lived on wind swept deserted beaches for almost two weeks and had grown a little tired of sand fleas and grit in our beds. When I announced we would head back to Honolulu and begin looking for a place to live, the children bounced in their seats and cheered.

"Dad, can we stay in a hotel with a pool, by the beach like we did before?" Ryan asked.

"Yes, one more time," I said, although I had gone over our finances and was beginning to get the budget blues.

The Holiday Surf welcomed us back and gave us the same corner room on the seventh floor. I registered for three nights, and while the kids swam in the pool, I itemized what I had to do next: find a home, get the children registered in school, send for the clock and the crate, and find a job. The first and second held the most risk. I dreaded the complications that lay ahead of me.

To rent an apartment, I needed complete identification, which I did not yet have, personal references, and sources for credit checks. I didn't even want to think about the most difficult task — entering Lori and Ryan into school. Could it even be done? The information and forms required by schools worried me. How could I make it through registration from their old school to a new school without someone detecting the phony records?

Okay, Lee, slow down. Deal with that matter when the time comes. First, we need to find a permanent home. Just knowing we were in one place for three nights had a hint of permanence. We might as well enjoy ourselves a while longer.

And we did, letting the excitement of Waikiki once again intoxicate us with its dazzling animation. Time passed as effortlessly as the swaying of palm trees and with such ease we were certain we'd remember every day forever. Being in the present we preferred; looking ahead was scary; looking back hurt too much. So we dove into the moment.

On our second day at the Holiday Surf, a hotel employee offered the kids a Siamese kitten. Though concerned the hotel management would object, I agreed. The little furball would replace Georgie Girl. And besides, we needed to begin building domestic permanency.

The maid gleefully helped us keep Georgie Girl II's presence a secret. I explained to her we were staying only another two nights. She said not to worry. "I clean this room, so no one needs to know except us." She emphasized the word *us.*

With that, Georgie Girl moved to center stage. We three were now four.

❧

"Money is your life blood," Sid had warned. "Without it, you're history. Dead."

I didn't need his warning to have the fear of running out of funds permeate my consciousness. Each purchase I made brought the fear of losing Lori and Ryan home that much closer.

Our next major expense would be renting an apartment. I had no idea what housing cost. I just knew paying too much in rent would rapidly consume our meager money supply, sharply reducing the time allowed for me to find a job. Under too much pressure, I might make mistakes and reveal our true identity.

One afternoon, I looked up an address for garden condominiums on the east side of Diamond Head, a neighborhood known as the Kahala area, one of the finest in the city. Almost directly across the street sat Wilson Elementary School, with its handsome open-air architecture and lush green lawns.

Waialua Garden Condominiums boasted rambling two-story buildings snuggled under huge, indigenous trees amidst tropical landscaping. With the kids trailing excitedly, the agent showed us a two-level, carpeted townhouse unit with two bedrooms, two baths, and patio onto a private lawn, $450 a month. The two-story floor plan came close to what we were accustomed to. While the kids whooped through the rooms, I gave the agent a $200 cash deposit. She told me to come into her office in the morning to sign the lease.

Faced with another identity challenge, I decided to use my Landel alias, despite the fact that much of the documentation was unfinished. The next morning, I greeted the agent, scared but determined to pull it off. We were from Denver, I told her, where my marriage had broken up because of my wife's drinking. Poor woman, the court had determined her unfit for custody. I planned to start a new life here in Hawaii, while she underwent treatment back in Denver.

The agent understood. Her sister had suffered similarly with a boozing husband. Keeping it conversational, I let her know my professional background, staying with the truth except geographical locations. The truth helped eased the sting of guilt I felt for being deceptive.

I paid the balance of the rent and deposits with $900 in cash. The next item on my agenda, I said, was to open a bank account. Did she know of a reliable bank? I would need it for making large financial transactions soon, some of which would be in her own field. She offered suggestions, responding to our lively discussion of development and real estate law, the angles, the loopholes. I didn't care for the flow of interwoven truth and fiction that spilled from me. I had always avoided deliberate distortions and their risks, yet here I spoke, ladling it out like an experienced con man.

Sid, I reflected, would be proud of me.

I felt ashamed, yet knew I had to do whatever it took to keep us afloat.

"Well, Mr. Landel," she said as we shook hands. She gave me a conspiratorial wink and for an instant, I wondered if she knew I was a semi-fraud. "I'm sure you and the children will be happy in your new place. I wish you well with your . . . enterprise. If I can be of any help, let me know."

As I drove to the hotel, I considered her ready acceptance of me without a glance at any credentials. The complex did have a number of vacancies, and I had paid in cash, but there are people who respect you for going after what you want even if you skirt normal channels. These people cultivate a high tolerance for BS, with no aversion to a little white-collar fraud, if it comes to that.

My view of the world had changed since leaving Atlanta, and

not all, it seemed to me, for the best. There was the possibility that in exploiting this harder edge of reality, I might come to accept it and be thrown off my moral balance even further. I didn't want that to happen. I wanted both the children and myself to come out of this with our souls intact.

In the meantime, forgetting the problem came easy. I collected the kids and rushed us off to our new home. A half hour later, I threw open the door and they ran through the empty rooms, deciding who would sleep where, then stripped to their suits and headed for the pool.

The place felt tranquilized — no furniture, no phone, no car; and so was my life — no job, no identity. And yet, as I gazed out the sliding doors, watching my two carefree porpoises take to the water, I decided we had what we needed to survive. We had each other. We also had completed the first step of our journey into the unknown.

Though meeting with the occasionally felonious survivor in me, I was also discovering a less guarded, more open and reflective self.

Family, I had been taught growing up in Fulda, is the only lasting confirmation of love. The three of us were reaffirming that, even if we didn't have the traditional complement of members. We three (and the cat) had found a new level of acceptance among us. Where had I been all those years? Was coming to know this darker side of myself also revealing its opposite, the gold and good within me I had previously not known?

And with that thought, I turned my attention to Wilson Elementary School, just across the street, where files, computers, and alert administrators waited.

In there, I would face the toughest challenge to date.

EIGHT

WHO ARE WE?

When a man undertakes to play a part on the stage . . . he is got into a track where he will find nothing but briars and thorns.

— William Hazlitt

A month had past since the children and I had arrived in Hawaii, and we were still camping in our Waialua Garden apartment, sleeping on the carpeted floor in sleeping bags, eating with plastic utensils off paper plates. We did have three folding chairs, and I had made each of us a desk from plywood and wooden sawhorses, small ones for them, a larger one for me.

I was sitting at it when Lori appeared in the open doorway, a beach towel around her, hair wet and tousled from swimming.

"Dad, who are we?"

I had wondered when this question might come since she and Ryan had heard me lease the Subaru at the airport.

"We're us," I answered. "You know, the Titanic Trio. We Three."

She sat down next to me. "I know. But those kids asked me my name, and I didn't want to say Coburn."

So typical of Lori to wait, think it out, but be ready. She had heard me introduce myself to the airport rental car agent as Lee Landel. When she had asked why then, I explained that in case they overcharged us and tried to contact me about payment, they wouldn't be able to.

She had also heard me use the name several times with the

rental agent. I had told her then that Val might be looking for us. Now, having been cornered by the neighborhood kids, she waited for me to make it all clear.

"What did you tell them?" I asked.

She giggled. "Puddin-tain, ask me again and I'll tell you the same." She grew serious. "It's bothering Ryan, Dad. And pretty soon we're going to school, aren't we?"

"You're right," I said, with an uncomfortable glance at the bogus documents spread out on my desk. "We have to decide." I shifted my chair to face her. "I think it would be best if we just changed our last name to Landel. Our first names will still be the same, but we should try to think of ourselves as Landel now and forget Coburn."

She tried the name several times out loud and frowned. "It sounds funny. Couldn't we think up a better one?"

I chuckled. "I should have thought of that. What an opportunity. Like maybe Rockefeller?"

"Or the Duke and Duchess of Windsor." She laughed. "Or we could be the Brady Bunch. I could be the mom, you dad, and Ryan that awful little boy, Whatshisname."

"Trouble is," I said, "it's too late." I pointed to the papers on the desk. "We need papers like this to get you in school. I've already talked to the superintendent, and he knows me as Mr. Landel, so you two have to be Lori Landel and Ryan Landel. Let's stick with that. It's important we keep anyone in Georgia from knowing where we are. You understand that, don't you?"

She nodded thoughtfully. "I think so. To keep Mom from putting you in jail."

"Well, that's pretty extreme, but it's possible. Mainly, it's so we can keep together and get things started here. Get you in school, get me a job. Is it okay, then?"

She nodded. I wondered how much she really did understand. She was always surprising me: one minute amazingly perceptive, almost adult, the next minute the little girl she had a right to be.

"It's part of making ourselves into a new family here," I said.

"And it's pretty nifty sounding once you get used to it. Lori Landel. Ryan Landel. They have a nice ring to them. So just keep practicing it in your mind, and then we'll practice out loud."

"But what about Ryan?"

"I'm hoping he'll pick it up from us the way he does a lot of things."

"Dad, I think I better get him to practice it out loud, too."

"Good idea," I said. "Make it into a kind of game."

"Okay, Dad." She romped out the door, her towel flying behind like a cape as she raced for the pool.

School began on September 2, only five days away. To register Lori and Ryan, I needed their previous health and grade records. If I used phony records and the local officials tried to contact Fair Oaks Elementary in Georgia, they would find no such school. On the other hand, if I used their bona fide records from Nancy Creek Elementary, I was setting up an easy trace for investigators, and the hounds would be upon us. I might even end up getting a free trip back to Georgia in handcuffs.

I decided to start at the top in getting a rundown on district registration requirements. Not only would it get me the right information, but I figured it might give me some influence with the school principal if he knew I had already talked to his superior. Honolulu School Superintendent Hatanoka turned out to be a genial man who was glad to brief me on the registration process and to welcome me to Hawaii with the traditional greeting.

Of course, I also remembered that Aloha could mean "so long."

A week after my talk with Hatanoka, I walked across the street to the school. At the administration counter, an alert and cheerful Mrs. Yokamora gave me a printed list of requirements for registration.

"Tell me," I said after I had the forms in my hand, "do you contact the previous school directly?"

Mrs. Yokamora had a beautiful smile, but it never varied, so it was difficult to tell what she was thinking.

"Because I hope you do," I added, looking very much the anxious parent. "The children's grades really ought to be better than they are, and if there's any question about their qualifications or anything, I would like the chance to call their teacher so you can talk to her."

Mrs. Yokamora smiled at this stateside dummy. "That won't be necessary, Mr. Landel. We don't often contact the previous school, but I can assure you that there will be no prejudice against your children because of their grades. A public school education is available to all in Hawaii, as everywhere else in the United States."

"Well, I still wish you'd talk to their teachers."

"I'm sorry, Mr. Landel, but we simply do not have the staff or budget for that sort of thing. I hope you understand."

It had been a roundabout way to find out, but it now seemed to me they were unlikely to check out the fake Landel school documents.

I breathed a sigh of relief as the fear quieted.

The printed list of requirements for registration looked easy at first.

Transcript of previous grades.

On my desk, I laid the multicolored transcripts I had put together in Atlanta, using the Landel name. They listed mostly A's and B's. Mrs. Yokamora would be pleased with her two new, bright students.

Birth certificates to verify age.

I studied the children's homemade Landel birth certificates, indicating their correct ages but locating their births in cities other than the actual St. Petersburg, Florida, and South Bend, Indiana.

Health records and results of recent physical exam.

Getting physical examinations meant getting past a doctor and possibly showing birth records. I did have their immunization history on a phony physician's form. The school requirements indicated evidence of a scheduled physical examination would be acceptable if time ran short. I looked up a nearby private physician in the yellow pages, phoned, and asked that appointment cards be made up.

Certificate of release from the previous school.

This one worried me. I reviewed the Landel certificates of transfer I had put together before we left. They were from that fictional Fair Oaks School in the nonexistent Stuart County, with counterfeit signatures of nonexistent school officials.

By some chance, Mrs. Yokamora might be wrong. Honolulu authorities might still decide to check the certificates' validity by mail. When the envelope came back "address unknown," I could rig up some kind of explanation, including vociferous complaints about the unreliable mail service. If they tried to check by telephone, I would explain Fair Oaks was a private school and the number must have recently been changed.

That was all too flimsy, and far from fail-safe. I decided to withhold my questionable certificates of transfer and see if I could slip by that requirement.

I worried for several days over the registration form itself. The form asked for names and addresses of both father and mother, including marital status.

Mother: Val Coburn, Rollingwood Apartments, Atlanta?

Not on your tintype.

I decided to use the name on the bogus birth certificates, Mary Landel, and drew a line through the spaces for the other information. For myself, I gave our new address but no telephone number. Occupation: "Presently being determined."

That at least wasn't a lie. I hadn't had a spare minute to work on my professional credentials and job presentation.

Marital status gave me concern. If I put married and indicated the mother had died, the children were likely to be asked about their mother by sympathetic teachers and schoolmates. If I put divorced, I might be asked to show a custody decree.

I decided divorce provided a common and ready explanation for the absence of the mother. Didn't fifty percent of all marriages end in divorce these days?

Looking over the papers, I understood why Sid Silano had placed so much emphasis on the problem of identity, and I wondered, as Lori had, just who were we?

But there wasn't time for contemplation. On August 26, I went by the doctor's office to pick up the appointment cards. The nurse's questions mostly concerned the children's past medical histories. I was happy to deal with measles and not divorce.

On Friday, August 28, I dressed in my best and walked across to the school. Mrs. Yokamora, smiling irrepressibly, shuffled through my stack of papers and asked where the skin test cards were.

I told her I didn't know about skin tests. Back downtown to the city health department, where the children's upper arms were pricked for a TB test. Later, back to the health center, where their tests showed negative.

Monday morning early, I faced Mrs. Yokamora again, handing her my file of papers. The applications lay on top. She flipped through the pile, using the eraser end of her pencil. Returning to review the applications, she looked up, smiling.

"Is there a telephone number where we can reach you in case of emergency, Mr. Landel?"

"I'll let you know the number as soon as the phone's installed."

Her eraser moved down the lines of the application, pausing at "marital status," moved on to divorce, paused there, then stopped after Mother: Mary Landel. Mrs. Yokamora looked up.

"You don't know the mother's address?"

I explained that my ex-wife was an incurable alcoholic under treatment in an institution, where she was kept incommunicado.

"So sad," Mrs. Yokamora murmured with a shake of her head. "So sad these days."

I agreed, cringing at the deception.

Next, the birth certificates. My best artwork. She glanced at them just long enough to write down the serial numbers, but not the city and state of the fictional births. Good.

She perused the immunization records, the vaccine cards, the physical exam appointment card.

Finally, at the bottom of the stack were the colorful grade transcripts, not as decorative as the birth certificates, but a far more complex job of counterfeiting. She barely noticed them before pushing them across the counter.

"These you can give to the children's teachers, if you wish."

"Oh. Well, okay."

Her face brightened. "Welcome to Wilson Elementary, Mr. Landel. I expect we'll see your children tomorrow?"

I wanted to hug her and get out, but there was the nagging matter of the Certificate of Release. I couldn't have it coming up some time in the future without warning.

"I'd like the names and room numbers of Lori and Ryan's teachers," I said.

She wrote them on a card and handed it to me, her smile faltering for the first time as she glanced at her watch. It was time for her coffee break.

"Oh, Mrs. Yokamora," I said, producing my copy of the registration requirements, "about the Certificate of Transfer, I'll have to send to the states for it."

"That's fine." She made an airy gesture of dismissal. "You can bring that in when you get around to it."

She smiled, nodded good-bye, and moved briskly toward the coffee machine.

That afternoon, I opened a bank account, relieved to have the cash in a safer place, but also alarmed at how quickly our funds had dwindled. With little more than three thousand remaining, I had to find a job fast. I still had work to do on my Landel credentials and job presentation, and I couldn't print a résumé until I had a telephone number.

Electric service began with no complications, but ordering a telephone might not go as smoothly. The questions I would be asked were to some extent regulated by the FCC, but I didn't know exactly what they would be. Dressed in my linen suit and tie, stomach churning, I drove downtown to Hawaii Bell. After a short wait, I drew a perky customer service representative, who introduced herself as Caroline CanIHelpYou.

"I'd like to begin phone service. One phone, single party line."

I told her I was Lee Landel, an attorney on the islands for the first time. A good home base for my new consulting business.

"I see. Will you be doing a lot of long distance calling?"

Experience told me that there would be an additional deposit if I said yes. Thank God I hadn't said I was in import-export as I had planned.

"No, not much," I answered. "Only personal and a few local business calls. Real estate, mostly."

"Where did you have prior telephone service, Mr. Landel?"

This one I'd expected. "I did a lot of continent hopping in my past business. Always used a forwarding message service. Unless you want to go back to Minneapolis about ten years ago."

She didn't look up from filling in her form; I sensed a silence I felt compelled to fill. "Now that I'm divorced and with my kids, I'm looking forward to settling down here."

"Is there someone we can contact in case of an emergency?"

This one I hadn't anticipated. As I thought frantically, Sid's warning nagged: "Luck won't always be with you."

Atlanta was out; my sister Randi was out; everyone I ever knew was out. I named my parents, using the Landel last name. From some obscure source, I dredged up the number 2430 and a street named Bayway Drive.

With my service order in hand, sighing relief, I exited into the sunshine. I had been lucky so far, but if the service representative checked my parents as a reference and discovered the address to be phony, there could be trouble.

Still the worst that could happen would be having the phone service refused.

When I could not give a reference or next of kin, I realized if something happened to the three of us, no one from our past life would know. We hadn't just disappeared off the continent, we had, in a sense, disappeared off the globe. Every tie to those who cared for us had been severed.

Alone, but together. That was enough for now. But as quickly as possible, I needed to establish a normal life for us. Once the kids were secure in that, any name would do.

On the night before they started school, I brought home a dozen donuts. After dinner, we made cocoa and dunked donuts and talked. The children were excited, anxious, wondered about their teachers and classmates. Lori hoped there would be an art room with a wall to paint on like the one at Nancy Creek. Ryan wondered if the school had baseball and football with real uniforms. Lori announced she planned to be an A student this year. Ryan said he hoped he wouldn't be the biggest boy in his class.

During a lull, I suggested they get their notebooks and write their names in the spaces provided on the covers.

"From tonight on, we're going to use our new last name, Landel."

Lori had obviously talked to Ryan about the name change, because his face immediately clouded over.

She brought the notebooks. I tore a piece of paper from one and printed their names. Lori Landel. Ryan Landel. I handed the paper to Ryan.

"What do you think, Ryan?"

"Why do we have to use a different name?"

"The point is, Ryan, we're starting a new life, so we should have a new name."

One thing about him, he never concealed his feelings. "If we change our names, how will Mom know where we are?"

Inside, I chuckled: he had hit the matter square in the head. "That's right," I said. "But if we use our old name, it might get back and then they could trace us here to Hawaii. If your mother finds out where we are, she will come and take you and Lori away. We won't be together anymore."

A heavy load for an eight-year-old. He was silent, his face drawn with a sorrow he didn't deserve. I put my arm around his shoulder.

"It will take a while to get used to. Remember when we decided we would stay in Hawaii? You got used to that after a while."

I gave the pen to him and helped him close his fingers on it. "Your printing is good, Ryan. Practice a few times, before putting the new name on your notebook. After that, we'll practice saying it. Then we'll lay out your clothes before going to bed. Big day tomorrow."

He bent over the paper, and as he laboriously printed Landel, his lips moved, rehearsing the new name.

The next thing I knew, 6:15 had arrived and early bird Lori was tugging at my sleeping bag, asking if it was time to get up. After orange juice and donuts for breakfast, I sent them to the bathroom to comb their hair and brush their teeth. As I passed the downstairs bathroom, I heard Ryan alternately spitting toothpaste into the sink and muttering to himself, "Ryan Landel, Ryan Landel."

I walked them to school and to their respective classrooms. Lori's teacher, Mrs. Nelson, exuded warmth, but we didn't have time to visit. We met Ryan's teacher, Mrs. Yamaguchi, a plump, pleasant woman in her forties. For a moment, she couldn't find his registration sheet but then located his name on her typed class roster. My small panic passed, only to return when she asked Ryan, "Where are you from?"

His face flushed.

"Georgia," I said quickly. "Ryan's just one of those shy, southern country boys."

She laughed and patted his shoulder. "Oh, I know about that, I married one. Not so shy once they get going, right, Ryan?"

I walked back to the quiet apartment. For the first time in over a month, I had a break from my minute-to-minute concern for the kids. I settled into my job-hunting materials but couldn't get my mind off the school and what might be happening.

At 2:30, I heard the front door open. Ryan came upstairs.

"I didn't like it."

Lori arrived shortly afterward, full of positive tidings. With orange juice and the last donuts, we sat on the floor of my room to talk over our day.

Ryan showed me the lunch menu. Lunches were better at Nancy Creek, he said, pouting. Lori didn't like the boys talking dirty, but she liked her teacher and had already made friends with one girl. They didn't have an art wall though.

"We can go to school barefoot," Ryan said, "but I'm not sure I want to."

In Lori's class, her first and last name had been called. She had given a speech about herself, saying she was from Atlanta and her father was an architect and lawyer. Ryan was glad that first names only were used. "I'm afraid I'll forget my new name," he said.

I unrolled a roll of white butcher paper I had purchased. "We'll tape this up in your bedroom and you two can have your own Scribble Wall to write or draw anything you want."

In chorus: "Allll right!"

❧

Day two of school, and still I felt uneasy. I wasn't worried about Lori, but what if Ryan's schoolmates pressed him? Where are you from? Who's your father? Where's your mother?

At 2:15, they came up the stairs to my room, smiling with excitement. Lori handed me a folded piece of paper.

A note from her teacher.

My adrenaline pulsed into red emergency before opening the mimeographed memo to all parents about the cafeteria program and school protocol. Relax.

Ryan showed me his first handwriting assignment. At the top of the paper, he had meticulously printed his name, Ryan Landel.

I asked Ryan if he wanted to shoot off the rocket he and I had built together the previous Christmas. That evening, we fired off the rocket, which took an alarming wind drift toward neighboring trees, then to our cheering relief, fell on the concrete beside the pool.

During the next week, I wandered into Lori and Ryan's room

to look over the Scribble Wall. Their drawings were everywhere: butterflies, Lori's specialty at the time; Ryan's jet planes and rocket ships, including what I took to be a Boeing 747 by the bulge on its brow. My favorite drawing featured three figures, recognizable as one adult male and two small children holding hands above arched red block letters: THE TITANIC TRIO.

Normalcy was my goal: school, the kitten, the comfort of daily routine. We made a work chart for all of us: my job hunting efforts, their homework, housework, everything portioned out, each according to abilities. We agreed on house rules: everybody picks up after himself and no swimming or cooking when I was gone. They had been shown the fire extinguisher and how to work it.

I wrote a letter to the south Atlanta storage place, requesting the grandfather clock and the large wood crate. I avoided phoning my Atlanta mail drop but knew I would have to make that dangerous contact soon. Meanwhile, I mailed an application to a New York city mail service, along with the small fee in cash.

On September 7, Lori began dance lessons. I registered the children in the Wilson Park youth program. Ryan had basketball on Mondays and Thursdays, with games Saturday mornings, football, Tuesday and Friday. Lori had cooking classes Tuesday afternoons, Girl Scout meetings after school on Thursdays.

I had turned in the Subaru to save money with plans to purchase a used car. Lori rode the Kahala No. 1 bus to her dance lessons; the park and playground activities were within easy walking distance. Scout meetings were at a church two blocks over.

Normalcy. We were getting there.

Meantime, I had to have the Landel Social Security card before I could accept any employment. Mustering my nerve, I called Atlanta on a morning when the kids were in school. I had led them to believe one could not telephone the mainland. I couldn't risk their trying to phone their mother.

It had been over six weeks since I applied for the Landel Social Security number. My Atlanta mail drop should have the card in hand. I dialed, the relays clicked, and the line hummed, reaching to the satellite and across those 6,000 miles. I pictured detectives and FBI agents crouched at their bugging stations.

A secretary answered. I identified myself and explained that I was calling from Los Angeles on my way back to home base in London. Had any mail come in?

One piece, she said. It had to be the card, since I was expecting nothing else.

I told her I was returning to London via Hawaii and to send the envelope to me at my temporary Hawaii address. She repeated my Wailaua Gardens address back to me. I detected no hint of suspicion in her voice. We said good-bye. In my case, I meant it. She would not be hearing from Lee Landel of London again.

While waiting for the card, I worked on my job interview presentation, changing the names from Landau to Landel. My bank account had shrunk drastically. I was running out of time.

Normalcy. I kept working on it, but touchy moments reminded me nothing was going to come easy.

Ryan's classmates called him names, hoping to start a fight. He soon figured out why. He and the other Caucasians were the racial minority. Some native Hawaiians carried their bitterness about their exploitation forward from previous generations. In his efforts to put up a brave front, Ryan had begun to swagger and swear. Inappropriate foul language perked from Lori at unexpected times as well.

I decided formalizing the swearing might clear up their confusion, and at the same time provide a way to let off steam. Not just for the children, but myself as well. On a Saturday morning, I announced our first five minute "Freak Out."

In it, the three of us would get together and for five minutes, let loose, saying every awful word we could think of as loud and furiously as we wanted. This allowed us to compress our baser verbal instincts into a short period. Then, for the rest of the time, we'd do our best to behave like a lady and gentlemen.

We squatted on our knees, like a small pack of wolves. Lori was hesitant at first. The first tasteless exclamations came interspersed with seizures of giggling, but once started, she and Ryan bayed and swore and pounded the floor with unexpected fervor.

I had neglected to notice that the gardener, a stout Australian I'd met earlier, happened to be trimming the hedge just outside our open patio door. When I called time, the kids collapsed on the rug, wheezing out their final profanities. At that moment, the gardener strolled past the open door, paused, and grinned in at us. He shook his head admiringly, gave a snip of his clippers. "Not bad, that. I've 'eard stronger, but never so colorful. In fact, I learned a few new ones. Thanks for that."

Tipping his cap, he moved on.

We repeated these swearing sessions for several weeks. Eventually, the vulgarisms lost their appeal; the coarse language, along with the discontent it often represents, slowly vanished from our lives.

During the second week of school, Ryan brought home a friend from his class. Blond and about Ryan's size, Dru said his family had been in Hawaii for two years. They lived two buildings away in the complex. Ryan's first friend and ally, also a mainlander, and too important not to invite in.

Dru looked around the apartment and asked where our furniture was.

"We don't have any yet," I said. "Lori and Ryan's new bunk beds are coming next week, right, Ryan?"

"Right, Dad."

They soon went off to Dru's, and when Ryan returned, he seemed in a more cheerful mood.

That night, as always, I tucked them into their sleeping bags. They clasped their hands and softly chanted the prayer they had been saying nightly for as long as they could remember.

"Great, great elephant, tiny yellow bee,
A tiny, purple violet, tall green tree,

A red and white sailboat on a blue sea,
All these things you gave to me,
When you made my eyes to see.
Thank you, God, amen.
And God bless my family."

Downstairs reading, a short while later, I heard Ryan shuffle down the stairs. He stopped in the doorway, his eyes gleaming with tears.

"I can't help it," he sobbed.

I held out my arms. "That's okay, come here."

He shook his head and turned away. Rising, I put my arm around him and drew him over to sit beside me on the floor.

"Ryan, tell me how you feel."

He buried his face in my chest and clutched my shirt in both hands, choking the words out one by one. His teacher had asked him why he was day dreaming in class. When he told her his parents were divorced, she said that wasn't so bad, seven other children in the room also had divorced parents.

"But that only makes it worse," he wailed. "I miss her. I miss Mommy!"

He leaned against me, crying. When he quieted, I spoke softly, "I miss Mommy too, Ryan. I miss us all being together like we used to be. I feel sad once in a while, too. It's okay to feel your feelings, Ryan. You'll be all right as long as there is someone to talk to and someone to hold you and love you."

There wasn't much else I could say but repeat the same thing in different ways. After a while, silence felt most nurturing. We held onto each other until we had the strength to separate again.

Later, I went upstairs and listened to him and Lori talking in the dark. They were discussing the color of the pistachio nut and why pistachio ice cream was green.

When the bunk beds arrived, we had a donut celebration, not so much because we were ashamed of not having furniture, but because the beds represented another step toward peace and permanence. We had acquired a little of the gypsy toughness in us by now. I wasn't as subject to social embarrassment. In Atlanta, having no furniture would have brought mortal shame; now, material trappings seemed unimportant compared to living from our hearts.

At school and on the playing field those first weeks, Ryan weathered more confrontations, coming home with a bruised cheek one afternoon and refusing to discuss it beyond mentioning that the other boy had received worse than a bruised cheek.

During our first hotel week in Honolulu, Ryan had wet his bed twice, but his sleeping bag had stayed dry all through our beach tour. When their new bunk beds arrived, he got the upper, and on the fifth morning, confessed to me he had wet it. I told him not to worry about it. It never happened again.

I wondered if his unexpressed feelings in Atlanta had found expression through his wetting the bed. Could the family bond we now shared help him feel loved regardless of his behavior?

Though our family grew more settled every day, I knew a crisis could be just around the corner. When the phone rang one night, my heart squeezed up against my ribs. The phone had not rung since it had been installed.

Who? Should I answer it? I lifted the receiver. Just a phone solicitor offering a carpet cleaning estimate.

I resisted the urge to go out and tell the kids about it. Remembering my parenting books, I tried to maintain an air of confidence to assure them they were safe. I would take care of things. Stay calm.

In order to find the peace I desperately needed, I often retreated to my journal, where I could expose and investigate my most secret feelings:

> *I used to get solicitation calls all the time, from being on different lists as an architect and attorney. I detested them, but was also flattered. Now, one call sets me on red alert to the danger of our situation. Yet strangely, I want to talk to some-*

one, anyone who doesn't know us, just to be totally honest, if only for a few minutes, without all this conniving and suspicion and lying. My paranoia mixed with the aloneness is exhausting. There's an older couple next door. The woman came knocking to give us a starter of ivy. I say hello to her in the mornings when she leaves for work. I'm cordial, but I don't linger, I can't risk it.

The feeling of being adrift, as I did in Atlanta, is gone. More than adrift, I felt destroyed, annihilated, dead. I do miss my friend and confidante, Sid Silano, the only one who knew it all and who inspired me to make my own justice. One of these days, I will phone him.

Meanwhile, I feel vulnerable and scared. But I have the children and the determination to make things work for us. In the past, I never really saw Lori and Ryan as individuals. Now I notice. Like when Lori doesn't like something, she wrinkles up her nose and makes a joke of her own annoyance, "Ooooh, burn!" she says. Ryan on his skateboard, swooping and spinning. And at football practice the other day, his tender face grimaced in fierce determination to make a tackle.

Sometimes, I think about Whatzername. I went through the files of our correspondence during the divorce proceedings and remembered feeling if she died, I would be relieved. I still feel rage and sadness. Lying in bed, with the children asleep in the next room, I imagine what she must be going through, and sometimes I feel for her, but mostly I imagine her agony of loss and am glad. I would write that letter telling her off and rubbing it in, if I didn't know it would only add fuel to whatever vengeance she is planning. It's a sick and sour feeling, this anger, but I can't deny it, I don't want to. I still need it to keep me going, to keep me from feeling how much I hurt. Maybe to keep me from looking inside myself.

As long as love is here and real in this house, I don't need it elsewhere. Acting out of anger maybe wasn't the most loving move, but taking action was what I knew best to do. I brought us here, and now have no grounds for complaint about loneliness or anything else. I am nobody, a man without a past. But I am the somebody I dreamed to be, father to Lori and Ryan. I'll make it work. I have to.

❧

In early September, I bought a used Rambler. Lori, Ryan, and I drove around downtown Saturday and then up the coast to Koko Head crater and Sandy Beach. Great to be on wheels again.

Airborne Freight called just as we walked in from our drive. I drove down, checked the crates, and requested their delivery to our address.

At the apartment, we removed the lid from the four-by-four crate. As if seeing into a time capsule of our history, we perused our only possessions, both trivial and treasured, artifacts of a world that seemed a century away, but now welcomed components of our new life. I uncrated the grandfather clock. Carefully, I set the glass and wood cabinet against the living room wall. I lifted the chimes into place, then stepped back to admire our vestige of family history before pushing the pendulum to swing. A familiar, reliable measure of my life, in motion once again.

❧

Monday morning, September 20, the kids were in school. Calling Sid and the thought of possible complications brought pangs of dread. It took me half an hour to calm myself before I dialed 1, then Sid Silano's home number.

Relays again, the satellite hum, imagined voices murmuring from space. FBI agents listening somewhere? *Nonsense,* I told myself. *Paranoia.* Ring. Sid's rumbling voice answering.

"Silano."

"This is Jack Taylor calling from Chicago."

His tone changed at the sound of my voice.

"Get off the damn phone!"

It was too sudden for belief. "I don't understand."

"I've been tailed. My phone is bugged. Gimme your number, quick!"

"I don't . . ."

"The number, damn it. I'll call you."

I started to say the number.

"No area code!"

I gave the Honolulu number.

He hung up.

Total shock, then the beginning of terror's nausea. You anticipate the worst, imagine it, plan and rehearse your responses. Your reactions are likely to be acceptable, but you never really know how it is going to feel until it happens.

The receiver rattled in its cradle as I fumbled it back into place. I trembled all over. Made small electric muscle jerks I couldn't control. I went into the bathroom to splash cold water on my face. After a few minutes, the shaking stopped.

I sat at my desk trying to work on my résumé. I couldn't concentrate. My whole body refused to believe what I had heard. The phone bugged, the FBI pushing to find us . . .

I paced onto the patio, wandered into the kitchen, then to my room. I had to know what was going on. Until I knew exactly what the situation was in Atlanta, how could I react, how could I plan any needed counter action?

The kids came home from school, and somehow I kept up the front through dinner and got them off to bed.

I decided to call Sid again at 2:30 a.m., Hawaii time. Maybe his Atlanta office number wasn't tapped.

I couldn't sleep. I checked on the kids. Lori slept curled into a neat bundle, her back snug against the two friends she kept lined up beside her pillow, Raggedy Ann and Andy. Ryan had kicked his covers off. I tugged them into place, automatically feeling the mattress. He muttered and rolled over onto his stomach.

I moved through the condo, dousing every light, drawing the darkness around me. I'd never felt such immense, all-embracing fear. In a matter of hours, at best days, they could be here.

I closed the blinds, crouched at the front window to peer out at the street, seeing shapes in the shadows. I hurried to lock the rear sliding door. Then back to the front, huddled, ready, watching, waiting.

NINE

A FAREWELL SALUTE

To accept imperfection as part
of your humanness is to grow.
When you can love the part of you
that you think is imperfect, then
the act of transformation can begin.
— Emmanuel's Book

The voice that answered at Sid's office wasn't his. Maybe a receptionist or sales manager. I told her I was Jack Gordon calling from Chicago. The change of code name was a haphazard attempt to throw off anybody monitoring the call. I hoped the Chicago origin would alert Sid it was me.

"Hello?"

"Sid, it's me. Don't hang up. What's going on?"

"I told you, I'll call."

Click.

I swore, pounding the table while the phone jumped and buzzed.

He didn't call that night. I was antsy, short with the kids. Lori showed me her new dance steps, but I had trouble paying attention. I moved in a fog. Dinner took forever, but finally, they climbed into their bunks. I sat in on their prayer.

"Great, great elephant, tiny yellow bee . . ."

"Dad, we're finished."

"Oh, amen, huh?" My laugh sounded hollow. I kissed them and turned out the light.

Had the FBI recorded our number on that first call? Even

though I hadn't given the area code, wasn't it possible for investigators to simply check the front pages of directories and separate the ones with a 737 exchange? Had they already done it? Was a plane on its way to Honolulu at this moment?

I didn't sleep.

At 2:15 a.m., the phone rang. It was Sid, his voice muffled and in a hurry.

"I'm calling from a pay phone. Got to make this quick, so listen up. I had visits from two different investigators, plain clothes. I don't think either knew about the other, but they could be working together and covering that up. One asked me if you used an alias and claimed he had turned up your Landau driver's license. The other was talking subpoena but wouldn't show it to me or even his badge or whatever, but he sure talked the language. I told them if they couldn't prove who and what they were, I didn't know them."

"I didn't tell them a thing, but my advice to you is get out of the country, Lee, get out of the country! It's your only chance. Remember what the authorities did to my brother in Los Angeles? And my aunt in Fort Myers? Six years later, Lee, and they're still harassing my family, trying to find Carrie and me. Your cover isn't good enough."

"A phone guy I know looked at my home phone, and I complained to the company, but I still don't know if I'm tapped or not. So don't call me there. Don't call me anywhere."

"But you're my only contact," I protested. "And the fifteen-hundred dollars . . ."

"Don't worry about that," he snapped. "I'll call, I'll call. But you better get out of the country. I may be in trouble now, too. At least you're still on the move . . ."

The operator cut in. "That will be seven dollars for three minutes."

"I'll call!" Sid shouted, and there was a descending clatter of relays.

"Operator!" I pleaded.

"Sorry, sir, your party has terminated."

I suppose murder mysteries and suspense films and cop shows are ways for us to exorcise our fears. Or maybe we half-consciously think they might somehow prepare us in case such things should happen to us. But they don't help. They only give us that many more possibilities to imagine.

I paced the empty apartment. I was certain from Sid's behavior and tone of voice he really was frightened. Two investigators suggested either Val had hired someone, the state had indicted me for interfering with custody, or the feds had brought a federal indictment on my PBC activities. A federal law concerning childnapping had been drafted, but it had been hung up somewhere in congress. Still, the federal indictment, if there was one, could mean the feds had stepped into the custody matter.

Either way, if one hound found me, the whole pack would close in. I would lose the kids, my freedom, everything.

"Get out of the country, Lee, it's your only chance," echoed in my mind.

❧

In the morning, I awoke, my stomach still a blender running on high. I found myself again at the front window, holding to the shadows and peering out at the grounds.

A dog barked.

I leaned closer to the blinds until their edges pressed into my brow and I was able to see through the hedge that separated our unit from the neighbors. A mailman was coming up the walk. But not our regular mailman — he came later in the morning. In his hand, just an envelope, no bag. Something wasn't right. I pressed my back against the wall, hoping he couldn't see in the window. Damn! Is this it? A subpoena? I had heard of process servers posing as mail carriers.

He glanced up from the envelope and squinted at our front door, then turned and approached the neighbor's entry. He slipped the letter through the slot in their door and turned away to walk down the sidewalk.

The dog stopped barking.

I could hear the sounds of children in the playground. I sagged back against the rough texture of the wall, feeling it rake my sunburn, but stayed there, unable to take my eyes from him. I watched him disappear, then slid down the wall and collapsed on the floor.

Every day at 2:30, I waited in front of the school. I worried about Lori and Ryan walking home by themselves.

Even though they walked only a short distance, I was afraid someone would snatch them from the street. It was a common enough occurrence, particularly in cases where parents wanted to deprogram children lost to certain cults. It also happened in custody disputes.

On Friday, nearly a week after my conversation with Sid, a man dressed in a business suit, looking uncomfortable in the midday sun, walked from behind the condos directly toward the school. He hurried across the lawn to the six-foot-high shrubbery that screened the private yards from the street. Peering through the bushes, he could almost touch the children as they walked along the other side.

He appeared to be hiding in the depths of the hedge, braced for action, as though ready to pull a child through the hedge as one walked by.

He was so intent on spying on the school kids, he hadn't noticed me sitting in my parked car. Though he stood closer to the crosswalk, I would see the children first.

To be even more certain they would hear me at that crucial moment when the man might jump out, I stepped from my car as if it were too hot inside and stood by my door.

Leaning against the fender, I glanced at my watch and made certain I kept my head down. If he were after the kids, he was likely to have a photograph of me as well.

The dismissal bell rang. The sound of schoolchildren filled the street. I looked up. Lori and Ryan walked toward the hedge, laughing and talking with three other kids. If the man hiding behind the bushes moved even an inch as they came near him, I would yell for them to run to me.

They were on this side now. At first, they walked the wrong way, then Lori took Ryan's hand and turned toward me. I stepped forward, ready to run, not wanting to warn the man of my presence, but knowing I had to get to them first. As they walked by the hedge, the man gave them a glance, but quickly switched his attention to a different group of children across the street.

As the youngsters stepped onto the sidewalk, a small boy slipped through a hole in the hedge and took the man's hand. Together they headed across the lawn toward one of the condos. Just a father waiting in the shade of the shrubbery for his son.

Leaving the car, I joined Lori and Ryan on the sidewalk. "Guess what, Dad. Today was 'Thank Your Parents Day' at school." Lori held up a folded piece of pink construction paper with a clown on the front. The figure's costume glittered with blue sequins. As she handed it to me, some of the sequins fell off.

"I'm sorry, Lori."

Her glance was puzzled. She smiled and reassuringly touched my arm. "That's okay, Dad. Are you going to read it?"

Inside the card, she had drawn a clown holding a big red parasol balanced on a tight rope, with a man below him holding up his arms. The inscription blurred as I tried to read it. Something about Dad being a safety net.

"That's super, Lori." Blinking fast, I hugged her.

❧

That night I struggled for hours, trying to think of another way, but in the end I saw no recourse; the risks of staying in Hawaii had become too great. We needed to leave the country. Our freedom depended on moving quickly.

To make our move we needed cash. We needed as much as we

could get, as quickly as possible. I started by cataloging our few possessions, priced each item, and called in an ad to the paper.

Next came a decision on our passport. I dared not make the mistakes I had made in Atlanta. From the D'Youville home phone, I had ordered a Honolulu directory from the local phone company to preview listings under real estate developers. Any investigator worth his pay would discover the item when going over my past telephone bills. Pilgrim Storage had the name Landau, and Sid had said investigators had discovered my Landau license.

If leaving Hawaii precipitously did prove necessary, I would use the Coburn passport, though by now, the name would be on a federal fugitive list. All things considered, the name Landel, which had not been used in Atlanta, provided the greatest security.

As I walked back and forth to the car to sell what little furniture we possessed, I kept a close eye on the gardener. Whenever possible, I said hello to him and his fellow workers as I walked by, then would casually look back to see if they had gone on with their work or were still looking at me.

I also took note of the cars that regularly parked on our street. If a new one appeared and stayed for any length of time, my suspicion increased. Vans parked anywhere within view of our place made me especially nervous, particularly those with curtains or tinted windows. Surveillance work is often done from a nondescript strategically parked van.

There were two vans on the street. One had curtains across all the windows. The other was an older window van. As I strolled toward the vans to get a closer look, I watched for anyone trying to slip away. Only a few tropical birds saw me press my face against the tinted glass to peer at carpenter tools, a stack of lumber, and two sawhorses. The other van was empty.

For the moment, the sleepy stillness continued along the street, but I felt little solace or safety as I returned to the urgent business of getting us to a foreign country.

The next morning, I studied the neighborhood closely again as

I walked Lori and Ryan to their classrooms. The street crawled with cars, any of which might be a private detective's perch to watch our movements in and out of the apartment. My anxiety ran high, and most nights, sleep eluded me.

I reasoned that once investigators in Atlanta learned my telephone number and address, they would hire a local detective to watch us. They would have to be certain it was Lori and Ryan before taking them back to Georgia.

They would also want to positively identify me as the children's father. Sid had cautioned me repeatedly of the complications I faced. He said even criminal charges, though unfounded and spurious, might be filed against me solely for the purpose of enlisting the services of the FBI.

Before leaving Atlanta, I had considered flying to Sydney, Australia, using the Coburn passports. Instead, we would travel to Auckland, New Zealand. Reading about both countries made me believe we would prefer the majestic beauty of New Zealand.

Obtaining Landel passports for the three of us, however, was another matter. I would have to submit documents that appeared to be originals. Perfect facsimiles. Producing documents on a Xerox copier would have been easy, but I needed more than that, much more. The graphic artwork alone was enough to keep me busy for a week. Did I even have a week?

Each day we remained in Hawaii increased our risk of being found. Also, our dwindling finances dictated a quick departure. Better to use our small resources to get to our next destination.

I hoped to complete our birth certificates and government identification in time to file for the passports on Monday. Just four days.

Thursday, seated at my desk, I laid out pens, paper, and press-on letters and set to work. By Saturday, after two days of tedious artwork, I completed my certificate. With its engraved emblem of the State of Minnesota, embossed red seal, and formal signature of the county deputy, the document looked as impressive as the original.

Pushing aside pangs of guilt and haunting fear, I rubbed my strained eyes and stretched my tense shoulders. "Not bad. Not bad at all."

Next, I turned to the children's. Theirs were dissimilar — Lori's from Indiana, Ryan's from Florida — but I decided to use Indiana's simpler format for both. Working into the early morning, I finished the original graphics on parchment paper. With the basic forms completed, I then needed the birth information typed onto the certificates.

Not having typed since college, I knew my typing would be an arduous and time-consuming task. Instead, I decided to use the public stenographer I had hired for typing my résumé. But how would I explain my request for typing on what appeared to be "official" documents?

Every possible excuse I thought of was so obviously false my frustration turned to fear. What if she reported me to the authorities? All those months in Atlanta, while I prepared for Launch Day, Sid had drummed into me one thought over and over again: "Lee, trust no one. No one!"

Finally, I decided it was a matter of attitude and presence.

Simple. Lori and Ryan were both in school plays and each needed a certificate to act the parts. Here were two different forms I had purchased at an office supply store. I included instructions for another draft of my résumé to help me treat the request for typing the certificates with a fatherly nonchalance.

The stenographer greeted the request casually, quelling my apprehension somewhat. Still, when I picked up the typing, I scouted the area, afraid she might have reported this unusual request. Not until I carried the documents in the front door of our condo did I relax.

At the desk, comparing my documents to the originals, I noted only one difference, that of age and wear. I folded the certificates in half numerous times to soften the fold crease and weathered the new edges by rubbing them on the desk top to make them appear used. A torn corner from Ryan's and a smudge on Lori's finished the aging process.

Next, I needed identification to prove I was the person named on the birth certificate, Leland Landel. The passport application requested either a military, federal, or state ID or a valid driver's license. For any of these, I needed a picture of myself and one with the three of us for the application.

I drove into the city to a passport photo shop. We had one picture taken of the three of us for the passport, and a single shot of me. For a corporate security pass, I explained to the disinterested photographer.

Within a few minutes, we were handed a black-and-white photo for the passport and the colored shot I needed for my ID card. Quite by accident, this miniature photo captured for a brief second, a picture of the inner man at a crucial time in his life.

The pressures of the moment prevented me from reflecting on what this picture revealed about a man who had kidnapped his own children. But for that brief second, time stopped for the person in the photo; bronzed by the tropical sun, serene and content, relaxed and smiling with a sparkle in his eyes as though indeed a happy man. He looked too much at peace to be a part of the drama that enfolded him.

Back at my desk, I began designing what I hoped would be my official State of Illinois government-issued identification card. By using color and format ideas from my Georgia driver's license, I designed a form that became an official state ID card and not a driver's license.

By Sunday night, right on schedule, I had the card completed. To my untrained eye, it looked credible. But would it pass inspection by an experienced passport agent?

Having the documents completed and ready to go gave me a feeling of accomplishment. My confidence, however, equaled that of a wounded rabbit fastly losing chase to a ravenous fox.

Early on Monday, the phone began ringing with people interested in buying our household items. Not wanting to miss any sales, I decided to postpone applying for a passport until Tuesday.

I was recovering from having just sold my rare coin collection to a bargain hunter when Lori and Ryan came in from school. They asked if we could go to the beach for a swim. A good idea. We played all afternoon with a feeling of newfound freedom.

On our way home, I noticed a voter registration booth and decided to give my new ID card a try. I felt relieved when the woman in the booth took the Illinois card and my social security card without question. But instead of the wallet-sized card I hoped would add to my Landel identification, she handed me the completed form on standard size paper. Not what I wanted, but it would help. And it validated my new ID.

Monday evening, while Lori and Ryan played at the playground, I filled out the passport application making sure the names coincided with the fictitious names on our birth certificates.

For Lori and Ryan's parents, I filled in Leland Lon Landel and entered deceased on the line provided for their mother's name, as I had for the Landau passport.

Tuesday morning, I awoke early to enjoy solitude before walking Lori and Ryan to school. Alone in the stillness of the apartment, the fresh mountain breezes spilling through the opened windows, I scrutinized each passport item for authenticity, cross-referencing the information on the documents as I placed them into a manila folder.

Included in the folder were our fabricated birth certificates. Mine had me two years younger with the false birth date of April 21, 1941. That moment of vanity in the midst of paranoia still amused me, though later made things difficult. At every chronological reference to an event in my past, I had to make quick calendar adjustments, too often ending up looking befuddled.

I studied Lori and Ryan's birth certificates one last time before placing them in the file folder. They appeared indistinguishable from Lori's original. With these, I added my voter registration and a Landel Associates letterhead I had quickly pasted together from the leftover press-on letters.

Additional identification would have been helpful. But my past identity with three state bar membership certificates, two state architect registrations and my National Counsel of Architects Registration Boards certificate, had not been graphically changed to Landel.

These, along with my two university degrees, would have been excellent ancillary material to have in the folder. There had not been time, however, to do the necessary graphic artwork to change these over. Finally, and most important, I placed the passport photograph with the application.

Since I had given my occupation as architect, I decided to wear my white linen suit with a designer knit tie. I hoped this would make me appear debonair and maybe even intimidating. Wearing the suit and tie might also make me feel more confident. Especially since I became more and more jittery as the morning wore on.

I decided to apply for the passport during the noon hour when the regular agent might be out to lunch, believing an inexperienced person filling in would be easier to fool with my forged documents.

I paused outside the door with the official gold letters that proclaimed: UNITED STATES OF AMERICA. Passports — Official Business Only

Taking a deep breath, I entered. One look at the dreadful scowl on the face of the matronly woman sitting behind the counter told me this was not going to be easy. With a quick sniff that I took to be a dismissal of my presence, she turned her attention to a young couple who stood at the counter.

I took a seat in the small, windowless waiting area. Faded green walls, frayed carpet, and queer yellowish light emanating from the flickering fluorescent bulbs added to the room's gloomy air. Hushed whispers blended with the rhythmic creak, creak of the wobbly ceiling fan.

I told myself to relax. Everything would go smoothly, as long as I appeared calm and confident.

The young couple stood at a small opening in the counter processing their application. I listened intently to pick up clues to what would happen when my turn came. I watched them lay out their driver's licenses and credit cards, and could hear muffled voices talking about identification. Everything seemed to be going routinely. They paid the passport fee and were told processing would take five to seven days.

The agent, with bushy eyebrows and a fierce, tight mouth, turned her iron gaze on me to inform me it was my turn.

I stepped to the window. From close range, her forbidding face made her look more qualified to be a drill sergeant for the Green Berets than a passport agent. Mustering my best business demeanor, I told her I needed to process a passport application, took out my completed form, and handed it to her.

"Photo," she said curtly.

I laid the contents of the folder on the counter and slid the black-and-white photo across to her.

"Birth certificates," her voice flat, devoid of emotion.

I leafed through the documents and pushed the certificates toward her. She inspected mine, looking at the embossed seal as she held it up to the light.

To help me relax and divert her attention from the birth certificate, I asked, "Is this a particularly busy season for you?"

Her steely gaze snapped toward me, then she looked away as if I didn't exist. The X-ray treatment of my certificate continued. I could see idle conversation wasn't going to prevent her from doing her job.

One at a time, she held Lori and Ryan's certificates, looking at them curiously under the light. With each one, she rubbed the parchment between her thumb and forefinger testing the quality of the paper.

Trying again, I offered, "The children are really looking forward to their trip to the . . . Orient. I think it will be a nice change for them."

Again she ignored me — busy inspecting the embossed seals of the certificates. She held them close to her face, squinting her eyes as she scrutinized the documents. Next, she turned the certificates over to look at the seals from the back side.

That young couple before me hadn't received this kind of treatment. I glanced at the door. Maybe I should grab my papers and make a quick exit. Even though she looked as if she ran the place, there might be a manager she could call. Then I'd be in hot soup.

Instead, I faked a yawn to force myself to remain calm.

What she did next made me certain I was in deep trouble.

Instead of writing her notes on the application which lay in front of her, she lifted the top edge of the application off the counter. She rolled it toward her to hide the lower portion of the paper as she noted something regarding Lori and Ryan's birth certificates. She's writing down the numbers on the birth certificates so she can verify them later, I realized. I gazed around the room, pretending not to notice.

When she finished making her confidential notes, she looked up. "Identification?" she demanded.

Reaching for my wallet as if I had done this a thousand times, I removed my State of Illinois identification card and handed it to her.

She glanced at it and then glared at me over the top of her glasses. "This is not a driver's license, is it?"

"No . . . no, it's a state identification card. They uh . . . issue them to people who don't drive." Adding that I didn't have a driver's license because many people like myself, who live in the heart of Chicago, find it safer and cheaper not to own an automobile. I told her I planned on obtaining a driver's license now that I had located in Hawaii.

Dropping the card on the counter, she snapped, "I have no way of verifying the ID card. This won't do."

My heart dropped. Now I'm finished, because she won't accept my false Illinois identification. Turning to the counter behind her, she mumbled, "Maybe I can check it another way."

On the counter in front of me, she placed a thick three-ring binder containing front and back photographs with a written description of every driver's license in the United States. Using this verification book, she could have, in a minute, confirmed the card to be an imitation. Had I attempted to produce a facsimile of a state driver's license, I could have been apprehended on the spot.

Fortunately, the book did not show every possible federal, state, and local identification card issued in the United States.

Her-wire rimmed glasses slipped lower on her nose. She glared over them. "Do you have any credit cards?"

"No," I said, "I've stopped using them. They were more trouble than they were worth."

She pressed her lips together. Doubt ran down her face. She appeared disturbed about the Illinois identification card.

"If there are any questions," speaking softly, determined to keep my composure as I opened my file folder, "here are my voter registration, my Landel Associates Architects letterhead, and correspondence with my signature at the bottom."

I commented again about preparing materials for my business trip to Japan.

The materials earned a cursory glance. We stood there silent. Now what? Quickly, she reached for my files. I saw a decision reflected in her face and wasn't sure I liked it. She slid the documents across the counter to me.

Holding the Illinois ID card under the light, she copied the registration number onto the passport application in the block for other identification. I knew there could be no checking the validity of the numbers she had just copied off the card. She placed the ID card and my forged birth certificates on top of the other materials. "Seven dollars registration fee."

Quivering inside, I handed her a twenty.

"Now raise your right hand," she ordered.

I hesitated.

"Your hand, your right hand," she repeated, holding hers in the air to demonstrate. "Do you solemnly swear this information is the truth and nothing but the truth, so help you God?"

"I . . . I do."

"Your signature on the photo please, along the left side," she said automatically as she made change for the twenty. "And there. This line . . . and here."

As she replaced the three-ring binder on the shelf behind her I flipped the application over to see what she had written so secretively at the bottom. A quick glance revealed she had jotted down the registration numbers and filing dates for both certificates. My worst fears confirmed — the documents were going to be verified.

"How long does it take to get the passport?" I asked as she handed me my change.

"Five to seven working days, if everything checks out," she said ominously.

I thanked her and turned to leave the room as casually as possible, the words "if everything checks out" pounding in my ears.

I walked to the car feeling I had just been freed from solitary confinement, but horrified that my effort to obtain a Landel passport might now backfire with serious consequences.

Trembling, I slipped behind the wheel. Everything had gone wrong from the moment I walked into the passport office. The experienced agent, trained to spot phony identification such as mine, had me pegged or at least was suspicious. She would likely verify everything before issuing a passport. She seemed visibly uncomfortable with all the documentation. An investigation was sure to follow. This I could be sure of. Thoughts of losing the children and my freedom raced through my mind.

She was probably on the phone right now, calling South Bend, Indiana. Passport offices, I assumed, were equipped with national "WATTS" telephone lines to facilitate calling county offices anywhere in the United States. Calling the counties shown on the birth certificates to verify names and dates would reveal no such birth records existed. She would discover that my application was fraudulent and take prompt action to have me apprehended.

No matter how I analyzed it, an investigation would be instigated.

I thought of one comforting detail. After she'd scrutinized the birth certificates and copied the data on the application, she had returned them to me. The spurious documents were in my hands.

She had only written information. Her first consideration might be that she had transferred the data incorrectly onto the application.

I reasoned, trying to muster a ray of optimism, that quite possibly before commencing an investigation, she would call or send a request for confirmation of the information. That would provide notice of imminent complications and give us time to disappear. But then their experience might have proven it to be more effective to send out investigators immediately, before the offender had time to react. At most, we had a couple days before they came to apprehend me.

How could we leave? We didn't have enough money. And now we didn't have passports. We couldn't get out of the country and away from the investigation that was sure to find us. If the federal agents hadn't been after me before, they would be now.

I felt my dream for a life with Lori and Ryan slipping away. I wouldn't be able to watch them grow up or help them in their life or share in their happiness. I would become a stranger to them. I leaned my head against the steering wheel, crying in defeat.

"Hey buddy, what's the problem? You okay?"

I wiped my eyes and looked to the sidewalk to see, inches from my face, a black leather harness holding a pistol.

The policeman placed his black gloved hand on the door and leaned closer, his face creased with concern. "You okay, mister? You been drinkin'?"

My stomach tightened. I shook my head. "No . . . I . . ." My throat too thick to speak.

"What's the problem?" he asked, his tone becoming harder, more official.

"I'm . . . divorced." Blurting the first thing that came to mind.

"Ahhh." He nodded. "Well, it happens to us all, sooner or later — especially policemen. Just remember one thing, don't give up. Life goes on."

I nodded, wiped my face again and sat up straighter.

"Listen," he said, leaning close to the car window, "one thing I learned. You survive. No woman's worth this. There's a lot of them out there. Right?"

Silent agreement showed on my face. Inside not so sure.

He stood back, hooked his thumbs in his pistol belt, and smiled down at me. "Pull yourself together. Go get drunk, whatever. But don't drive. Okay? And remember, you'll get over it, so don't do anything you'd regret. Take care. I wouldn't want to see you again for the wrong reason." He touched the bill of his motorcycle helmet in a farewell salute and walked back to his machine.

I tipped him a wave as he roared past. He was right about one thing — nothing gained by giving up now. As long as I was running free and Lori and Ryan were still with me, I wouldn't quit. I turned the key. The engine caught. I eased into the downtown traffic. I would be back in time for Lori and Ryan when they came home from school.

TEN

SUDDEN DEPARTURE

So, I would suggest that one should sit quietly and see, "As long as I have bitterness or hate in me, I am not at peace."

— Tara Singh, *Love Holds No Grievances*

No matter how hard I tried to think of other things, my mind kept returning to the disaster of the passports. In the midst of my misery, one comforting thought came to me. If Eagle Eyes had been certain about my material being fraudulent, she wouldn't have accepted the application. But suspicious she had been. Most likely she'll have the data on the application checked, but that will take time. I had two to five days before their investigators came for us. And who knows, maybe I was imagining things. If the passport did arrive, we had a good chance of getting to New Zealand.

I paced around the apartment, trying to think straight. I had to remain calm and relaxed with Lori and Ryan. No matter how bad things were, I had to appear in command. They needed to feel sure that everything was on course. Could I stay in balance? I had to.

Doing something productive would quiet my nerves. I began packing two boxes for shipment to New Zealand. It wasn't easy deciding what to send, what to carry with us and what to leave behind. I wanted our treasured belongings out of the apartment. Most of all, the birth certificates, in case the investigators asked to see them again to verify the information.

I packed the electric train I had received when I was ten. Into other boxes went files containing the essence of the work I had done as an attorney, photographs of architectural projects and materials for my career portfolio. I held onto these as my lifeline to future income.

All day Wednesday, I sorted our belongings, hoping to mail them no later than Thursday morning. As the day wore on, I looked forward to evening's calm. Darkness would provide a welcome illusion of safety.

We relaxed playing checkers, ate popcorn and talked into the evening. Huddled around the checker board, entrenched in our temporary seclusion, hidden from our pursuers, I felt free to pause and rest at least momentarily. While Lori and Ryan played, I formed plans for the following two days.

Tomorrow, I could either stay home and answer the phone if someone called with questions about the passport application, or I could leave and avoid all calls and unwanted visitors. I didn't dare be taken in for questioning. My story had too many holes.

Six days had passed since I had made the fateful call to Sid. No one had appeared to apprehend me or the children. Still, I continued my watch for lurking detectives after school each day.

The dark shawl of night masquerading as momentary protection did not quiet my fears of remaining in the apartment.

We walked across the street to the playground so Ryan could practice his skateboarding. As he practiced his jumps and wheelies under the flood lights, Lori and I took turns on the swings, climbing bars, and slide. From our swings, we listened to the spirited sounds of a nearby softball game.

My watch read 8:00. We decided to walk through the school yard to a creek, where we had previously discovered a couple of large frogs.

The children had developed an affection for the creatures and wanted to find their friends. None could be seen. Ryan said they must have gone under the building to sleep. He and Lori were disappointed but suggested a game of hide-and-seek instead. They appointed me "It." As I stood counting near one of the school buildings, I heard two men talking inside.

As their low voices drifted to me on the evening breeze, I momentarily forgot the game.

I heard one of them say, ". . . and they are cute kids, too. Brother and sister, you know?"

Edging closer in the shadows of the office window, I strained to hear more. The district superintendent, whom I met when I enrolled Lori and Ryan, sat behind his desk. The other man, wearing a suit and hat, unusual for casual Hawaii, stood before the desk. The tone of their voices and the looks on their faces told me they were discussing a serious matter.

I moved as near as I dared, annoyed by the brightness of the full moon and the glow from the softball field. I heard the superintendent say, "In one case like this, the court granted custody to the school until the matter was worked out."

They spoke in low secretive tones. The word *custody* set my nerves tingling. They must be talking about Lori and Ryan. The passport application must had given us away, and during the day, investigators had tracked down the Landel children.

Minutes later, the man in the suit took off his hat and wiped the sweatband with his handkerchief. I heard him say, "That's all I need for now. I'll take care of everything tomorrow."

Was he going to pick up Lori and Ryan?

My heart pounded. This might be the end.

"Dad!" Lori called. I jumped, then edged away from the window and ran toward her voice.

"Daddy, you're not playing," she said. "Who were you listening to?"

"We'll talk about it later. Where's Ryan?" I asked, hoping to mask my fear.

"Here." He hung back by the tree he had been hiding behind. "I can still run to base and be free."

"Ryan, we have to go now. There's something important we have to talk about."

"A family conference?" he asked, rather serious for an eight-year-old.

"Yes," I agreed. "A family conference."

We walked back to the apartment in silence. On the way I argued against my fear. The meeting I overheard could have been about anybody's children; Lori and Ryan weren't the only brother and sister in school.

We went upstairs to their bedroom and sat on the floor. Their bunk beds had been sold the week before; now we were sleeping on the carpet again. The streetlight painted an eerie glow in the room. I explained about the passport and birth certificates, then told them what I had heard at the school.

"Each passing hour increases the chance that someone will come to our door and ask about the passport. It would be the end of our being together." I took their hands in mine. "The thing that matters most is for us to be together."

They nodded in agreement with a seriousness in their faces I had not seen before.

"Maybe we should consider leaving the house now. That way if they come in the morning, we'll be gone."

Lori stared at the floor in contemplation, then looked at me. "Dad? If there's a chance someone will take you from us, then we better go now."

"You're right, Lori," I said. Ryan nodded in agreement.

"If we're going, here's what we'll do," I said. We'll drive to the north end of the island, find a campground, and hide. That will give us time to decide what to do next."

Ryan glanced around the room, then gave a half shrug. "Okay, Dad," he said bravely. "I'm ready."

Relieved at making a decision, I said, "I don't think we have to leave this very minute. When they come for us in the morning . . ." I paused, suddenly aware of how strongly I believed the investigators would be at our door at sunrise. "I'm certain we have time." Glancing at my watch in the dim light, I made out 10:00.

"When we leave," I cautioned, "we might never come back. We have to make sure to take everything we're going to need, but only what we need. Some of our favorite things will have to be left behind."

"That's okay, Dad," said Ryan. "We already left a lot behind in Atlanta, and we had fun anyway."

"Good, Ryan. Then let's divide up the packing and get busy."

Suddenly, lights from a car pulling into the back lot swept across the bedroom walls. Instinctively, I pushed Lori and Ryan below the window level. Their hearts beat against my hand. The car's motor grew louder. We dropped even lower, holding our breaths, listening.

A car door opened, then slammed shut. Seconds later, the door opened again and closed. Its wheels then crunched out of the driveway.

I sat up, forcing my voice to be calm. "Okay, now we can get to work."

We worked using only flashlights. Ryan complained he couldn't find anything. We turned the lights on and rushed through the apartment, packing and cleaning. Even though we weren't coming back, I wanted to leave the place orderly.

Decisions had to be made — what to take, what to leave. They packed their clothes first. It didn't take long, since they didn't have many. Certain things were discarded without question: files, school papers, books.

Knowing he couldn't take his half-finished model airplane, Ryan chose to throw it away rather than leave it behind. He placed the Cessna scale model in a box, and under his other arm, he carried the three-foot-high model V2 rocket we had built and flown together.

We walked across the street to the dumpster behind the elementary school. Ryan heaved the models into the dumpster.

In an instant, a shared love of our lives became a memory. We spoke not a word. We couldn't. We had given up so much, and now our pride and joy, the models that represented cherished time together, thrown away like so much unwanted garbage.

Blinking back tears, he led the way to the apartment. I put my arm around his shoulder.

"I promise, Ryan," I said, "someday there will be another model, and you and I will see it fly." I wondered if he heard my vow and would remember it.

As the boxes were packed, I carried them out to the car and placed them among the tent and camping gear. We loaded the suitcases last. Lori laid her doll on the front seat; Ryan carried his blue blanket, his symbol for safety and security.

We walked through the apartment for one last look. We were leaving behind the teak and leather chairs, the stereo, numerous small items, and the one thing that had made this hideout a home, the grandfather clock. This important link to our past now became expendable. Anything, everything, we were willing to leave behind, if it meant we could stay together.

One thing we had forgotten to consider, Georgie Girl II. We had no choice. We would take her with us. Maybe we could find her a home somewhere.

Lori carried the litter box, Ryan the bag of kitty litter, and I carried Georgie Girl.

It had taken us a little over an hour to pack, organize the apartment and load the car. By 11:30 Wednesday night, September 29, we drove off. Another home abandoned, another curtain drawn.

❧

Before entering the freeway, I stopped to buy gas. Stations along the coast would be closed this time of night, and the last thing I wanted was to be stranded and have a police car find us.

"Ten dollars regular," I said.

Another attendant saw Georgie Girl standing in my lap. He

reached out and teased her with his rag. "She sure is cute. My wife and I have been wanting a cat. You wouldn't want to give him away, would you?

"He's a she," I corrected. "Her name is Georgie Girl." I handed her to him through the window.

He held her close to his chest, rubbing her ears.

"If you want her, she's yours," I said.

His eyes lit up. "Are you serious?

He was still thanking us as we drove away.

Previously, Ryan and Lori said they would be sad if we gave Georgie Girl away. Now even they felt a sense of relief over her unexpected departure.

We took the Lunalilo Freeway through Honolulu to Like Like Highway, over the mountain and up the windward north shore to Kahaluu. I remembered Kaaawa Park for its shade trees, lawns, and better bath facilities than most we'd been to.

In the pale moonlight, under the shadowed palms along the beach, I pitched the tent and helped Lori and Ryan into their sleeping bags. We fell asleep listening to the surf wash onto the beach just yards away.

We awoke to cool ocean air rippling past the tent flaps onto our faces. Yellow light seeped through the canvas, telling me morning had grown up fresh and clear. Beyond the surf, I could hear seagulls quibbling for their morning morsels.

Lori and Ryan soon joined me by the morning fire. We walked through the deserted park and back along the beach as the breeze cleared our minds and prepared us for another day. Here I felt safe, certain no one would find us, at least for a while.

While I prepared breakfast, Ryan asked, "Dad, what about our not being in school today?"

"I think it's okay not to be there today, Ryan. We'll give them a call tomorrow and tell them something. All right?"

"Sure. Great, Dad."

We loaded into the car, and drove back to Honolulu.

First, I had banking to do.

I closed the checking account by writing a check to cash for $500. The teller handed me the money in twenty-dollar bills. I had one check outstanding, the rent payment for the coming month, but I countered the twinge of guilt with the knowledge that the landlord held a month's security deposit for unannounced departures. *Unannounced departures, how appropriate.*

I had earlier withdrawn our $2,500 from savings, receiving a cashier's check made out to Leland Landel. Cashing it in another country would create a trail to us. I wanted no links, not even the most tenuous, pointing to our new location.

To cash the $2,500 check, I went to another branch to avoid being recognized by personnel at the original bank, in case an investigation moved in behind us. I told the teller I was buying a car, and the man wanted cash.

"May I see your identification, please?" she asked.

I gave her my State of Illinois identification card. *Very official looking,* I thought.

She cashed the check with an apology. "I'm sorry, but we only have twenty-dollar bills, nothing larger."

"That's fine," I said. "The man selling his car won't mind," thinking as she counted the bills for me that I could obtain one hundred dollar bills at any bank. Two banks later and still no one hundreds. I decided it didn't matter and would just carry the hundred and fifty twenties.

For safe keeping, I hid the stacks of new twenties in the most inconspicuous place I could think of, the dirty clothes bag stuffed in a corner of the trunk.

Later, at a Laundromat, we inadvertently put the twenties in a top-loading washing machine. We returned to discover we had washed the entire $3,000 along with the clothes. Lori and Ryan thought it was a good joke on Dad.

I had to agree — one hundred and fifty bills swirling in the soapy water did look strange. We had no choice except to dry them in the dryer.

I told the kids, "This is what you call laundering your money." They didn't understand the pun.

We loaded our clothes and the money into the car and headed for the beach. I drove with caution, keeping with the flow of traffic and in strict obedience to the laws, aware that a simple traffic ticket could mean the end of being together as a family.

I pulled into a less populated section of the beach park, still concerned that we might be seen here by someone from Atlanta. Lori asked if we could get ice cream cones. I bought them a single dip cone each, conscious about conserving money and sent them to play along the beach while I made a phone call. This wasn't just any call, but a call to Sid in Atlanta.

As I waited for the call to go through, I calculated what time it would be in Atlanta. 3:20. Would he be in the office?

His secretary answered. Using our prearranged code name, I said, "This is Mr. Taylor calling from Chicago."

She put me through to Sid.

"Sid, it's me." My voice almost at a whisper.

"Right," was all he said.

"I'm taking your advice. I'm moving us to New Zealand. Do you understand?"

"Right."

"I'm going to move quickly on this. The fifteen hundred dollars, Sid, I need it. We can't leave without the money."

"Okay, great. I'm glad you're taking my advice; its the only way. I'll get it to you right away, old buddy. The weather is warm here, in fact, too warm. You're doing the right thing. I'll forward it to you right away."

"Thanks," I said, hearing the relief in my voice. "I couldn't have done any of this without you, Sid. You're the only person I have to rely on."

"Don't think about it. Remember, we're both in the same boat. Right?"

"You can say that again," I said with a lift.

"I'm going to sign off now, buddy. You understand?"

"I know Sid. You're right."

"Do everything I told you, and you'll make it. And remember; trust no one, Lee. No one."

"Okay, buddy. Good-bye and good luck."

A click and the line went dead. I hung up and turned to look for the kids. Lori and Ryan were on the sea wall, throwing the last bits of their cones to the gulls. *What a beautiful sight,* I thought. *We're going to make it.* And what a friend Sid has been. Thanks to him, the three of us were together.

I walked with a bounce, feeling a sense of renewed confidence, as I went to get the kids.

Our next stop, a freight forwarder to ship our few remaining possessions to New Zealand. After three carriers and two wrong addresses, a shipping clerk looked at the boxes in the trunk and asked what the contents were. I told him books, files, a few personal items.

He lodged his pencil stub behind his ear. "Want to know the cheapest way to ship this stuff, mister? Postal Service. The U.S. Mail." He nodded in self-agreement. "Yup, just tell them they're books, that's the cheapest way."

We had spent the better part of the day trying to find the right shipper, but it made sense. It just hadn't occurred to me to send them by mail.

At the Kahala Branch Post Office, on our way back to our campground, I mailed the boxes to Leland Landel, General Delivery, Auckland, New Zealand.

The receiving post office would hold general delivery mail for thirty days before returning to the sender. To avoid alerting anyone of our destination, I fabricated a return address to put on the boxes. I had to take the chance the boxes would arrive, and we would be there to receive them.

We drove north along the tree-lined Pali Pali Highway, speeding through late afternoon shadows as we climbed over the mountains to the windward side. We looked forward to the quiet park and a meal cooked on the fire at our campsite, but we had one last thing to accomplish: We had to sell our car, without a telephone.

Lori suggested using the telephone at the campground. We could stay at camp all day and take turns listening for the ring.

We would try it.

Lori and Ryan were glad to be "home" after a long day riding in the car. I gathered wood to build a fire for dinner, while they ran to toss the Frisbee on the beach. They relished the excuse to run through the water to reach an errant throw. They seemed free, filled with a lightness I hadn't noticed before. I wondered if we could have been this content and happy had we stayed in Atlanta. Perhaps given more time, we would have.

As I stoked the burning fire, a realization stirred within me that everything we had left behind, everything I had sacrificed, my career, friends, family, possessions, meant little when compared with the love my children and I now shared. But what price were we really paying? Could a solution without revenge have brought the same sense of love and joy with less pain and loss to everyone? I hoped in time I would know the answer. In solitude, I prepared our primitive supper. This time alone helped me renew my resolve to discover a new life with Lori and Ryan.

After dinner, as they played on the beach, I strolled down to the shore. The moon had risen into the fading dusk, spreading a sequined swath of glitter across the water.

How like us, I thought to myself. As if all the world had conspired to hold us back, to keep us from a purposeful, loving life. And we, like the moon, now traveled in darkness yet led by a light we did not understand.

I considered our future, trying to map out what we would do, where we would go, what life would be like for us in New Zealand. My earlier sense of confidence waned. How would we cope with so many unknowns? Standing there, isolated, hearing only the slap of the waves, I knew I had no one to turn to. "But that's what you wanted, Lee, to be a dad to your children," I reminded myself, speaking to the waves and the moon.

"Dad! Dad!"

The children's voices drew me back. I took a deep breath and turned my back on the moon, the sea, and my past.

"Look down the beach," called Ryan. "Let's go see what the lights are."

We started down the beach to investigate the flickering orange. Ryan sloshed through the water, keeping pace with Lori and me as we trudged in the soft sand. We came to a small group of natives night fishing for squid. Their candled Japanese lanterns bobbed mysteriously on the bows of their small fishing craft.

We listened to the guttural chattering as the fishermen hung their catch on racks above the fires. The squid sizzled, and smoke drifted to where we stood, carrying us away to a different land. Finally, we turned and stole in silence back to our camp. At our tent, we talked for a while before I brought up my mission for the night.

"I'm going back to the apartment," I said.

"But why?" Lori asked. "You said it was dangerous."

"I want to get those two chairs. A man offered to buy them. He'll pay us two hundred dollars. I won't be gone long."

"Daddy," Lori said, "be careful, won't you?"

I hugged her. "I promise."

Ryan moved closer. I included him in the hug.

"What about the police, Dad?" he asked. "Won't they be there?"

"I don't think so, Ryan." But maybe some kind of investigator will be.

I settled them in our tent. In spite of what I told them, I was concerned. Anxious for myself and worried about leaving them alone for what could be as long as two hours. I considered waiting until early morning. But someone might see me. I had to go tonight.

ELEVEN

SHELTERED HAVEN

A conscious being simply sees, with a compassion that is born of insight and perspective, that everyone is on the road to awakening.

— Ken Keyes

I drove over the mountain into Honolulu, arriving at Kahala Mall parking lot just two blocks from the apartment. In a dark corner I organized the back seat and trunk before going to retrieve the chairs. As I dug through my trunk, a white car pulled up close behind me.

The driver leaned out his window. "Everything all right?"

"Everything's fine." I said.

Then I noticed the badge on his shirt, an undercover police officer driving an unmarked patrol car. Someone rummaging through a trunk at one-thirty in the morning was cause for suspicion. Damn! Why hadn't I done this at the beach?

"Okay, you take care." He swung the wheel and pulled away.

Shaking from the close call, I slammed the trunk shut and took a circuitous route to the apartment, in case he followed me. No headlights appeared in my rear view mirror.

In the parking lot behind the apartment, I doused the lights and coasted to a stop, then disconnected the overhead dome light. Everything seemed quiet. Not a person in sight.

Inside the dimly lit apartment, shadowed cadavers of our prior existence lay about. Nothing appeared disturbed. After loading both chairs, a few decorator accessories, and the stereo, I locked the apartment door and slipped across the lawn to the car. In the glow of distant lights, I checked my watch. 2:00.

The engine growled as I rolled onto the main street. My adrenaline and my thoughts kept me awake driving back to Ryan and Lori.

How much better it would have been to have flown to New Zealand using the Coburn passport. I felt trapped, desperate, hiding in a deserted campground.

When I pulled into camp, a sharp tapping noise in the engine shattered the thick silence. The engine, another problem to deal with before selling the car. Too tired to worry about that now.

In the morning, I awoke to a crystalline sea and a surf less vocal than the evening before. I crawled from the tent into the cool stillness. The early morning sun sparkled through palm branches, splintering artful shadows across our tent. I retrieved toiletries and fresh clothes from the car. We would be meeting people during the day.

Lori and Ryan walked along the beach to wake up. Exhausted from the previous night, I was tempted to spend the morning at camp, but we had too much to do.

We drove into the city, stopping to call the man about the chairs.

At his building, we took the chairs to his office. A brief chat before walking out of his office with two crisp one-hundred dollar bills in my wallet. At a used furniture store, we sold the stereo receiver and household accessories for $125. Good. New Zealand closer and our burden of possessions diminished.

In Ala Moana Park, we found a telephone booth next to a shaded green lawn alongside tennis courts. With the telephone number, we drove to the Honolulu News Building to place the ad.

A call to Wilson Elementary School had to be made before the school day ended. Lori and Ryan had been absent Thursday and now Friday without the expected explanation from a parent. I didn't want the school making inquiries. If the investigators had moved quickly, my call would also explain our absence. The quiver in my stomach reminded me I had better not blunder this call.

When the receptionist put me through to the principal, I pretended to be calling from San Francisco. I told her the children had come with me on the trip and apologized for not informing her on Wednesday before we left. I explained to her about my considering a job offer on the mainland and asked what would be involved in transferring the children's records if I decided to take the position. She said it was simply a matter of signing a release card to be sent to their new school.

I said we were undecided at this time but would let her know. I spoke highly of the children's teachers and how much Lori and Ryan had enjoyed their classes. She wished us a nice weekend before saying good-bye.

The principal came across as cordial and helpful on the telephone, something I would not have expected if the federal investigators had been snooping around asking questions about the Landels.

Sitting in the car after the phone call, I felt immensely relieved knowing they had not moved so rapidly in their investigation as to involve the school.

Ryan jumped onto the front seat. "Okay, Dad, what's next?"

"If we're going to be spending time by this phone, we need a campground closer to the city. Where would you two bunnies like to live next?"

"We've never stayed at Hanauma Bay." Lori said as she joined us. "That's the prettiest place on the island."

Twenty minutes later, we pulled into the parking lot above the bay. Before us lay the blue coral reef, white sand beach, and a secluded campground. The park, filled with people, made a perfect place to hide.

We walked to the camping area, picked a site, and pitched our tent under a myrtle tree.

Ryan started the charcoal.

Later, we sat around the fire savoring the spareribs, while the moonlight danced across the bay. In our frantic packing, we had forgotten plates and silverware. We ate with our fingers. Ryan said it improved the flavor.

Over the embers, we popped popcorn. Speaking in whispered tones, we ate our popcorn as the waves slapped at our feet. After a while, we strolled along the moonlit shore, feeling for the moment safe and thankful to be together.

The next morning, I slipped from the tent to discover a brilliant pre-dawn horizon shimmering across the silvery bay. Waking Lori and Ryan, I suggested a walk along the beach to enjoy the sunrise. While we walked, I photographed the volcanic rock emblazoned in shades of crimson by the early morning light.

Lori and Ryan threw bread crumbs to the brightly colored fish feeding near the shore. As I watched the children, I thought about the turmoil of the past days and marveled once again at their joyfulness, their resilience.

Here with them in this sheltered haven, I felt at peace, calmed by the timelessness of our surroundings.

Returning to our campsite, Lori and Ryan left to explore the beach in the other direction. While taking more pictures of the unusual morning light, I pondered what lessons we might be learning by our experience here. In my journal, I noted the events of the past several days, along with this poem:

Hanauma Bay
Morning came
light radiating on my heart.
Dawning deep within me
that all I would ever have,
could ever have
was each precious
passing moment.
And to live my life as though these

passing moments were
my last . . .

I put down my journal when I saw Lori and Ryan running toward me holding in their hands treasures they had found.

After another day of playing and beachcombing, I decided to attempt another furniture run, this time to retrieve the grandfather clock.

We first drove to Honolulu to browse in the bookstore at Ala Moana Shopping Center. Believing that my omnivorous reading had contributed to the breakup of my marriage, as a single parent I now seldom read. Since then, I made sure my reading did not get in the way of what I valued most, my two children, but the bookstore remained my favorite place to visit.

Lori and Ryan loved the place, especially the children's corner. They would sit on the small stools used for reaching the upper shelves and read the books of their choice for hours, with nary a word between them. Two children, sun-bronzed, with golden hair, peering into their books, looked the picture of contentment. The store manager, I noticed, acquiesced in their pleasure.

The early morning hours would be the safest time to retrieve the clock from the apartment, so when the shopping center closed, we drove to Kapliolani Park. It had a merry-go-round the children liked. Lori pleaded for me to spin her and Ryan around, which I did, prompting screams of delight. I hopped on but got too dizzy and jumped off. But for them, the faster it went, the more they liked it.

We took turns on the slide and swung high on the swings. They scaled the climbing bars; I worried about their falling. Fortunately, it was soon time to leave.

In the car, we curled onto the seats and slept. I woke at 2:00. The time had come to recover the grandfather clock.

Following the same approach I had used the previous trip, I entered the rear parking lot and coasted to a silent stop. In the back seat, the kids lay sound asleep.

I slipped inside the apartment. Nothing had been touched. The moonlight in the living room provided enough light to disassemble the clock. The work required care and concentration. I was especially careful with the tubular chimes. If they touched against anything, the resounding tones would betray my presence. I stayed alert for sounds of approaching footsteps.

Laying the parts on the living room floor, I wrapped the chimes, weights and pendulum into towels. I nestled each bundle in the trunk, then returned quietly along the dark, hedge-lined sidewalk to the apartment to retrieve my tools, my briefcase, anything that could be sold. Once these were in the car, I faced the challenge of moving the clock cabinet.

Its face and sides were made of quarter-inch-thick beveled glass inside an ash wood cabinet that stood nearly six feet high. I opened the rear door of the apartment and scanned the darkness. Seeing nothing, I returned to the living room. As I lifted the cabinet through the door to the walk, I let the screen door slam.

Bang!

I froze. When no sounds came, I locked the apartment door behind me.

I hoisted the cabinet piggyback and shuffled through the shadows to the car. After standing the case up, I woke Lori and Ryan. With their help, I laid the clock across the top of the car seats. It looked like a casket. They squeezed in beneath and draped it with a sheet.

Mission accomplished, we drove the deserted road back to the park. We walked down the hill to the tent and slipped into our sleeping bags. Another tension-filled day and still together.

❧

The next morning, after cinnamon rolls and juice, we trooped up the steep path to the car. The cabinet, under its white sheet, made it appear we were in the funeral business.

At the Pacific Consignment Center, I asked the man, who

appeared as ancient as the scarred rolltop desk he worked on, if Mr. Ming was in. A few days earlier, I had shown Mr. Ming a photograph of the clock to determine his interest. He said if it was in good condition, he would look at it.

The weathered little man finished another line of numbers in his ledger before studiously capping his ink pen and placing it on the desk. He turned in his rickety chair to consider our arrival, himself appearing on the verge of tumbling off his ancient perch.

"Not here. He come at ten o'clock."

I glanced at my wrist. 9:15. "We'll wait. Is it all right if we look around?"

"Sure, help yourself." He pointed his pen at Lori and Ryan. "These kids break anything, you pay."

We passed the time with a tour of the consignment center. Everything imaginable had been brought to the shop from around the world. Our curiosity and amazement kept us occupied until Mr. Ming's arrival.

On first impression, Su Ming appeared to be a congenial man, perhaps thirty years old, with short, dark hair. I introduced myself, reminding him of my purpose for being there.

"Oh yes," he said, sucking his teeth while sorting through a mess of papers as if our presence didn't matter.

"The clock is in our car," I said, wondering if I would have to give the grandfather clock away just to be rid of it.

I led him to the car and pulled the sheet off the clock. "The cabinet is in mint condition."

"And it works?" he asked.

"Perfectly."

Rubbing his chin, he said, "Five hundred dollars for the clock. Do you have anything else?"

I showed him the power tools, stereo, and lamp in the trunk.

"Six hundred for all of it." he said.

I feigned disbelief at being offered such a low price. I didn't want to arouse suspicion that something might be wrong with the goods and have him retract his offer. He suggested we go think about it and return the same day if we were interested.

Lori and Ryan climbed into the front seat under the clock for our drive to the farmer's market. We would look around for an hour and then return to accept Ming's offer.

We toured the native craft center, then returned to Su Ming's consignment center. Once again, the old man told us Mr. Ming was gone but would return shortly. We found a worn, dusty couch to lounge in.

As we sat down, the real estate woman who had leased us the condominium walked into the shop. If she saw the clock in the car and us here, she might become suspicious enough to call our landlord. I grabbed the kids and led them to the back of the store.

Slipping out a side door, we hurried to the car and left. When we returned thirty minutes later, her car was gone. Su Ming had returned.

"Ahh, you have changed your mind, then?" he asked.

"I checked with the other two parties that had expressed interest in the clock," I lied, "but neither of them were willing to make an offer today. I've decided to accept your offer."

"Good. Now let's see . . . that was five hundred, wasn't it?"

"No. Six hundred for everything."

"Ahh, yes. Of course."

Lori and Ryan helped unload the clock, my briefcase, and the tools. I stood the cabinet upright before carrying it inside. My real name had been engraved on a brass plate and affixed on the inside of the door. I ran my fingers across the plate. The clock had been a family keepsake, to be passed on to my children and then to their children.

I removed the name plate. It glimmered in the afternoon sun as I held it in my hand.

I was struck by a strange feeling of weightlessness. I felt as if I were ready to take my first solo flight. Here we would take leave of our last worldly possessions.

Only weeks before, I had owned a beautifully furnished contemporary home that had been featured in *Atlanta Magazine* as one of Atlanta's newest luxury townhouses. Among other photographs in the article had been a picture of my wife and me sitting in our luxurious living room with our prizewinning Burmese cat, our images reflected in the full-length mirrors on either side of the stone fireplace.

The grandfather clock represented the material life I had so carefully constructed: the handsomely appointed home, elaborate offices with framed professional certificates hanging in the library, the latest model luxury sedan, an attractive wife, the latter as much a part as the hand-blown glass collection by the internationally famous artist, Hans Frable.

Today, I stood outside a musty pawn shop, sweltering in the scorching sun, surrounded by swarming flies. The last remains of that exquisitely orchestrated facade of my previous life I now held in the palm of my hand. Selling the clock symbolized my abandonment of a burdensome, lifeless, and often loveless material world.

Along with the possessions, I was unloading outdated and misapplied values, enabling me to begin experiencing life very differently. A giant leap in my consciousness was occurring. How limited and narrow had been my appreciation of the world around me and of the people in my life. How distorted and inappropriate had been my value system — worldly, educated, proud, and yet so blind.

Revelations rushed over me like giant waves one after another. The striving, achieving, collecting, suddenly meant nothing. Stripped of the material remnants of my self-delusion, my inner being revealed the shallow, insecure person I had been.

I slipped the brass plate into my pocket.

The next item to be carried into the pawn shop had long been a symbol of my self-image. No aspiring attorney savoring prominence and success would be without his leather briefcase.

Bulging with memories of difficult cases, of ambitions for national recognition as one of the few attorney-architect specialists in the country, the briefcase had become stuffed full of disillusionment. Bewilderment oozed from its hinges.

The briefcase represented the quintessence of my professional dreams. As Ryan carried the case into the shop, I felt exposed, naked. I hadn't planned to disrobe in front of Ming's Consignment Center, but unloading the car was as much an undressing of a poorly arranged, overstuffed self as one could imagine.

Inside, I instructed Ming's assistant on the installation of the weights and pendulum in the clock. Once he saw that everything was in order, he wrote a check for $600 to Leland Landel.

Pleasantries said, we left. The transaction had taken the better part of the day, but now we had six hundred dollars more for our move to New Zealand.

We drove through Kapiolani Park to catch the high road around Diamond Head. As the Pacific Ocean revealed its haunting presence, we could see, far below, wind surfers riding the white-capped surf. Stopping to watch, we sat on the stone wall high above the beach, Diamond Head Crater towering like a great sphinx behind us. Each time we came, the power of the place affected us and provided, at least for me, a sense of renewed hope.

I hoped they, too, felt the lift in their hearts after nine months of being pushed and pulled and stretched by the pressures of the dissolution of their family.

There were times, of course, when each of us would be overcome with sadness, times when the memory of what we had left behind was too strong to deny, times when we would cry our souls out like dammed up rivers bursting loose. I believed if we were to know peace within ourselves, we had to accept all our feelings, especially those of immense anger and loss. I wondered whether Lori and Ryan seemed happy and content in our flight to a new life because they had been allowed to be themselves and experience these feelings directly and honestly.

Listening to Ryan, trying to sense what he felt, I heard no signs of anxiety resulting from the fear of our being caught. Perhaps the physical presence of his sister and his dad were all he needed to feel secure.

He and Lori were informed of what we were doing and that I could be taken away if I were caught using false identification. How much of this could Ryan understand? It was as though he were on an exciting voyage, enjoying himself with his sister and father.

Of the two children, Ryan was the one who would express his feelings about missing his mother. He would announce almost in passing, "Dad, I miss Mommy." But then he would play hard all day, saying nothing more. I sometimes wondered, when I allowed myself to feel beneath my anger, which one of us longed for her the most.

Leaving the stone wall perch, our spirits ran high as we headed back to camp. We looked forward to a swim before dinner and an evening spent around the fire as dusk settled in around us.

❧

At dawn, a fresh bouquet of sunlight cast crimson hues across the glimmering bay, bringing another balmy day.

Awake with a start, we raced to the water for an early morning swim. While Lori and Ryan continued their snorkeling I walked to my favorite rock to write in my journal. Feelings had surfaced I wanted to record. Even with the tension, anxiety and fear, each day became a gift shared and enjoyed. How could we not be changed by our stay in this tropical sanctuary?

We hiked to the parked car. Today, people interested in purchasing our Rambler would be calling the public telephone at Ala Moana Park. We looked forward to picnicking and swimming while waiting for inquiries.

The car wouldn't start. Each time I turned the ignition, we heard only a clicking sound. Maddening, especially since we wanted to be at Ala Moana Park by nine o'clock to begin receiving calls at the pay phone.

Ryan and I headed out to find help, while Lori stayed with the car. On the main road, we hitchhiked. Surely, on a Sunday morning, someone would offer a father and his small son a ride.

A half dozen cars went by before two men in a jeep gave us a lift to the service station two miles down the hill from the park. Inside, a highway patrolman spoke on the telephone. My first sensation was panic. He hung up and came out.

"You folks need help?"

"We're up at the park," I said, "and the car won't start. A dead battery, I think. Is there a park ranger that you could call on your radio? Or maybe a number I could call for road service?"

"No park rangers, but maybe I can help. I have jumper cables in the cruiser."

We climbed into his patrol car. As soon as he slammed his door, he asked my name. His voice was stern and official.

I realized that being caught by a police officer with a wallet full of phony ID could be trouble. Thinking quickly, I said, "Landel, Lee Landel. And this is my son, Ryan."

As he spun the car out onto the road, he lifted his microphone. "Number 435 en route to Hanauma Bay parking lot to assist distressed motorist named Landau."

He had misunderstood Landel for Landau. *What if he asks for identification?* I worried. I had a Landau driver's license, but it was a direct link to Georgia. I still had no Landel license.

Fortunately, he didn't ask.

He seemed friendlier once he had completed his call to the dispatcher. "That's funny."

"What is?" I asked.

"Your name."

"My name?" I asked, expecting him to say it was on some kind of watch list.

"Its the same as my new car, Mercury Landau. You know, the one with the leather roof? Isn't that something?"

We turned into the parking lot and coasted to the Rambler. Lori hopped out when she saw us inside the police car. She behaved as if there were nothing to be afraid of as we attached the jumper cables.

I slipped behind the wheel, praying the engine would catch, and turned the key. The engine caught and idled perfectly.

Cables free, we slammed the hoods shut and walked back to our respective cars. I waved to him as he backed away, one hand on his wheel, one on the microphone.

Lori settled into the seat beside me. "He was nice, wasn't he, Dad?"

"Yes, but he made me a little nervous." We headed into the city and our designated telephone booth.

As we set up our picnic near the phone booth, I missed hearing the telephone ring, but heard a tennis player say, "This is a park, buddy, not a car dealership."

At least, now we knew the ad had been published.

We waited all morning. Lori read on the blanket. Ryan practiced his skateboarding. They kept asking how much longer. To pass the time, we played mumblety-peg in the grass, tossed the Frisbee, and counted out-of-state license plates. Ryan kept beating me in jacks. Lori sketched in her notebook. Still the afternoon dragged on. No calls.

Selling the car was all that remained for us to leave Hawaii. If it didn't sell, I planned to abandon it in the airport parking lot on the day of our flight.

By 6:00, we'd had all the waiting we could take. We packed up and headed back to camp. I pulled into a station to have the battery charged so it would start the next morning. I turned the motor off. Nothing would make it go back on. The station lights blinked for closing. Too late to buy a new battery.

Discouraged, we rode the bus to the end of the route. We would have to hike the last two and a half miles to the park.

We walked in silence, at peace despite our difficulties, calmed perhaps by the mysterious presence of Koko Crater silhouetted against the luminous night. In forty-five minutes, we reached our tent and went directly to bed.

❧

Waking the next morning, thinking we had overslept, I nudged Lori and Ryan.

"We have to go to the city. We're going to be gone all day; I want you two to organize the camp area."

Lori crawled out of her sleeping bag, then went outside the tent to look for her tennis shoes. As she retrieved her shoes from the beach, Ryan darted past her, kicking sand to show off his enthusiasm on his way to a morning dip.

Lori yelled, "Dad, let's go swim with Ryan."

We raced to see who could get wet first.

After our swim and eating breakfast, I purchased a new battery. When the engine started, rousing cheers came from the backseat. We had wheels again.

The teller cashing Mr. Ming's check told us his account showed insufficient funds. Hopefully, the lack of funds was an innocent oversight by his bookkeeper and not an attempt to swindle me. We drove to Ming's Consignment Center.

Ming glanced at the check. The grimaced look on his face showed he would have preferred that we had not returned.

"If you'll return in thirty minutes, I will take care of it," he said with an air of dismissal.

Half an hour later, I walked into his office.

This time, he looked squarely at me. "There are dents in the clock's brass weights."

So this was his ploy. If he thought he was going to get away with paying less than the agreed amount, he was wrong.

"There were no dents when I sold the clock to you. If there are dents now, they happened after you bought it."

He rocked in his chair, clenching his jaw. His eyes flicked to me, then to Lori and Ryan. Dusty sunlight streamed across the floor. A fly buzzed around Ming's head.

At last, he shrugged, opened a desk drawer, and pawed through a clutter of papers. From an envelope, he withdrew six one hundred dollar bills and tossed them on the desk, stood, and brushed past me, to disappear into the shadows of his store.

I wondered, as we drove away, if we had come close to being taken by a local swindler. Could Lori and Ryan have cast a fortuitous spell on Mr. Ming, swaying him toward honesty? Maybe he did have some scruples.

I called the public stenographer to inquire about using her telephone number in an ad to sell the car, explaining I was away from the apartment most of the time. She said she'd be happy to provide answering service at fifty cents a call.

That done, I placed the ad, which completed our last official business for the day. We headed to the campsite to begin enjoying our few remaining days in Hawaii. On the way, we stopped at the apartment for the mail.

Arriving in daylight made me nervous. Driving into the parking area, I envisioned the grounds swarming with investigators.

I walked a circuitous route to the mail boxes, occasionally looking back to see if an investigator trailed me. Finding the box empty withered me with disappointment.

I walked back to the car, forgetting to be on guard. Lori and Ryan asked to go snorkeling. With the pace of our past week and the strain of living like stalked criminals, we hadn't had time to relax in the sun. For the afternoon, we would be vacationers and blend into the ambiance of the island and Hanauma Bay Park.

Certain that an investigation had been instituted by the authorities, I no longer expected to receive a passport. Without one, how could we leave the country? Using our Coburn passport entailed too much risk. As soon as we sold the car, we would have enough money, certainly enough when the funds arrived from Sid. But without the money, New Zealand, with its promise of freedom, safety, and an end to my constant fear of discovery and arrest, no longer seemed possible.

Of course, we could leave now using the Coburn passport. But if the car sold and the money arrived from Sid, our life would be much safer wherever we went. I decided to stay another couple of days at Hanauma Bay, checking the mail nightly for Sid's letter and the passport and keeping in touch with the secretary in hopes of selling the Rambler.

The day passed as we each enjoyed our own time. A brief shower scattered the tourists and cooled the beaches, while the natives, accustomed to rain spilling over the mountains, ignored the changed conditions.

As the afternoon waned, the towering lava cliffs around the bay cast purple shadows across the water and onto the beach. Scorched tourists trudged up the incline and disappeared over the stone wall. Peace returned to the stately grounds to be savored by those who remained.

As the moon spun a silver cord across the bay to the waves slapping into shore, the children and I sat around the fire telling stories.

Later, I popped popcorn, while Lori dug holes in the sand with her heels and talked about what it would be like to be back in Georgia. She wished she could have her musical jewelry box, and she remembered her shells and silver ring and most of all, her canopy bed.

"I miss Emily," she said. "She was the best friend I ever had."

Prompted by his sister's lead, Ryan said, "You know what I miss? Not having a baseball glove and my leather football. And I miss Mommy, too."

I remained silent to allow Ryan the room to say what was in his heart, but he returned to poking the fire with his marshmallow stick in silence.

"I don't really miss Mommy," Lori said. "What I miss is our home at D'Youville and the friends I made before we left."

I added more branches to the coals, and we wrapped ourselves in reminiscences of our life in Georgia. Lori and Ryan, I hoped, would feel more secure being able to share their longing for the only existence they'd known.

As we finished the popcorn, we took turns seeing who could remember things about a certain place or event. We turned it into a game that even years later, in a slow moment, one of us would start, just for fun.

We crunched on old maids as the fire died out, quieting to our own thoughts. Lori and Ryan crawled into their sleeping bags, falling asleep before I could say good night.

❧

Startled by the brightly tinted morning air streaming into the tent, I remembered today we could sleep late.

I looked at Lori and Ryan and a comfortable feeling moved over me. Would they remember the undaunted joyfulness of this moment and how we treasured one another? In their later life, would they retain their indomitable spirits, so strong now, as to seemingly dissolve the tragedy of their personal loss? As for myself, how long would I struggle with a sense of guilt for having denied Lori and Ryan their mother? I had put their emotional lives on the line and now felt immensely responsible for them.

Together we were learning to accept sorrow and finding its reward, forgiveness and peace. When sadness overwhelmed Ryan, I held him close and trusted he could feel my love for him. Lori, too, found comfort in our hugs.

For each of us, memory of the vanished life cut deep, bringing pain we thought would never leave. And yet each morning they began the day as though it were the first day of a great adventure.

Watching them in the soft early light, their hair wild around their faces, I knew this morning, as every morning since leaving Atlanta, they would wake up happy with anticipation for the day. Why was it so?

I decided someday they should know they have written within them an amazingly joyful spirit.

Today, we would remain at the campground to wait for calls to the stenographer. Until the car sold, we had nothing more to do before departure.

Lost among the snorkeling tourists and glazed bathers, we relished our seclusion. Here at least, people didn't notice or weren't concerned about the children not attending school.

I needed a day to lie and rest on the warm sand. Continuous vigilance against discovery and constant concern for Lori and Ryan had drained me, emotionally and physically. Here, I could rest and become restored for the unknowns that lay ahead.

Late afternoon, I called Ryan in to tell him we were going into the city to eat as soon as he and Lori had showered and changed into clean clothes.

He must have liked the idea because he darted head first into the water to tell Lori. We all met under the open-air shower where the cold water got us jumping as we cringed to adapt. We hadn't had a hot shower in more days than I wanted to think about.

A water fight started.

"Wash the sand out of your hair," I shouted above their giggling.

"Dad, dirty is just as good as clean for me," Ryan announced.

Lori tried her best to stay clean using the limited facilities, but in the stench of the dank public restroom, she could do little.

We drove into Honolulu.

Feeling roasted from too much sun, sand and saltwater, but clean, refreshed, and energized by our day on the beach, we waited for our dinner in an air-conditioned restaurant.

For an after-dinner treat, we went to the bookstore. The children went immediately to find footstools. I hoped the evening staff hadn't noticed our frequent patronage and the two whispering elves perched with books on their laps.

In the travel section, I thumbed through books. Where might we hide besides New Zealand that would cost less to get to and be an English-speaking country? The need to learn a foreign language would be a barrier against establishing a new life.

Our resources were too limited to exist for long. After paying the airfare to Auckland, New Zealand, we would have only enough money to support us for a week.

What then?

As three aliens, penniless, unemployed, and without friends, our freedom might be jeopardized. Once our presence in the country was brought to the attention of the authorities, I might cease to have a voice in our future.

We could, perhaps, find our way into a network of underground people, but this would require time, which we wouldn't have because of our limited funds. Besides that, receiving help from people in the underworld, I presumed, was not as simple as stepping through a door. It was more likely accomplished by a slow seepage through quiet word of mouth, not easily done without money while caring for two children.

I continued to weigh carefully the risks of being without funds and becoming dependent, desperate in a foreign country.

As I flipped through the pages of world travel books, in my mind, a distant chorus of bloodhounds bayed louder and louder. From Hawaii, I must leave no prints.

Break the scent. Stop the deafening cry.

But they never stopped.

Years did not quiet the hounds barking in tireless chase. With every unanswered click of the telephone, every flashing light of a patrol car, the incessant howl evoked panic and the urge to flee again.

Standing in the aisle between travel and physical fitness, I pondered the advice Sid had given me before we left Atlanta. "You must know how to survive as a fugitive; it's your only chance," he said, certain that any way but his was doomed to fail.

But the more I thought about his way, the more I realized its moral cost was too high. He had shown me a series of survival moves: how to leave a restaurant without paying, how to travel first-class anywhere in the world at no cost, even with two small children. He had also taught me how to set up and use dummy bank accounts, to "kite" checks, and to use more than one alias to the best advantage. He even had advice on the use of people: "If you need a woman's help, screw her first, no matter how ugly she is. That way she'll be grateful and won't stand in your way." But even now, when I felt most threatened, I realized there had to be another way.

I accepted a change of identity in order to stay with Lori and Ryan, but I resisted becoming a common criminal; nor did I feel I had to treat people like pawns to be manipulated for my own gain. I was, after all, a parent and wanted to be a positive role model. Silently, I dismissed Sid's methods as the furtive deeds of a madman.

My back ached from standing. I switched my weight to the other foot. Determination bristled through me. Whatever the hardships, we would proceed with honor.

Flickering lights reminded customers the store closed in ten minutes. Reluctantly, Lori and Ryan abandoned their books, and we joined the stream of late-night shoppers in the mall. Outside, we sat on the bench beside the fish pond, wondering if the spotted carp knew the mall had closed.

Lori suggested we head back to our campsite and, on the way, stop to watch the night surfers. We took the high ocean drive toward Kahala around Diamond Head Crater. Tonight, the overlook was deserted and darkness engulfed us. We sat on the stone wall separating the road from the park, watching from afar miniature surfers riding sequined waves rolling into shore.

The drive to our campsite took us within two blocks of our abandoned apartment. I pulled in to check the mail. The letter from Sid, with the fifteen hundred dollars, could arrive any day.

As for the passport, the normal processing period had passed. In a way, checking the mailbox had become a fantasy. Like a child making repeated trips to an empty cookie jar, hope makes a better companion than resignation and despair. Watching the mail kept hope alive.

I slipped through a hedge to reach the mailbox, staying clear of the apartment, in case an all night surveillance team waited inside for our return.

The mailbox numbers were barely visible in the dim light. I ran my fingers along the row and found number 137. Opening the small door, I stuck my hand all the way to the back. An envelope! I pulled it out and held it up to catch the faint light from the distant street lamp. An odd size, not a letter from Sid. My heart fell. It looked more like an official manila envelope. Could it be the passport office requesting confirmation of the erroneous birth information?

The contents could mean even deeper trouble for us.

I ripped open the envelope. In my hand lay a thin, small book with a dark cover and gold insignia on the front. The passport! On the inside, I could make out our picture and the name, Leland Landel.

I ran down the sidewalk to the parked car to show Lori and Ryan. They were sound asleep in the back seat. I shook them awake.

"Lori! Ryan! The passport."

They sat up slowly.

"It's here!" I repeated. "We have our passport. See, here's our picture. Here's the official stamp. We're safe. We can go to New Zealand!"

They jumped from the car and hugged me. We danced around the Rambler in the moonlight, giddy with relief.

"This means we're not being stalked by federal agents," I said to Lori and Ryan, both still dancing around the parking lot. "We can stop hiding like desperadoes."

Lori slowed her jumping. "Does this mean we can move back to the apartment?"

"That's right," I said, suddenly realizing the significance of it all. "We can move back tonight if we want."

She tugged me toward the car. "Let's go get our sleeping bags."

"That way," I added, "we can shower and enjoy a good night's sleep . . . clean for once."

"I'm pretty clean, Dad," said Ryan, looking himself up and down.

"Well, I'm not," Lori said. "Come on, let's go!"

We drove the deserted highway to the park. Even with the late hour, we were wide awake. Our feet seemed so light, we almost ran up the steep incline out of the campground.

TWELVE

ALOHA

The greatest challenge is to accept the tattered remnants of your life. For there you'll find the golden threads to weave the silken tapestry of who you are.

— Lee Coburn

"Money, it's the life's blood of your escape."

Sid's words stayed on my mind as we drove back to our Waialua Garden apartment. Ironically, he held our life's blood in his hands, the fifteen hundred dollars I had left with him. We were in a double bind. Not only were we in the worst financial shape we'd been in thus far, but also the worst predicament, needing to get out of Hawaii and the country fast.

At least our luck had turned with the arrival of the passport. Saved by the mail. Once again, free to fight to be free. I threw open the condominium door, and the kids ran in.

No furniture, of course, but after our weeks of camping on the sand, bare carpet never looked so inviting. Lori and Ryan debated who would shower first. I located the broom, and they drew straws from my hand. She got the short one, and within minutes Ryan whooped happily under the shower, while Lori hopped barefoot on the tiles and shouted for him to hurry up, this was not his "Morning Business."

The inevitable water fight began, but the sounds revealed contentment, and I figured I'd let them have this one. We had a mop for cleanup later.

I slid my tired body down the wall, stretched my legs out on the carpet, and reached for the manila envelope. The passport felt solid in my hands. I opened it. The paper was crisp; the ink smelled fresh. The embossed seal with its familiar eagle exuded authority, security, approval, or at least permission to exist as a family.

Citizen Landel.

And two children.

We'd made one giant step away from that bottomless pit, where a man has no name, no future. And another giant step ahead of the legal forces that could rip the children from me and leave me alone with the struggle to rebuild my life and my self.

Our plight was not over, but better. Good enough for now. I closed my eyes, and that steel coil inside me loosened a little. The children's voices reached me through the soothing echo of midnight surf.

Ryan appeared, swathed in an enormous bath towel, his head shining like a seal's back. "Dad, Lori says I can't take my skateboard into the shower to practice balancing. Dad? Dad, are you asleep!"

❧

The phone's ring jolted me awake. I experienced the fugitive's conditioned reaction: Wake up, clear your head, get set for anything. Maybe it was Sid replying to my letter, maybe the police. My watch read 7:00 a.m.; we'd finally gotten to bed at 1:00 a.m. I feigned an alert hello. The landlord, his voice serious.

"That rent check, Mr. Landel, it was returned. Insufficient funds."

He sounded puzzled but not really annoyed.

"There's been a mix-up at the bank," I said. "I'm terribly sorry," my heart pounding.

"That's okay. But I'd like to come by this evening, if you don't mind."

I couldn't refuse. He owned the condominium. I would have to fake it through somehow. "Sure."

"I'll bring my wife," he said.

"Good. It will be nice to meet her, and I'll write you a new check."

I hung up, thinking if necessary I could wave my passport at them. You see, your tenants are real after all, Mrs. Robinson. Smell that ink, look at that eagle!

But the one phrase nagged me — "insufficient funds." True as far as the account was concerned, but not for fugitives on the move to New Zealand.

Fortunately, the kids awoke in joyous commotion, interrupting my train of thought. Ryan pretended to trample on me while I remained snuggled in my sleeping bag.

"Last one out of bed is a mudpie," he announced and then sat on me to keep me from getting up.

While they renewed their battle over who showered first, I shuffled to the kitchen, trying to ignore the latest problems. Insufficient funds. Insufficient eggs. Insufficient bread. Why hadn't I heard from Sid? Where was that fifteen hundred?

Two slices of bread under the oven broiler made toast. I scrambled the two remaining eggs so neither of the kids would sacrifice for me.

"Dad, not scrambled!" Lori pleaded.

"I'm sorry, but we only had two so I scrambled them."

"That's okay," she said, "divide it in half, I'm not hungry."

"No sir," said Ryan. "Thirds, right, Dad?"

"Right, thirds."

Once I had sold the car and paid the rent and other minor costs, we would have enough for the airfare to New Zealand. But there'd be only a few hundred dollars left over, certainly not enough to establish ourselves in a strange country. I would need weeks or even months to find a job paying enough for us to live on. Damn it, when would I get that money from Sid? Three weeks has passed since I'd asked him to send it.

I remembered his rumbling voice caressing the Trans-Pacific line, reaching out, always reaching, as though he couldn't let you get away, had to make you like him.

"Right away, old buddy, I'll send a cashier's check immediately. Made out to cash, you bet. And remember, we're in the same boat. And don't forget. Trust no one, Lee. Don't trust those bastards!"

Once again, I pondered the irony in his final admonition. I reran the memory, concentrating on the peculiar way his manner could shift unhesitatingly from smooth, equanimous assurance to venomous distrust and rage. Again, I considered the danger implicit in such a mercurial personality. Like the wayward wind, it could turn on you.

I would give the check two more days to arrive, then phone him. The thought of calling him prompted a sense of renewed haste and even pleasurable excitement, as if one phase of our odyssey neared completion. I needed to act quickly and decisively or risk losing hard-won momentum.

After lunch, I told the kids we were going to have to leave Hawaii. This time, Ryan seemed to take it better than Lori. They both wanted to know where we were going.

"Maybe New Zealand," I told them. "It's a beautiful place. Here, see for yourselves."

I showed them the travel brochures and read them clips from my research. Ryan liked the pictures of soaring green mountains and shepherds on horseback.

Lori asked about a photo of a handsome, tattooed Maori chieftain, but said she would miss her friends at her dance class and didn't like having to make new friends all the time.

"Me either," I said. "And I can't even tell you for sure if it will be New Zealand until the car sells and I make an important phone call. Tell you what, let's not worry about it. We have to go back to Hanauma Bay to get the tent. On the way, we'll talk about what we want to do during our last days in Hawaii. While we're there, you two can do a little snorkeling."

As we drove, they enjoyed naming their favorite beaches and planned excursions for the next week. With the pressure off for the moment, we would play vacationers again.

At the beach, we gathered up our tent and other equipment before the kids ran off to goggle, nose to nose with the colored fish. I took pictures and sat on the sand, reflecting that if we had to, we could retreat to the beaches again for our last week. We really had become gypsies, able to take it day by day, adjusting to changes in fortune as they came. We existed adventurously, despite our losses.

By late afternoon, I still hadn't thought of what to tell the landlord when he saw the house devoid of furniture. I just knew I would say or do whatever necessary to protect us.

Stuffed pork chops for our dinner were simmering in the oven when the doorbell rang. I had met Mr. Johnson before, a fussy, balding little man with a perpetual worried look.

Now I figured I was meeting the real power in the relationship, his petite Japanese wife. He introduced her as Kimsu. She smiled and gave a modified formal bow, her eyes swiftly taking in the emptiness of the room.

"I'm afraid this will have to be a stand-up visit." The bizarre situation had one advantage: If they couldn't sit down, they weren't likely to stay long. "As you can see, we're still rattling around here like dried peas in a pod. I think I told you I was waiting to hear from stateside and the shippers?"

Mr. Johnson nodded vaguely, an apparent attempt to conceal his shock over the empty apartment. "Oh yes, on the phone. About your furniture being delayed."

"Right. Well, my worst fears were confirmed yesterday. They sent our stuff to Alaska by mistake to another Landel family." I appealed to Mrs. Johnson. "I tell you, they're getting worse than the airlines."

"Yes," she said, her smile bright, her eyes alert and unimpressed.

"I don't know whether to file an insurance claim or start buying new furniture right now." I turned to Johnson. "I was wondering if you know a furniture dealer who might, well, you know, not be adverse to giving a small discount on a houseful of furniture."

He tugged a card from a small leather case, making an effort not to seem eager. "An old friend. Tell him I sent you, and he'll give you a break."

I chattered on about how it pays to know the right people and how I looked forward to the day when we were established here, with helpful contacts for my consulting business. I wrote out the rent check, while Johnson nervously shifted his feet and his wife stood immobile, her dark eyes riveted on my writing hand and the check.

"There you are. I called the bank this morning, and this time there will be no more computer mix-ups." I handed the check to Mr. Johnson and turned to call toward the kitchen,

"Lori, set our places for dinner, I'll be right there."

The kids were, in fact, out back playing. I turned back and smiled at Mrs. Johnson, "They're a great help to me."

"Yes," she said. "I hope you won't have to get by like this for long."

"Oh no." I gave her a reassuring smile. "Not for long at all."

I watched her eyes as she cast about for further reassurance but found none. She bowed again. "I am sure you will take good care of our condominium, Mr. Landel. We're glad we can leave your deposit intact, although, of course, next month's rent is now due in two weeks. Thank you."

"Thank you for being so patient."

Cheery good-byes, and the two departed. I peeked through the blinds as Mr. Johnson handed the check to Mrs. Johnson. She scrutinized it as they walked to their BMW.

❧

Thursday morning, October 7. The alarm jangled me awake and all the things yet to be done rose up in my consciousness, like one of those Waemia killer waves. With the house silent and the kids not up yet, I found I couldn't move. Too comfortable. I lay back, giving in for the moment, letting my senses awaken at their own pace, and my thoughts just followed along.

The neighborhood was waking up. Our flimsily built condo units stood cheek by jowl, windows open to gather the ocean breezes. Sounds came sharply and sometimes intimately. The family next door turned on their TV, and the program's host greeted the whole street. Somebody's dog barked. Other dogs chimed in.

A traffic helicopter wackered somewhere distant. A diesel engine revved, then idled in the driveway, pinging. A garbage truck beep-beeped as it backed to the dumpsters. Dogs again. A baby cried; a woman sang. Children shrilled off down the street, wrong direction for school, maybe going to the store. What day was it?

I had listened to these morning sounds before, but with distracted annoyance or suspicious attention. Now, I relished them, picturing the participants, wondering who they were, how they lived, rather than whether they were agents or detectives. Though we did not know one another, their smiles came easily on the street and gave me a sense of belonging.

Now, I allowed myself a cautious yearning toward people and the normalcy I hoped somehow to find again for myself and the kids. I felt the nostalgia return for Atlanta and for the sense of honest identity and purpose I had there, for the social comfort we call happiness.

But had that really been happiness or just an illusion leaving us all in pursuit of a deeper meaning to "happiness" and satisfaction in our lives?

Our isolation and the need to be alert had sharpened my sense of the world and myself. Had I ever listened to a suburban Atlanta morning with this attention? Had I really listened to my wife? Did I even know Val? If I had taken more time to understand her, if I had opened into myself more deeply, could we have experienced true intimacy and forestalled this emotional ruin? Had I been afraid to look at who I really was?

I pushed those thoughts away. My healing process had barely begun. Not even the U.S. State Department could issue a passport to inner peace. Besides, inner peace threatened my anger and rage, which I still needed in order to get through this latest crisis. I had to phone and confront Sid once and for all. We had to have that money to get off the island.

I pried myself from my sleeping bag, rekindled the bitter anger as an inner resource, and went to wake the kids.

Nonetheless, in those brief moments on that clamorous Honolulu morning, I had my first glimpse beyond my rage and the pressures of the escape. I now knew that once we were safe — if ever we were — deep and painful inner repairs needed to be made. They would be the hardest work of all.

❧

Lori and Ryan had been away from classes for ten days. The time had come for a formal withdrawal from Wilson Elementary. If there were official papers to be issued, I would need them for their next enrollment.

They had grown fond of their teachers and wanted to say proper good-byes. Dressed suitably, we walked to the school the next afternoon at 2:30 when classes were over.

Mrs. Nelson and Lori had become friends. I explained to her that I had received an attractive job offer in San Francisco. She sighed regrets.

"Hate to lose her, but Lori will do well wherever she is. I'll make sure her next teacher knows what a gem she's getting."

She made out copies of Lori's preliminary grades and some notes on her progress and handed them to me.

"Good luck, Mr. Landel." Her blue eyes twinkled behind her glasses as she held Lori at arms' length. "One last quiz, young lady. Who is buried in Grant's tomb?"

"Oh, burn," said Lori, and they hugged, both laughing, both with tears in their eyes.

Next, we sought out Mrs. Yamaguchi, who had been especially insightful with Ryan, taking note of his shyness and occasional melancholy, getting him through the afternoon when he had wept openly over the divorce. She had also helped him adjust to being a racial minority for the first time in his life. I thanked her the best way I knew how. She gave me copies of Ryan's progress reports. Scarcely as tall as Ryan, she shook his hand briskly. "Will you remember me?"

Ryan looked down at his feet. "Yes, ma'am. Always."

"Good. That's the reason for being a teacher." She sat down, readjusting her eyeglasses. "Well, at least in San Francisco, you won't have to put up with Hawaii's monotonous weather."

"Yes ma'am."

"But we do have a good word." Her eyes twinkled. "Aloha! Good-bye. At the same time, and I hope so, hello again."

At the administration office, a new woman behind the counter said the children did not need to make a formal withdrawal. When their new school requested a discharge certificate, it would be sent.

One document I wouldn't have to counterfeit.

❧

Sunday, October 10, we received a promising call from a man interested in the Rambler. He lived in Barbaras Point, and since we had never seen that corner of the island, I agreed to bring the car to his house the next morning. Money. Life's blood. Maybe this would be the sale I'd been hoping for.

We took Farrington Highway through sugar cane fields twenty-five miles to the southwest tip of the island. Here was an area the tourist industry had missed, or had selectively ignored. Still wild and verdant, it was a hint of what had been here when the island's ancient culture had thrived.

Our customer proved to be a grubby, surly character who perused, asked a few cursory questions and announced he didn't care for Ramblers. They tended to kite at high speeds.

What kind of turkey was this? Why hadn't he mentioned that on the phone? Kite. Smite. I was tempted to tell him to do more than go fly a kite.

To use our gorgeous day, we drove north past Barking Sands to Kaena Point. We saw fishermen balanced precariously on volcanic lava above the surf and native boys spring from high rock cliffs to make long, silent dives to the sea. How far back in time had natives used these majestic cliffs above the ocean? I had no way of knowing, but somehow our being here made us a part of their history, and our own as well.

Perhaps, the timelessness of the beaches we'd shared before had joined into this moment, because something within us shifted along this remote beach. I wondered if the simplicity of our existence these past months had brought us in touch with nature's most primitive urge, survival. Had our giving up everything, except what we had in our hearts, altered the image we had of ourselves and each other, and of the world as well?

Leaving now, we would have time to drive north up the coast to Sandy Beach.

Here, weeks earlier, Ryan and I had come within a fish gill of drowning. Even so, we were drawn to the golden sand and the killer waves. Our favorite beach on the island provided a kaleidoscope of body surfers riding the big waves.

Lori chased ocean suds, and Ryan built a sand castle. I photographed close-ups of their sand-blown faces as they dug caves in the dunes. By afternoon, our feet sizzled on the hot beach, and the time had come to leave.

"I don't want to leave — I mean Hawaii, Dad." pleaded Lori.

"I know," I said, brushing off the impact I knew this island had had on us. I took her hand to walk along the shore one more time, before catching up to Ryan.

Days passed and still no response to our car ad. I decided we had to resist beaches and stay around the apartment, hoping for a call. None came. I made frequent trips to rear and front windows, peering through the blinds, watching passersby suspiciously, worrying about parked vans.

I found myself yearning for a thunderstorm, a burst of hail or a snow blizzard. But instead, only the blinding sun, the heat, the waiting.

Columbus Day, when people were home, I was sure someone would call. If no calls, I would sell the car for a major loss at a lot .

We had to get moving. It could take us a month or even two to establish a new home. If necessary, I would begin a tutoring program in reading, writing, and math to keep the children ahead of any lag in their learning curves. But they were still losing precious school time.

New home, but where? Without selling the car, we wouldn't have enough money to settle in New Zealand. An alternative was Canada, but even that was too close to Atlanta for comfort, and if the Feds really were after us, their reach went around the world.

By evening, no calls about the car had come. I put the kids to bed, set the alarm for 2:30 a.m., crawled into my sleeping bag and tried to sleep. Eventually I did; the alarm tore me awake. I fumbled around the kitchen, making a cup of instant coffee. At 3:00, I took a deep breath and dialed Sid at home.

I had stopped listening for any telltale sounds of surveillance equipment. I didn't care. The phone rang eight times, then a click, and Sid's muffled "Hello."

"Don't hang up, Sid," I said quickly. "It's me, Lee. I have to have the money. We can't move without it."

Silence. Was he waking up or stalling? Finally, "Where?" he asked.

He could guess that. We had discussed New Zealand and Australia back in Atlanta. "I won't tell you. Did you get my letter?"

"Yeah." His tone, was flat, indifferent. "I sent you a cashier's check a week ago."

"To the address in the letter?"

"Right," he said. "That's where I sent it. Gotta go now, Lee."

"Wait!" I reached across the thousands of miles, not just for the money but for some remnant of the old emotional connection. I would even have welcomed sharing some anger again.

"Things are tough here, Sid, very tough."

"Sorry about that. But I took some risks myself, you know. I'm changing this number this afternoon. Don't bother to try to get me at work; you won't. I got my own troubles now. In fact, some people might say you owe me that fifteen hundred. Consider this a cutoff, Lee. Good luck. Good-bye."

With shaking hands, I dialed his number again. This time I counted fifteen rings before I put the receiver back.

I sat for a long time, trying to puzzle it out.

He'd spoken of his own troubles. While trying to trace me, had investigators become suspicious of him and Carrie? That would explain his turning on me, his feeling I owed him. Or maybe he needed the money as much as I and figured I wouldn't be back to Atlanta anytime soon to collect.

That thought hurt. Sid had been a friend when I most needed one. The tenderness between him and his daughter, her healthy cheerful personality, had quieted my doubts about raising children on my own. His friendship, assurance, and advice had just cost me fifteen hundred dollars. My mistake had been not listening to his most often spoken words: Trust nobody. Nobody.

Still, he had said he mailed the check.

Before noon, I was at the post office, asking for our mailman. He said he knew the mail drop location, but could recall only a small manila envelope with a see-through address window.

If he could remember a single piece, then surely he would have remembered a second larger manila envelope.

"Is there any way I can put a tracer on this?" I asked. "It's important to me."

The little mailman seemed worried that the service might have somehow failed. "I'm sorry. This doesn't happen often, but you can try this." He suggested I contact the dead letter office in San Francisco and gave me the number.

At the apartment, as I dialed, I imagined Sid deciding to keep my fifteen hundred dollars, giving the same wolfish smile he had when he described conning a free trip in first class, walking out on a restaurant bill, backing out with the advance on a script he never intended to write.

Getting one up on the world. Paying it back. For what?

Sometimes, I had forced a cynical smile of my own to mirror and acknowledge his.

"Description of the search item, please."

I gave the woman the details I had: large manila envelope, date sent, the address, the contents.

And my future, I wanted to add, *and the future and safety of my children.*

They had nothing fitting that description.

Nothing.

Our veins had just been emptied of fifteen hundred dollars in life's blood. I had barely enough to pay the airfare to New Zealand, and I needed enough to cover rent and food until I found a job. We could no longer afford to linger at Wailae Gardens. The electricity and phone bills were overdue, and the intrepid Mrs. Johnson would come for the rent in twelve hours or less.

I considered using Sid's method for flying first class without paying. But it was risky. And, to my fleeting puzzlement, I found myself deciding I had done enough wrong changing identities and didn't want any more guilt.

That evening we packed. I told Lori and Ryan we were going to bide our time at their favorite beaches. That cheered them up.

The next morning, the phone rang. A woman said her husband was interested in looking at the car. He would be home on his noon hour, if we could bring the Rambler over then.

We swept the sand out of the car and removed our beach gear from the back seat. Lori cleaned the windows inside while I wiped the outside. I figured by the time we reached the caller's house, the hot engine would make the tapping sound barely noticeable.

We pulled into their driveway at noon. A pleasant, casually dressed man about my age came out. An English professor at the

University of Hawaii, we learned, and no automotive idiot, either. He checked the car over with the thoroughness of a forensic lab technician. On a test drive, he said he heard a tapping sound in the engine. Also that the car needed new brakes, shocks, and a muffler. He talked a lot, mostly about how much the car needed fixing. None of which I noticed when I purchased it.

"There's another car I want to look at," he said. "I'll give you a call later to let you know what I decide."

Aloha, Professor.

We stopped at the beach before returning home. As we walked into the apartment, the phone rang. It was our forensic expert calling. He offered me five hundred dollars for the Rambler.

"Tell you what," I told him, "if it doesn't sell this weekend, I'll accept your offer on Monday."

"I'll call you then, Mr. Landel. Cheers."

Five hundred wasn't much to cheer about, but at least it would be better than the three hundred we would get at a used car lot.

Time pressed in on us, as the tension of doing nothing became a waiting time bomb. The police could drive up at any minute. I sought avoidance by napping in the shade on our patio while the kids played with their new travel books.

An hour later, I sat bolt upright, sure I had heard knocking at the front door. I listened again. Just Ryan and Lori pounding the table pasting paper shapes.

After dinner, we drove to the bookstore and left Ryan sitting on his favorite stool, gobbling up aerospace books. Lori and I toured the jewelry counters and finally found tiger-eye earrings and a matching necklace with a gold chain for five dollars.

Later, after the children slept, I looked through my world travel books to decide where we would go. Using money as a major determinant, I chose Vancouver, British Columbia. The closest English-speaking foreign city within reach of our budget, Vancouver offered the only promising choice. In the morning over pancakes, I told Lori and Ryan.

She said if we had to leave Hawaii, she didn't care where we went as long as we were together. Ryan's lower lip thrust out, but this time there were no tears. He just didn't understand why we couldn't stay where we were.

I had explained earlier; I explained again.

"I really do think this will be the last big move for us," I said. "And I promise wherever we go, we'll make a happy home. We have so far, haven't we?"

He had to acknowledge that much, but his gloom didn't lift until I asked if he had found any aerospace books he liked.

He named several.

"Okay. Lori got earrings, you get a book to read on the plane. Then, when you become an astronaut, you can pay me back."

Finally a grin. "You can't bribe astronauts."

"Oh well," I said, "in that case, forget it."

"Wait," he said. "I'm not an astronaut yet!"

Friday, October 15, I called Pan Am's reservation desk and learned that flying direct to Seattle was the cheapest way to reach the continent. We would rent or buy a car and drive north across the border to Vancouver.

I made reservations for Mrs. Mary Bernard and her two children, Susan, 10, and John 8. Three days to another Launch Day. After covering the airfares, little remained of our reserves. I wondered what kind of public assistance Vancouver offered. In Canada, welfare was called The Dole. God help us if we had to try for that with my questionable history.

I wanted to make the most of our last weekend on the island. Friday night, I scarcely slept. Saturday, at dawn, I left the kids asleep and took my camera to catch the sunrise behind the Diamond Head lighthouse. An indigo and crimson blaze had risen up to paint a watercolorist's dream across the horizon. The soft morning light calmed my restlessness and gave me hope for what lay ahead.

After breakfast, we loaded the car with our remaining saleable items: the folding chairs, two speakers, a lamp. I had already sold my boyhood stamp and coin collections and a dozen other small but personally precious things. First stop, the pawn shop, where we got forty dollars for the common household stuff.

Cherishing our memories of Hawaii, we toured the island, taking pictures of our favorite spots, lingering at the Pali lookout and marveling one last time at the panoramic vista of windward Oahu. On our return to Honolulu, we celebrated our last weekend in Hawaii by eating dinner out.

Saturday morning, we stayed close to the apartment, hoping someone would call and buy the car. We cleaned the apartment until it was as spotless as when we moved in. More waiting, pacing the carpet, peering nervously out at the street. Around eleven, a woman called. I described the car. She said she would talk it over with her father and call back. She didn't.

The kids squabbled over a box of raisins. I had them count them out: twenty-seven, an uneven number.

"What shall we do, oh wise one?" Lori asked.

I popped the spare raisin into my mouth. "I'm on a raisin diet. When my spirits are down, I raisin . . ."

They groaned gleeful criticism of my terrible pun.

Later in the afternoon, I called the professor and told him I accepted his offer. He said he was pleased but had thought it over and decided he would pay only four hundred fifty dollars. He added that he planned to look at a couple of other cars Sunday morning unless I accepted his offer.

The professor was getting to be a pain in the ass. I gave him the registration numbers and other information. We agreed to meet at his bank at 9:30 Monday morning, only a few hours before our Pan Am flight was to leave for Seattle.

I reviewed our finances. With luck and care, we had enough to carry us six weeks once we reached Vancouver.

Our last day, we walked along the Waikiki pier, where we had first enjoyed the sun and bright throngs of tourists. Out of fear, I still watched passing faces, letting the kids gambol on ahead. I felt more comfortable separated from them, as though any pounce by police might get only me and somehow leave them unscathed.

Monday morning, we were up at 7:00, had breakfast, cleaned the kitchen, carried the bags to the car. The kids asked me to take pictures of Wilson Elementary. There were brief tears in Lori's eyes.

"I'm so tired of moving, Dad," she said.

"Me too," Ryan added.

Again, I held their hands and told them in heartfelt truth that I also hated to leave, but that we had to get on with our lives.

At 9:30, we met the professor at the bank. After completing the deal, I went to a teller's window, intending to change some loose coins into thirteen precious one-dollar bills. The professor, relaxed and even more loquacious than before, assumed I was buying traveler's checks.

"Listen, Lee, I have a friend at the Cook agency who can give you traveler's checks at no cost. Just a few blocks away."

Reluctantly, I consented to his taking us to his friend. I didn't want traveler's checks. They would provide a link connecting us from Hawaii to Seattle.

Another possible mistake because I couldn't speak of our situation.

With two thousand dollars in traveler's checks made out to Lee Landel, and ready to bid farewell, the professor, still persisting in being helpful, asked where he could take us. Again, not thinking, I told him we were on our way to the airport. He asked what airline.

I tried to cover our tracks. "United."

"I'll drive you out."

It was 10:15, our Pan Am departure time was 11:00. A taxi could get us to the airport in fifteen minutes, but only if the traffic didn't jam up, which it sometimes did. Again, his friendly insistence persuaded me. I had lived in lonely fear so long, a little casual kindness swept away my usual defenses.

Once in the Rambler and on our way, he asked, "Where you bound for?"

I tried to cover my previous lapse by saying San Francisco, a new job in real estate development there.

Real estate, now that was interesting. He had investments of his own, which he described at length as he drove. At least he asked no more questions about us.

We pulled alongside the United departure curb, but still he lingered, helping us unload the luggage. Either he felt guilty about chiseling us on the car, or he just couldn't stand to be alone. Maybe he was just a nice man. With the cases on the curb, I turned to shake his hand and thank him, but he already had two suitcases in his hands and was heading toward the United counter.

We joined him at the end of the line. He started a conversation with Lori, asking if she had read *The House With Green Gables.*

The ticket line diminished rapidly, moving us closer to the TV monitor and the United schedule, which showed no flight to San Francisco.

I grasped the professor's hand and pumped it hard. "I want to thank you very much. Very, very much!"

Perhaps it was the preternatural loudness of my voice, or the vice-like grip of my hand. Something signaled him that finally, we wanted to be alone. He shrugged, bent to say good-bye to Lori and Ryan, gave me a final smile of immense good will, then waved and walked to his Rambler.

"Come on!" I whispered to the kids. "Let's get over to the right airline."

As we abandoned the United line and labored toward the distant Pan Am desk, I had a sudden sense of being out of my body, somewhere high above, against the ceiling, looking down at this harried father lurching along with a bulging suitcase in each hand, trailed by an equally burdened and struggling girl and boy. I thought, if I were God observing this scene, I would have to be gently amused by this befuddled and determined trio, maybe even a little forgiving from now on.

"Boy," Ryan puffed from behind me somewhere, "that professor sure takes up a lot of talking space."

"You can say that again," I gasped.

"Boy," my two cute angels chirped in chorus, "that professor sure takes up a lot . . ."

THIRTEEN

A CLEAN SLATE

Children are surely one of God's greatest gifts and truest challenges. To share your life with a child is to humble yourself...

— Kathleen Tierney Crilly

As the plane gained altitude and began its interminable drone, I slowly relaxed. Surely, in a plane full of strangers flying at twenty thousand feet, we could be safe from anyone trailing us. Just to make sure, I took a stroll through the tourist compartment to check for any suspicious looking faces.

Seeing none, I slid into my seat, luxuriating in a bath of peace and anonymity. Lori and Ryan wasted no time asking for a deck of cards for a game of Spoon. By now, they were accomplished travelers and expert at amusing themselves.

At least for a few hours, I could let go long enough to relax and come to grips with what had happened to us these past months, then brace myself for our future.

I ordered a soft drink and nuts and reached into my travel bag for my pen and note pad. Inside the notebook, I discovered the brass name plate from the grandfather clock.

The weeks had passed quickly since that day in the pawn shop when we had reluctantly sold our most substantial and beloved symbol of family. At least I had the name plate. I rubbed its face on my pant leg to restore the luster; its smooth metal warmed in my hand. My real name, engraved in bold capital letters, flashed up at me.

Yes, Lee Coburn, you've been away only months, yet you've traveled far from your real identity. But how real was that identity? Running to elude your pursuers has put the old self into sharper focus. But were you really running from someone, or instead running from looking at your own empty, unknown self. Yes, Lee, you have experienced the darkest period of your life. You've been through the fire and have been affected in ways yet to be discovered.

I studied the children's faces out of the corner of my eye: suntanned, eager, absorbed in their game. They didn't understand that Hawaii had cost us everything. We had only a suitcase each of clothes and a small cash reserve. No home, no assets, no professional standing, no job prospects, no friends, no family waiting for us in Seattle.

And yet, our "nothing" was not the everyday world's "nothing." Stripped of our identity, fugitives, threatened with separation, we somehow had gained a deeper appreciation of each other, and of something greater than ourselves, which we had never known before.

Was experiencing the truth of our emotions and accepting our feelings showing us a way to beyond ourselves? This would account for Lori and Ryan's ability to live eagerly in the moment. For them, living more emotionally honest made them feel safer, no matter how threatening, just as long as we stayed together. My mind worked to comprehend and accept what they knew instinctively. In this, they became my teachers. Never in my old life, when ambition clouded my vision, would I have understood, much less have accepted the lessons offered from others. The children, once again, were my spirited guides to this emerging man.

They drew me into conversation about their card game. The words were only a way to touch, as a family of cats will move about, periodically touching, reaffirming the bond. Then my thoughts returned to our future.

What frightened me most was running out of money. Coping with the moment-to-moment situation was complicated enough; without money, things would become so difficult my entire effort might fall apart. How long did I have before becoming desperate? I visualized each step to be made once the plane deposited us on the mainland. On a piece of paper, I wrote a budget of anticipated expenses.

Motel — Seattle five days to buy car — $175.
Rent a car — five days at $20/day — $100.
Purchase car — $400.
Food — sixty days to first pay check, $20/day — $1200.
Housing — eight weeks 200 per month — $400.
Gasoline, cloths and sundries — $250.
Contingency — $100.
Total for sixty days — $3025.
Available Funds — $3000.

It would be tight, but if we were frugal, we could make it to the end of December.

In Seattle, our first priority would be to find a motel, then a car. The sooner we had transportation, the sooner we could cross the border and begin our life in Canada. Every day consumed a portion of our precious reserves.

Thinking about how quickly we could become financially desperate stirred my anger at Sid Salano. I needed the fifteen hundred dollars he owed me. Remembering his callous farewell made my blood boil again.

"I got my own troubles now," he said. "In fact, some might say you owe me that fifteen hundred, Lee . . ."

That son of a bitch. Yet I'd ignored his continual warning to trust no one. He had never included himself among the untrustworthy, but hadn't the implication always been there?

"Trust nobody, (not even me)."

It was possible he had set me up all along. I would soon be a fugitive, possibly in some foreign country under a false identity. He knew better than I what it was like to be anonymous and legally helpless.

Had it all been lies, his warnings about the two investigators and the federal indictment? Had he planned to panic me so I'd feel too helpless to retrieve what he owed me?

My hand clenched the brass plate so hard the flesh turned white. Something else made me hate his memory even more. I recalled the prurient, obliquely sexual urgency of his voice, that salesman's need to reach out, manipulate, compel. His "charm" couldn't conceal his venomous anger and rage. "Don't trust the bastards. It's a snakepit out there. . ."

Perhaps it was. If you needed your anger to hide from your fear of healing the wounds of your past. If you could not forgive yourself or your ex-wife for actions long since over.

Six years after kidnapping his daughter, he was still as angry as the night he fled Los Angeles. Our angers had met like two lost brothers uniting. And in that madness, we became comrades, fellow conspirators against the world and all its ills. Our conspiracy lasted as long as it served to feed his inner turmoil and to justify his dark view of humanity and himself. But worst of all, I had become a pawn in his hatred of women.

"Screw 'em and use 'em, Lee, or they'll use you."

No, I would not become like that, no matter how hard things got. The time had come to let go of the bilious memory of Sid Salano, along with the fifteen hundred dollars. God knew I was bitter enough. But beyond the walls of jealousy and anger, I glimpsed the promise of another more honest light. I had only to look at my children to know love existed.

My grip loosened on the brass plate; saw the blood flow again. Yes, we had to start all over, but at least we would do it with a clean slate.

So long, Sid. There isn't even any need for vengeance against you. You will take care of that. You will fester yourself sick with anger for all the rest of your poisoned life. True, my rage has propelled us to keep going, but I don't want to be forever angry.

As the plane began its descent, the kids pressed their noses to the window to gasp at the vast lights of Seattle. My tension returned, and with it the strain of constant caring for Lori and Ryan and my unrelenting worry that one crucial mistake would unravel our cover.

We continued dropping fifty feet a second into the heart of a dense, unknown jungle. Dwelling on my difficulties wouldn't help. *One step at a time, Lee. Don't forget, in the constant looking over your shoulder, how far you've come.*

The panel overhead winked on: Fasten Seats Belts. Lori and Ryan chattered with anticipation of a new adventure.

I restored the brass plate to my bag. Someday, I would attach it to a new grandfather clock and openly proclaim: Our family is back, wiser and a lot more accepting.

❧

October 19, Tuesday, one year minus nine days since Val told me she was leaving. Three months since Launch Day, a lifetime and a half. Yet, as we took in our first deep breath of Seattle, I experienced a surge of optimism I hadn't felt since our arrival in Hawaii.

We hopped a shuttle bus to Motel 6, just outside Sea-Tac Airport.

After allowing ourselves the luxury of sleeping in, we found a restaurant with a $1.95 breakfast. From here on, money would be my constant concern, yet the simple meal lifted our spirits.

We returned to the motel under somber gray skies, breathing in the thick autumn air. That faint scent of burning leaves carried me back to when I was a boy raking lawns to earn a dollar. I remembered darting through the smoke with my eyes closed, challenging my limits.

Now my limits had met another challenge, moving around by bus in a strange city to buy a car. The casual friendliness of everyone eased our entry into the sprawling metropolis.

I spent the day standing in a phone booth, calling car ads. I also phoned the British Colombia Tourist Bureau to inquire about jobs and living in Vancouver. Restrictions were minimal. Good. We would continue with our plans to hide in Canada.

For dinner, we found a restaurant with all you could eat for $2.50. As we discussed our first day in Seattle, I wrote in my budget book our daily expenses. We had already run over my twenty dollar per day survival budget.

I had never known destitution. To my knowledge, eighty percent of Americans have never known endemic, persistent poverty, though everywhere the threat of it persists. Fear of financial desolation becomes the whip of a modern industrial society. Coming to the edge was one thing, but to feel the precipice under my toes, not just momentarily, but day after day, was quite another. I did not take lightly the power of privation's crushing hand.

But that wouldn't happen to me, I told myself. My responsibility to the children assured me of not giving up. Things becoming more difficult only added to my determination. We would survive. Somehow.

On Wednesday, we took the bus to West Seattle to look at a used car. The '65 Rambler Classic advertised for $400 might be just the car. Two hours and three bus transfers later put us inside the Rambler, inspecting its rather tattered interior.

Offered $300.

Owner held firm.

No sale.

Back on the bus.

Our return bus ride brought us into downtown Seattle. We found a diner and had chili and milk shakes. At Penney's, we bought Ryan a coat and gloves, and Lori a knitted hat. Second day gone and still no transportation. In my journal that night, I wrote: "By now I'm used to everything coming hard. Just keep going, somehow we have to make this work."

Up early on Thursday. We had to keep pushing. While the kids watched morning cartoons, I used the lobby pay phone to make calls. My fifth call turned up a 1960 Chrysler New Yorker in my price range. The owner offered to drive it over for us to look at. By

11:00, I had taken it for a test drive. An elephant of a car, but it ran well as near as I could tell. The mileage would be bad, but time was wasting. We could get a better car later. The seller wanted $500. I offered $400. Settled on $450. Fifty over my budget.

We returned to his house, where I gave him cash and received the signed title in return. By noon, we had wheels of our own, just in time to check out before 1:00.

We headed north. Crossing into Canada, I told the border patrol we were from Seattle. Through fog and intermittent rain, we drove into Vancouver. I checked us into a budget-fitting motel of prehistoric vintage. The room was filthy.

The next morning, I called the Canadian Immigration Service. My enthusiastic tourist bureau ambassador back in Seattle had not told me everything.

For temporary residency in Canada, I needed a letter of acceptance from the Immigration Office. This would be issued only after receiving the appropriate forms from my intended employer. The process took about two months, sometimes three.

To become a permanent resident, I had to apply from outside Canada. This would take eight months. Any deviation, such as trying to work without a permit, was punishable by deportation at best, and possibly stiff fines and/or imprisonment.

And certainly an investigation into my past activities, such as abducting my children, I thought to myself.

I hung up. Frustration sank through me. My knees turned limp as I stared at the torn phone book. We couldn't chance living in Vancouver.

At the motel, I explained to Lori and Ryan why we had to leave, then waited for their reactions. I felt silly bringing us all the way to Canada to learn we couldn't risk staying.

They sat on the sagging bed, back to back. Lori looked up from her book, and in the dim light, her pretty face looked older, weary. Her small smile lit up the room.

"It's okay," she said. "I liked Seattle better anyway."

Ryan's brow puckered; his silent wide-eyed stare needed no words. It said simply, "When will we have a home?"

As we crossed back into the U.S. that afternoon, the Border Patrol officer asked if I had accepted employment or bought anything. "Neither," I said.

We drove south though gray, drifting drizzle. The kids dozed, Lori's head against Ryan's shoulder, while the wipers thumped and scraped. When we reached the outskirts of Seattle's north end, I exited I-5 over to U.S. Highway 99, also known as Aurora Avenue. In its prime, this had been the main arterial through Seattle, but now it had become car lot city, dotted with tired vintage motels and restaurants, their signs as worn as their mattresses. Names like "Nights Inn," "Rodeside Lodge," "Wagon Wheel Motel" and "Twin Tepees" welcomed us as we drove.

I called to check rates, settling on the Golden West Motel. Weekly rate, $10 per night, one double and one single bed, color TV, a desk, lamps, kitchenette with utensils, a parking area for Ryan to practice skate boarding, and best of all, a free telephone in working order. One hundred dollars per month over budget.

I handed the money for two nights through metal bars in the window of the locked motel office door.

That night, the kids slept soundly in the double bed while I lay in the single, drifting off for a few hours, awakening periodically to make plans, as blue neon light flickered through the curtain.

In the morning, with the help of the yellow pages, I called to inquire about stationery stores and prices, printers, and a secretary to pull my résumé materials together. In the afternoon, we went exploring to learn more about the city.

Halloween had also been on my mind, since it had always been a special time in our family. I worried about it being a disappointment for the kids this year.

As we drove south on Aurora, they spotted a pumpkin stand. The search for the right pumpkin turned hilarious when I told them we'd buy as big a pumpkin as Ryan could lift.

In the car, they drew faces in a notebook to decide on their favorite design for the pumpkin. They agreed on a smiling face with one tooth missing.

Continuing south, we located Gasworks Park. I had read about the place in a Seattle Guide Book. On a prominent point of land on the northern shore of Lake Union, a retired city gasworks plant had been converted into a city park. The aging steel boilers, catwalk, and now brightly painted machinery had become the focal point of a new park, which included a panoramic view of Seattle's downtown skyline.

On the highest knoll, we braved the evening chill to fly the delta kite we had brought from Hawaii. We took turns holding the taut line. Looking south across the lake, we watched city lights sparkling on the skyline as marbled silver skies faded into darkness. Pleasure boats slid past slowly. As the quieting breeze lowered the kite, Lori and Ryan huddled against me in the cool night air.

"Well," I said, "this is it, kids. What do you think?"

"Can we go on a boat, Dad?" Ryan asked.

"Just as soon as we get to know someone who owns one."

"I'm going to learn to sail," he said.

"It won't be as hot as in Hawaii," Lori said, always looking for the positive angle, but also alert to the realities of our situation. "And look." She pointed to a distant shoreline. "There are a lot more trees here, Dad."

"I'm going to buy a kite," said Ryan. "It will be a dragon kite, and it will have a fifty-foot tail."

Holding hands, thankful to be together, we crossed the dark lawn to the car.

We parked in front of Unit 5, Golden West Motel. Ryan got the pumpkin out, staggered a little under its load. "I guess we're kind of lucky," he allowed.

Lori added, "Sometimes."

The next morning we awoke to cool air rippling past the open curtains. Sunlight streamed through the window onto the bed.

I left the kids in the room while I headed downtown to the post office.

In Atlanta, though comfortable and reasonably sure of what I wanted for my future, a vast, amorphous sense of discontent troubled me. With my growing disillusionment, I had inflated the rewards I thought I deserved: a large home, national recognition, some earth-rattling grand destiny. Somewhere in my marriage to Val, we had set our goals so high, we had lost touch with each other and the things that really mattered.

Now, small things brought me joy, like helping to find just the right pumpkin. When you're destitute, there's little time for big dreams. You inch along from crisis to recovery, and small setbacks can get you down, while incidental joys, one sunny morning out of five, can make you feel blessed and thankful.

I stood in line at General Delivery for almost an hour, only to be told that two of the three boxes I had requested from New Zealand were missing. I needed certain items for my job portfolio; the missing boxes probably held them. Damn.

When I returned to the car, a ten dollar parking ticket had been placed under my wiper. Five breakfasts! Damn.

On the way home, the car overheated. I pulled into a service station. The attendant, shaking his head over the engine, said I needed a new thermostat. If I had the tools, I could replace it myself, but the tools alone would cost double what the mechanic wanted for the job. I decided to chance letting it go for a while.

As I drove up in front of our motel room, clouds of steam rolled from beneath the Chrysler's hood. Lori and Ryan came out, restless and cranky, complaining I had been gone too long. Inside, the balloons I had given them lay punctured and discarded on the furniture.

"Clean this mess up," I said more curtly than I intended.

"I want to go out with my skateboard," Ryan muttered.

"No!" I snapped. "There are too many cars out there."

He stared, wide-eyed. Lori sulked from my shouting.

"I'm sorry," I muttered. "Bad morning. I don't think I have my stuff in here . . ."

I pried at the stubborn wrapping on the box. Even the tape seemed bent on thwarting me. Swearing, I clawed it open. On top, in one thick, neat packet sat the documents I needed for my presentation: the PBC brochure, my color negatives of architectural jobs, limited partnership memorandums, et cetera.

"Damn it," I snapped. "Would you believe, it was here all along?" I turned to blink at the children. "I'm sorry I blew my stack."

Lori put her arm across my shoulder as I kneeled at the box. "I'm glad you have your stuff, Dad."

Ryan flung the ruptured balloons and bounced on the bed. "Let's eat."

Let the Chrysler steam; we weren't going far. We found a small park on a back street, and Ryan whizzed around on his board for half an hour while Lori and I pumped on the swings.

At the restaurant, we sat in a corner booth, which the kids liked because we could see the Pink Elephant Car Wash sign and the big turning world globe atop the Post Intelligencer newspaper building. We opted for the evening special, creamed chicken a la king. At our request the waitress brought two delicacies that had eluded us in Hawaii: green olives for Sassafras, watermelon for the Melon Kid.

Our royal feast. Dinner for three, $12.50.

The next day, I worked on my résumé and made plans for getting the children started on a home-learning program. With a roof over our heads and transportation, I could concentrate on reducing our housing cost and finding a job. My failing budget hinted of complications ahead.

FOURTEEN

GYPSIES IN SEATTLE

"I never think about the past,"
Lucy tells Charlie Brown.
"Also, I never worry about the future."
"What about the present?" he asks her.
"The present drives me crazy!" she howls.

— Charles M. Schulz

Sunday morning, October 31, Halloween. Lori and Ryan began tickling each other before their feet hit the floor. Tonight, they were going trick-or-treating. Reason to rejoice, indeed. We spent the day making costumes and makeup and readying the shopping bags for the night with ghosts and goblins. Lori prepared to go as a black cat and Ryan talked the cleaning woman into giving him an old sheet for his ghost outfit.

As dusk settled and street lights came on, we drove to a neighborhood in nearby Richmond Beach. We had earlier discovered this area of large homes with sidewalks along lush green lawns, and tonight, yellow lights hallooed every porch.

Wrapped in the glow of early darkness, parents waited as masqueraded little people rang door bells. Shrill voices chanted the magic words, "Trick or treat, money or eats," each masked goblin counting on immediate reward like no other time of year. I joined the fun as just another father out with his children. We walked the streets for an hour and a half until the bags of one cat and a ghost bulged full.

Eventually, the streets quieted as porch lights, one by one, blinked dark, sending us to our car amidst raves of who got the most candy. Ryan couldn't wait to get home to inspect his loot.

At our room, they spread their sweet surprises out on the bed. The children's eyes glowed wide — treasure hunters discovering a chest of gold. Methodically, they counted and compared their cache. Eating popcorn balls, they carefully stored the rest for future rewards. Soon they clamored into bed, saving the half-finished balls for tomorrow.

"Thanks for a great Halloween, Dad," Lori said as she pulled the blanket up to her nose.

"I'll share my candy with you, Dad," Ryan offered. "Goodnight."

I listened to whisperings of this latest adventure as I sat in the corner under a dim light, trying to read.

My mind kept returning to the neighborhood of homes we had just pretended to be a part of. So reminiscent of our own neighborhood in north Atlanta. How strange it had felt to mingle among affluent and stable and law-abiding parents my age. The camaraderie of Halloween had made me, for the moment, one of them, a member of the legitimate human race. Would I ever again have security and the respect of friends and community?

I brushed the thought from my mind. A more pressing concern had to be faced. Our budget. Our motel costs were running too high.

❧

On the first of November, we moved to a new motel farther south on Aurora, the Skyline Motel.

Two double beds dominated the small room which offered a single window looking out onto a greasy, pot-holed parking lot. An old black and white television, the lower half of the screen black, rested on a wobbly, 1940s motel dresser. The closet-sized kitchen provided a small table where I could work, though the cabinets were bare of utensils. Lori inspected the cramped bathroom and volunteered to clean the shower stall. Bolstering her morale, I offered, "I know it's not much. But at least it's within our budget at a hundred and eighty-five a month.

On Tuesday, while I worked on my résumé, I listened to the election returns. In the beginning, few had believed Carter could win the Democratic nomination, let alone the presidency. If he won the election, our neighbor at D'Youville, Jody Powell, would no doubt move to Washington to continue as Carter's press secretary. I didn't dare send him a letter of congratulation.

Working on the bed with her new math book, Lori mused, "Maybe Emily will move to Washington D.C. Do you think so, Dad?"

"Most likely," I replied.

"Now I know I'll never see her again," she said.

"You'll be in school soon. You'll have new friends."

Her glance sought the dim light of the window. Rain spilled softly down the window panes, blurring our view.

"But I'll never have another friend like Emily. Dad?" The rise in her voice prepared me for another question. "Are we going to live in a motel forever?"

I told her I didn't know how long it would be, but I hoped to get a job by the end of November.

When they had completed their math, I gave them each a story to write about themselves as practice for essays they would be assigned once back in school.

After a few minutes, Lori asked if she should put down she had a mother.

"You do have a mother," I said, and added lightly, "You couldn't be born without one, you know."

She didn't smile. "I mean now."

"The answer is still yes, except she isn't able to be with us."

"I mean in describing my family. I mean, to me, family doesn't include having a mother now." The light from the lamp accentuated the pout of her mouth. I couldn't see her eyes. Ryan didn't look up.

"I agree with that," I finally murmured, and returned to my papers.

Half an hour later, Lori took a new tack. "What would each of us want if we could have only one thing?"

"Popcorn," spouted Ryan.

"Let's assume," I said as I got up to start some popcorn, "that we have food and shelter," realizing that this could be a big assumption. "What would you want next? You first, Lori."

This time, I could see her eyes. They gleamed with held back tears; she mustered her bright chin-up smile.

"A family."

"Ryan, what about you?"

"A family," he echoed, his solemn gaze fixed on his sister.

"Well, good," I said. "The same for me. But you two are my family. And I can be a father to you every day, instead of only on weekends." Silently, I was afraid to feel their loss I knew I was responsible for.

Lori nodded. Her small brow lines deepened as she looked at her paper. Ryan stared mournfully at her.

"And I'm grateful for that," I said. "Very grateful."

I stayed at the stove, feeling forlorn and a failure. The popcorn began to pop. Lori came in to melt the butter, and as I handed her the pan, she pushed against me and said softly, "We're glad, too, Dad."

❧

Wednesday, November 3. As President-elect Jimmy Carter received the press on the morning news, I figured out how to make coffee in a peanut butter jar by using a paper towel as a filter. Not bad coffee, either.

After telling the kids I would be back by eleven or call them on the pay phone in the parking lot at five after, I left to locate Highland Terrace Elementary School.

Mabelle, manager of the motel, with a couple of school children of her own and a little wild around the edges herself, had told me which school Lori and Ryan should attend. I found it, a contemporary cluster of red brick and glass buildings surrounded by green lawns and a large playfield. The school was nestled into a neighborhood of small homes with painted shutters and blooming flower beds. I could picture Lori and Ryan going to school here at Highland Terrace.

To my chagrin, Mr. Patelles, the principal, had left for the day, so I spoke with his administrative assistant.

Mrs. Olson, a pert woman in her mid-fifties, polite and a little brusque, asked if she could help. Behind her strict "toe the line" approach, I sensed a kind and generous person. Even so, I couldn't help but notice that the deep concentration lines between her brows seldom softened.

I told her an unexpected job change had prompted our moving to Seattle from Hawaii and we were temporarily housed at the Skyline Motel. As a result, my children had been out of school for a couple of weeks. (By now, it was closer to a month.)

"Fine, Mr. Landel. Just fill out these forms, please."

I hadn't expected an application so soon. Methodically, I began filling in the forms, but my alarm skills were rusty, and I couldn't remember the first name I had given for their mother on the fake birth certificates. Mary? Joyce? It wouldn't do to back out now. I wrote in Joyce and ignored marital status for the moment.

Mrs. Olson handed me a booklet. As she explained about the school, her firm face changed to one of animated delight. She handed me another form. This one requested records from Wilson Elementary in Honolulu and required my signature to authorize their release.

I had to sign. But looking up at her, I said, "Actually, a special situation exists here. I'd like to talk to Mr. Patelle about it."

"That can be arranged, Mr. Landel," she said calmly.

I sensed the quiet stirring of questions raised in her mind. She made some note on her calendar and gave me an appointment to talk with Mr. Patelle at 9:00 on Lori and Ryan's first day of school.

Driving back to Skyline, an all too familiar panic returned

when I checked their birth certificates and found their mother's name was Mary Joyce Landel, not just Joyce.

I'd almost forgotten who we were: strangers in a strange land. Too many names and too much stress. Never mind, I consoled myself, lots of people go by their middle names.

Thursday, we got up early for the kids to get their hair washed and wiggle into their best school clothes.

On the way, I drove, my stomach churned, they giggled.

While Lori and Ryan waited in the outside office, Mr. Patelle received me in his inner sanctum.

"Well, Mr. Landel, Mrs. Olson says you have a special situation?"

He was a small-framed man in his late fifties with a distinguished air about him. His gray eyes, behind rimless glasses, suggested a cautious but kind individual. His words drifted across his desk like pieces of velvet tailored for the moment.

"I've been on a consultation assignment in Hawaii," I explained, "and needed more time than I expected, so I enrolled the kids in Wilson Elementary in Honolulu. Since my divorce, there's been a difficult situation with my former wife, and I don't want them disturbed by that sort of thing here."

His glance flickered over the enrollment application. "You said you and your wife are divorced?"

I hesitated, then assumed a posture of remorse, of a man about to confess a painful truth. "She drinks. By at least two doctors' definitions, she's an alcoholic. I don't know about that, I'm no expert. I'm in Seattle to start over, and this time I intend to do it right and without any painful scenes. She's under treatment, but she has money and means of finding us. I don't want her jumping the court order to come in here and, excuse me, raise hell."

"Hmmm." It was clear he didn't much care for that possibility, himself. "You mean she doesn't know where you are?"

"It's in the best interests of the children that she doesn't," I said, "at least, until she finishes her treatment. Meanwhile, we'll have the opportunity to get settled before putting up with any more of the turmoil we've had in the past year and a half."

Nodding in apparent sympathy, he made a note on a yellow legal pad.

"We had a similar situation here last year, but in reverse, so to speak. It was the husband who came barging in. For our protection, we'll need a copy of that restraining order you mentioned."

I had talked myself into soup. I couldn't back out now, if I tried. "That's a rather remote possibility right now. My attorney is away in Europe."

"Remote perhaps," he put in, "but you are asking us not to contact the school in Hawaii for a reason, and I have to have something in my file to justify that special consideration. Not necessarily notarized, just the original order."

Further hesitation would only make him suspicious. "I'll telegram his office tomorrow. They must have it in their file."

His smile returned. He stood, and we shook hands on the deal. "Now let's get your children to their classes."

This latest requirement appeared to be the toughest one so far. After seeing the kids to their rooms, I headed to the motel to search my files for anything that would get me started on the production of a court restraining order.

Nothing. But one thing we learned in law school: whatever the question, somewhere there's a book with the answer.

At the University of Washington Law Library, I found the books I needed. After writing six pages of notes I returned to the school, where I hoped to buy a little more time.

Mrs. Olson listened to my explanation about two of my three boxes of files not arriving yet from Hawaii and to my surprise, offered sympathy. It seemed most people had in common a story about slow mail service. On my way out, I encountered Mr. Patelle, who accepted my explanation almost indifferently. He was more interested in telling me that Lori and Ryan had tested well above their grade levels and seemed well adjusted despite the divorce problems.

I thanked him for that, and we talked about camping. He told me about his camper and described its telescoping top. "Easier to get your pants on when you can stand up."

As I headed down the hall, he called cheerfully after me, "And don't worry, we aren't going to take your children away from you."

I still had to get the fake restraining order past him. I hoped that once I gave it to him, it would go in the file and that would be that.

The weekend ahead looked busy. Lori and Ryan wanted to stay home to play with friends they'd made at the motel. They also pored over the newspaper classifieds, looking for a Siamese cat to replace Georgie Girl II.

By Sunday afternoon, I had drafted the completed document and still had time for clothes shopping with Lori and Ryan.

The next day, I found a public stenographer to type my rough draft. She didn't ask any questions, and I didn't have to use my explanation that I was a writer doing an article on divorce.

Tuesday morning, with damp palms, I pushed the document across the counter to Mrs. Olson, along with Ryan and Lori's birth certificates and immunization records.

"Well, Mr. Landel, sooner than expected."

"I didn't have to wire the lawyer after all," I said. "The missing boxes arrived on Saturday."

Chuckling, she shook her head. "I wonder if we can thank President Carter for that."

Better to thank my angels, I thought, watching her scan the documents, then slip them into Lori and Ryan's files.

That evening, we drove to a house on Lake Washington Boulevard, whose owner had three Siamese kittens for sale. An hour later, Georgie Girl III slept in her box in the car while we dined at a Denny's restaurant. The kids took turns telling how much they liked their new teachers, and this time no tearful reports from Ryan of bullying.

At our motel room, Georgie Girl received a warm awakening

with her first bath, followed by considerable attention from Lori and Ryan, thankful to have a new kitten.

Once the kitten had fallen asleep, I lay pondering the events of the day. Feeling relieved, thoughts floated by, *Will there ever be an end to this deception,* before falling into my most peaceful sleep in weeks.

❧

The next day, staring out into Seattle's November fog, gray and gauzy, I forced myself to detail our expenses. The dank weather seemed to fit my mood. We were under budget for transportation, despite the cost of a new water pump. We balanced on rent and were over on food. I decided to cook more at home, despite our poorly equipped kitchen. I had not allotted enough for incidentals such as clothing and household goods. Overall, we had fallen behind nearly two hundred dollars. I foresaw deep trouble if I didn't have a job in a month. If I was still unemployed by December 25, we would be literally out in the cold and hungry on Christmas.

Looking for a job required every ounce of optimism I could muster. I had to find work, without references and using a false identity in a city that had more than its share of job-seekers, thanks to a slump in new construction due to high interest rates and drastic layoffs at the Boeing Aircraft Company.

By day, Lee Landel, architect/attorney/consultant offered himself for work in real estate development, while at night, Lori and Ryan helped me collate résumés and a cover letter under my new letterhead. By November 10, we had stuffed, stamped and mailed 64 letters to Seattle construction and real estate development companies.

In less than a week, I received replies from two companies offering interviews. I phoned on Friday, but both individuals were out until Monday. Damn.

Another weekend. My first priority went to helping Ryan and Lori feel content and entertained, yet the weekends were hells of waiting, fear, and agonizing delays toward landing employment.

At least the children had their new dachshund puppy to pamper.

The previous Thursday, while amusing ourselves at a dog show at the Seattle Center Exhibition Hall, we purchased, much to our surprise and delight, the puppy. Having stopped for groceries on the way home, Ryan suggested we name her Crinkle, after seeing Crinkle-Cut French Fries in the freezer section. Groceries, a kitten, and now a puppy to make another demand on the budget. But I knew we were creating what we needed and wanted most— a family.

From my journal for Saturday, November 20:

> *While still in bed at 8:00, Crinkle messed Number Two twice. Got up and spanked her, went back to bed. Up at nine, coffee, walked Crinkle. Helped the boy in the next unit adjust his 10-speed bike. Ryan wants a bike. I'm sick of being poor. At least I have him registered for basketball at the Recreation Center, and Lori begins ballet lessons next week. Finished off the rice pudding for breakfast.*

On Monday, I drove downtown, parked, and walked the four blocks to Vance's office. Vance Martin, a local real estate developer, had responded to one of my job inquiry letters. Cordial, about my age, he told me he didn't have anything for me, but as part owner and manager of a small shopping center, he sometimes needed architectural advice. I asked him if he would go over my list of job leads in the Seattle area. He took time to point out the key players in Seattle real estate. At the reception room door, he shook my hand. "Keep me posted, Lee."

I thanked him warmly, but I doubted he knew how much his easy generosity had done for me. His generous assistance boosted my morale. My first positive contact, the first indication we had a chance to get up and out of the hole we were in.

At the parking lot, I discovered my car had been towed away.

I found a pay phone, located the towing service, talked with the dispatcher, found the correct bus, rode for an hour, walked seven blocks, paid thirty dollars, and drove wearily home to find the kids trying to cook. It was against my rules, but by then they were hungry. We ate wieners, sauerkraut, and bread. Ryan reported his new corduroy pants had shrunk so badly in the dryer he couldn't get them on.

Tuesday morning, I returned to the library for research on the movers and shakers in Seattle development. Back to Skyline by one. I called my answering service. Two calls, one from a Mr. Bill Dahl, telling me he was not the Bill Dahl in construction, the other from a Mr. Bill Greenwood of Greenwood Construction, who wanted to meet as soon as possible.

Encouraged again, I made myself relax: I cleaned up after Crinkle, then worked on a thank-you letter to Vance and six letters destined for real estate firms he had recommended.

After an hour of driving around the waterfront industrial area, I found Mr. Greenwood's office in a huge, gutted warehouse on Alaskan Way, just south of downtown.

Greenwood, a burly man in a suit and no tie, greeted me effusively, too eagerly, it seemed to me.

He led me into the warehouse, where I received a swift tour around the empty building. Our voices echoed in the large timbered space. Overhead, flaking dust-laden beams held a sagging roof while lights dimly filtered through a clerestory of cobwebbed broken windows. He babbled of clever gentrification projects like Ghiardelli Square in San Francisco and asked if I had any ideas.

I asked if he had a job for me.

"Well, fact is, Lee, I'm not hiring yet," he said. "But one day, Lee, one day . . ." He waved his thick arm, and his voice echoed hollow in the ramshackled shell. "All this will be ramped and partitioned. Boutiques that won't quit along both sides and on two levels. Food of all nations. Greenwood Square. It'll be a goddamn modern-day marketing miracle!"

I thanked him, and as I headed for the door, glanced back. Standing in a shaft of dusty light, he pulled a silver flask from his hip pocket.

I stopped by the library for more research. Then downhill to the County Courthouse, where I made six follow-up calls. Five secretaries put me off, and the one man I talked to said he was cutting back on his company staff. *Keep going,* I reminded myself.

As I emerged onto the street, I bumped into a panhandler. His clothes frayed but clean, he had the leather face of a man who had lived in the sun. He stepped back, held out his hat, feigned a smile that showed brown teeth while a deadness beyond anger shown in his pale eyes.

"Can you spare a quarter for a carpenter, lost my tools in Cincinnati . . .?"

I dropped a quarter in his hat and continued on, his spiel trailing me.

Walking to my car parked on First Avenue, I remembered Lori reading aloud from a guide book about how logs had once been skidded down First Avenue to Henry Yesler's lumber mill on Elliot Bay. With the arrival of that first industry had come the bars and brothels. And then came a preacher, Doc Maynard, who had upended an empty beer barrel for his pulpit and stood at the top of the avenue to issue his famous sermons.

Since then, Seattle's popular Pike Place Market and what used to be called skid road had been gentrified, while its defeated and broken folk had dispersed to wherever they could.

As I made my way to the car, it seemed I was seeing more than the usual number of winos slouched in doorways on soggy bed rolls; bedraggled homeless with their sorrowful, stunned faces, sallow-faced teenage girls in mini-skirts whispering as I passed, and old women wrapped in frayed mufflers, crouched beside bag-filled shopping carts, muttered to themselves. I fought the fear that rushed through me wondering how close might I be to joining them.

When I returned to Skyline, I found that Crinkle had been busy, and in their attempts to clean up, Ryan and Lori had gotten into a squabble. Lori was sulking in the kitchen. Ryan had gone to the Pizza Hut parking lot with his skateboard, against my express order not to wander off after school.

My temples pounded as I prepared to go after him. Plastic

wheels rattled on the pavement. He bounced in, saw me, and instantly turned sullen.

I struggled to put my impatience aside, clapped my hands, and mustered a cheerful tone. "I think we're all a little tired. Let's go to the Pancake House and celebrate."

"Celebrate what?" Lori asked glumly.

"Us." I put a hand on her shoulder. Neither of them would look at me. "Please, I need cheering up tonight myself."

"Oh, okay," Lori got to her feet.

"I want strawberries on my pancakes," Ryan said.

We climbed into the Chrysler. Having them there beside me felt comforting.

"Blueberries," I said. "I want blueberries."

I turned the key. The starter ground for twenty seconds, then stopped. Another dead battery. The only Skyline tenant home with his car didn't have jumper cables. The nearest service station was half a mile north on the opposite side of Aurora Avenue. To walk there seemed like miles along the hurling rush hour traffic.

Under the hood, I scraped corrosion from the cables, tried to loosen them and stripped the threads off one nut. Finally it came loose. Ryan helped me lift the battery up and onto the fender. Just then, the door to our unit popped open, and Crinkle scooted down the drive toward the highway. I raced after her, catching her three feet from a passing car. Lori took her from me as we walked back to the Chrysler. I slumped on the bumper, my face in my hands.

"Your hands are dirty, Dad." Lori said.

"I know."

"What's wrong?" she asked.

"Everything." I sensed their bewilderment. "Just resting my eyes." My attempt to smile felt unconvincing. These children depended on me alone. I was losing heart, failing them.

Ryan perked up, determination showing in his face. "I've got an idea. We can take the battery on my skateboard."

"Come on, Dad, say yes." Lori begged, excited by the idea.

They tugged at me, their enthusiasm hauling me out of my depression. "Come on, Dad, we can do it." Ryan assured.

And we did. I led the procession. The bedraggled father in his rumpled tweed business suit, tie tugged to one side, grease smears on his forehead, used a clothesline rope to pull the skateboard with the car battery tied to it. Ryan hobbled behind, keeping the battery balanced with one hand while Lori, her blonde hair knotting in the wind of passing cars, took up the rear, hugging a wriggling, peeing dachshund puppy.

We were gypsies in Seattle, trundling down the weedy shoulder of the highway, inching our way around the safer side of the telephone poles, gathering finally across from a Chevron station, balked by six screaming lanes of speeding cars.

"No way," I murmured.

"Maybe," faintly from Lori, as she eyed the traffic.

We held hands. I held the rope. Ryan steadied the battery. Choking exhaust fumes pushed us back. Crinkle squirmed and whimpered, her brown eyes dark with fear.

We waited at the shoulder's edge. A car in the nearest lane slowed, then moved on. The next car came to a halt. Its driver smiled and waved to us to give it a try.

We eased the teetering skateboard over the curb. A car in the second lane braked. Horns honked from behind, and other drivers shouted encouragement from open windows as the whole flow slowed and stopped: two lanes, then three. Northbound cars saw us crossing. One lane stopped, then another.

"Charge the brigade!" someone shouted.

Ryan laughed and took one hand off the battery long enough to wave. From the corner of my eye, I saw a blue and white police car farther down in the northbound lane. My stomach tightened. An arrest could mean the end. One lane still blocked us. The police cruiser rolled onto the shoulder and stopped. The officer stepped out scowling. He lifted his hands directing traffic. I took a deep breath.

"We've got it made," shrilled Ryan.

As we pulled our skateboard and battery past the policeman, he glowered down his shoulder. "What kind of trick was that, you three? We don't jaywalk in Seattle."

"We're not jaywalking, we're jay running," Lori laughed, and we pushed the board up and over the curb and onto the gas station's macadam.

"Everybody's a wise guy," grumbled the officer, shaking his head as he went to his patrol car, unable to suppress a smile.

FIFTEEN

BOARDWALK

When the shoe fits the foot is forgotten. When the belt fits the belly is forgotten. When the heart is right 'for' and 'against' is forgotten.

— Thomas Merton

During our first week at Skyline Motel I had bought a Monopoly game. It became one of our favorite games. Lori went for the utilities, while Ryan blew on the dice to win Park Place or Boardwalk. The game, of course, is about property, and our discussions during play often measured the children's shifting values. My own, too.

One night while we played, Lori announced she no longer wanted to marry a doctor. She preferred a millionaire. "Millionaires' cars don't break down." she said.

Another time, Ryan wondered how much money surgeons made.

I told him some made a lot, but they worked long hours. How about hotel owners? I named the only one I knew, Conrad Hilton. Ryan thought that if he couldn't be a surgeon, he wanted to be like Mr. Hilton when he grew up. "I'll bet Mr. Hilton doesn't have to live in a motel."

That afternoon, we parked along First Avenue to read our guide book. A panhandler pushed his nose against the window at Lori. She made a face at him, and he turned away. She let out a shriek of giggles. The beggar had dropped a dime on the sidewalk. She opened the door, scooped up the dime, and ducked back in. "Now I can afford B & O Railroad," she said.

A joke and yet not a joke. Despite their irrepressible optimism, I wondered if, at another level, our situation affected them.

A few days before Thanksgiving, I called the last name on my priority list, Warren Roth, president of the investment management division of Safeco. According to Bill Vance, Roth "knows everybody in town."

To my astonishment, he answered his own phone. I introduced myself.

"Yes, I remember your résumé." His barrel voice, formal and direct, tempered by a southern politeness, intimidated me. "We aren't in need of anyone at the moment, Lee, but I sent your résumé to Frank Orrico, President of Winmar, our real estate division. They are in the market for new people."

"Thank you," I said, encouraged by his directness. "If you have any questions yourself, I'd be pleased to answer them."

Paper rattled. "Hmmm." Apparently, he had a copy of my résumé on his desk. "Well, you certainly are qualified. The résumé doesn't say where you're from."

Stay calm, urged my books on job interviewing. Listen; when there is an opening, don't let it pass.

"Atlanta."

"New territory for you then. Why Seattle, Lee?"

I rambled something about the livability of the city and wanting a better environment for my two children.

"Two?" His formal approach loosened a bit: maybe a father himself, perhaps a grandfather. "How old?"

"A son eight and a daughter ten."

"Wonderful ages, Lee. What is the minimum salary you can get along on?"

His directness took me by surprise. And talk about my minimum income level didn't appeal to me.

"Twenty thousand, but it would be difficult."

"What is PBC?"

Don't hesitate, my books said.

"A company I founded in 1970. Small limited partnerships to invest in real estate."

"Hmm. Are they doing that much anymore?"

I laughed. "We did well. But no, you're right, the SEC has closed it off by making small syndications into securities." A clumsy explanation, but good enough.

"Tell you what," he said, "let's meet. I'm out of town all next week. What about Wednesday, December 8th?"

"Fine," I said. "Do you have your calendar there?"

His voice returned to that ostensibly easy, but firm southern politeness. "You take care of your end, Lee, I'll take care of mine. Nine in the morning, and please phone me to confirm."

"I will. Thanks."

"My pleasure. And enjoy the children. Believe me, when they reach adolescence, you'll yearn for the younger days."

I hung up, pleased to have made a contact that could lead to employment, but concerned that I might be in over my head.

New anxiety stirred through me. PBC on the résumé meant little as long as it could not be located. But I had said Atlanta. An important man like Warren Roth could easily order an investigation through the national offices of Safeco. Under Georgia corporations, PBC Inc. would show no stockholder by the name of Lee Landel. By checking with the other two listed stockholders, anyone could easily check out the Coburn name and discover my Georgia architect's registration and Georgia Bar membership. The qualifications and experience on my résumé were true, only my name and those of clients and companies had been changed.

Any investigation would conclude that Lee Landel was a fabrication, resulting in further inquiry.

Damn, damn, damn.

On the brighter side, I had just arranged my first important interview. An investigation was unlikely unless they became serious about employing me. That would come later, if ever. In the meantime, I could decide whether to meet Mr. Roth or just forget our scheduled conference and avoid going to Winmar.

One thing was for certain, after this I would no longer claim to be from Atlanta, Georgia. A nice city, but so was Jacksonville, Florida, and Jacksonville was a lot safer hometown for Lee Landel.

❧

With the arrival of Thanksgiving I could at least pause long enough to get better prepared for more interviews.

Our dismal motel room, reeking from untrained pets, seemed a sorry setting for the holiday. But what did surroundings have to do with being thankful, anyway? The real riches in life, I was learning, begin from inside ourselves. That day, I felt more thankful than at any time in my life.

We talked of roasting our own turkey, but we had no oven. We voted on going to the Golden Turkey restaurant for hot turkey sandwiches and cranberry sauce. After ordering, I asked the waitress how she planned to celebrate. She shrugged and gave a peculiar answer.

"Today we eat hamburger, tomorrow we have turkey."

On the way home, Lori commented that Mommy and Dr. Reynolds probably went to Grandma's for Thanksgiving.

"That could be," I said, thinking of at least three disparaging remarks I might have said. I could feel that old anger stirring inside me like a cancer consuming me. For now, I just know she doesn't exist, that's all. Whatzername is how I think of her, and she is out of our world, hopefully never to return. Perhaps a new mother for the children would be nice, but it will only be if it happens, and I'm not at all sure I want it to happen.

Alone after the kids had gone to sleep, I felt my stomach still churning from just thinking about last year's Thanksgiving when she had just left me. A year later in this cramped and dismal motel room something made me more thankful than any time in my life.

While installing a fan belt on the Chrysler, it occurred to me what the waitress meant by her remark. She dined on leftovers, hamburger on Thanksgiving, turkey the day after. When you're at the bottom, you begin giving thanks for the small things in life.

A trivial insight, but I wondered if I would have caught it had I still been Lee Coburn, Atlanta lawyer/architect.

On Wednesday, November 30, I had three interviews. None had any openings but each gave me the names of other people to see. I told them I had moved here from Jacksonville. At least I was moving, even if I hadn't yet arrived anywhere.

I had set the first of December as my deadline for a job. We had two hundred and eighty-six dollars in the bank. Lori wondered what it was like to have Christmas in a motel. I didn't say it aloud, but I wondered what it would be like to have Christmas on the street.

A few evenings later, a report on the news showed a man standing in an airport concourse with a boy about six or seven. Something about the boy's expression made me lean forward and ease the volume up.

The anchorwoman explained the mother had childnapped the boy from his father, who had won custody in a contested divorce. The man, searching for the child had spent over $50,000 and had reunited with his son after five years.

Bedclothes rustled, and Lori sat up in bed.

"How much is fifty thousand dollars?" she asked.

"Enough to buy four big cars or a house."

"Wow." She slid under the covers and put her arms behind her head. "Dad, are we poor?"

I hesitated. Why did it hurt so much to own up to our poverty?

Pride. Embarrassment. Despite my protestations, society's money-success programming still influenced my self-image.

"Yes, we are," I told her, "in money, and I'm working to change that. But we're not poor in spirit. Because we have love in our hearts, we'll always be rich."

Solemn consideration showed on her face. She seemed prepared to accept whatever came; she only wanted to understand.

"Are Mommy and Dr. Reynolds rich?"

"Maybe not big rich," I said, "but they have money to spare."

She lay silent for awhile, then turned, pulled the sheet over her shoulder, and curled into her usual sleeping position.

"I can't wait until tomorrow," she said. "Sally is bringing a friend to show us break dancing."

My humiliation suddenly lifted, freed by her positive spirit. Whatever pleasure or difficulties life offered, large or small, she accepted our life without reservation and without rancor.

That night, I dreamed someone from Atlanta captured the three of us. Val stood before me.

"You will never see these children again," she said.

She led them off, I was standing in a hedge beside a school. Lori and Ryan came out, but I couldn't take them. I hadn't changed my name, didn't have a car to drive away. Val walked to them, then looked straight at me and laughed.

In the dream, my scheming continued: how to establish a complete new identity beforehand. Every new scheme brought objections and faults in my plans, but I continued to calculate, consider every possible risk. I had to get them back, had to wipe that superior, condescending smile off Val's face.

I woke to dusty, orange light of dawn; my blanket twisted around my body and damp with sweat. I felt as if I had struggled and clawed my way to reach a mountain peak, only to find an even higher mountain beyond. An anxious sense of crisis and pending loss persisted all that day.

My December first deadline came and went and still no job. New leads continued to develop, and I sensed I was close, very close.

Interviews had been going well. At least in the sense the more contacts I made, the more interview leads I received. Still no offers, although Weyerhauser has scheduled another interview. They were impressed with my background, but it could take a month or more to work up the interview ladder to a solid offer. I couldn't wait that long.

Wednesday, I met with Mr. Roth at Safeco. He was what I

expected: tall, squarely built, with a tough, hearty handshake to go with his baritone voice. His deliberate speech and slow movements put me at ease, yet suggested a sternness that also intimidated. In American history, he could have been a railroad baron heading the quest to the west or a builder of industrial empires, the one in the field who confronts the work directly, knows his workers personally.

He came straight at me about my résumé, chuckling over my listing myself as president of PBC. "You're no president, Lee. At least, not yet."

With anyone else, I would have felt angry or defensive. Instead, I smiled, not certain I understood what he meant. He asked questions about my history. I told him as much as I could without actual admissions, backing up my experience and credentials with demonstration of specific knowledge.

He talked about some of his own experiences during the Great Depression: how he had picked coal from the railroad tracks, how his family home had burned to the ground. He asked if I were scared.

I thought for a minute, then said, "No."

He startled me when he asked if the children and I would like to come over for dinner. I said we would be glad to come. He said he'd check with Mrs. Roth and give me a call.

He dictated a letter to Frank Orrico of Winmar, advising Mr. Orrico we had met and recommended he schedule an appointment to interview me.

I left his office bewildered. Here I was, living in a motel with no job prospect in sight, invited to the home of a major figure in the Seattle business community. I thought about my answer to Roth's question about being scared. What sensible man wouldn't be scared facing Christmas with two hungry kids, the rent due, a fugitive on the run, and down to my last one hundred dollars?

Lee Coburn, well off Atlanta attorney, would have denied his feelings to maintain his illusion of control. But something changed in me while lying on the beaches of Hawaii. Our ordeal had forced me to face my anger and feel the fear beneath it that had driven me to this costly response.

That evening, I relaxed on the bed while Lori walked Crinkle. From my journal, Monday December 7:

> *Lori was elected president of her special reading class. She has started to make cranberry and popcorn ropes for our tree, and she's looking forward to her dance recital at the Seattle Opera House tomorrow tonight. Ryan is at basketball practice mastering jumpshots. Not easy for a kid who's only four-foot-ten. He grunts when he goes up with the ball, just like Julius Irving.*
>
> *I'm worried about Christmas presents. Trying to figure out how to come close to what the kids want without spending much money. Each has to get at least one big box, and it has to rattle interestingly so they can try to guess what's in there.*
>
> *Crinkle and Georgie Girl III are curled up together on the bed beside Lori. Christmas carols coming from the TV help drown out the traffic noise on Aurora Avenue. The cost to all of us for what I've done weighs heavy on my shoulders. Will we ever know real peace?*

Ryan started coughing after his practice and continued through the night. I barely slept, feeling his misery.

In the morning, I located a pediatrician in the Richmond Beach area and made an appointment. When we arrived, the nurse handed me a form. I gave my name as Lee Landel and my parents' address in Escondido. No credit cards, no references. Employment? I wrote down attorney. The nurse studied me. I looked straight back and told her we were new in town and getting established. I said I didn't have a checkbook or money with me, but I would come by later in the day and pay in cash.

"My son's sick," I said. "There's a scary sound from his lungs. He needs to be checked."

She tried staring me down, but her gaze broke, and she turned the half-filled-in card in her hands as if there might be some answer to her problem on its back.

"Well . . ."

"Good," I said and led Ryan toward the examination room.

The doctor diagnosed a bad chest cold and prescribed antibiotics and bed rest. Ryan fell asleep on the way to the motel, took a pill, and conked out on the bed.

From the bank, I withdrew thirty dollars, which I took to the doctor's office. Ryan slept until nine the next morning. The cough lessened over the next few days, and he returned to school on Friday. We now had a family doctor.

❧

Christmas danced near and splendid in Lori and Ryan's imaginations. Too near. No job, barely enough money for food, and I couldn't pay next month's motel rent. And yet my journal was more densely packed than ever with the everyday details of our life.

> *Less than two weeks to Christmas. Carl, the man in the room next to ours, told me he knows of a used 10-speed bike for Ryan that can be spray-painted and made like new. Didn't want to tell him I'm ashamed to give Ryan something used for Christmas. Even more ashamed to not have enough money to buy my son a used bike.*
>
> *We talked about what we each wanted for Christmas. Ryan was in one of his deep moods. He said what he wanted for Christmas was not to have his dad die. It caught me off balance for a minute, but I sat next to him on the bed and got him into a conversation about the airplane model we planned to build together. That seemed to bring him out of it.*
>
> *I worked on a new batch of letters and résumés while Ryan watched a Christmas program on TV. Only the top half of the black and white screen has a picture. But enough for him to join in singing Silent Night. Lori is hanging little*

branches of pine we picked up at the park. She's tied them together with red ribbon. They're to take the place of mistletoe, she said, and are to be responded to in the same manner.

Job hunting, like all selling, whether it's a product, a service, or yourself, can be seen as a numbers game. The more numbers you play, the better your odds. Still, I wasn't prepared for the incredible week that began on that Friday, the seventeenth, just eight days before Christmas.

In the morning, I attended an interview at the SATO Corporation, one of the fastest growing development firms in the Northwest. For an hour, I faced John Sato, its president, and his two key associates. They told me they wanted to expand their operation into larger projects, a major step. They asked questions designed to test both my architectural background and my legal knowledge in the real estate field, where I was on fairly sure ground.

Self-possessed and watchful, John Sato asked penetrating questions to test my technical knowledge. I wondered if he ever smiled, but at last he did as he shook my hand and told me he and his associates would now arrange to meet with the economist who headed their consulting division. Either I would be called into that meeting or Mr. Sato would meet with me alone.

"I know it's Christmas, but we're on the move and must keep the momentum. I hope you'll have the time," he said.

I assured him I would make myself available. I spent the afternoon interviewing at the offices of Winmar, which my research told me did three hundred million a year in real estate development. Another hour of testing and another warm reception. The two executives who grilled me announced they would arrange for me to meet their president, Frank Orrico, the next week.

After the meeting, I browsed through one of the city's major department stores, checked the prices of children's clothes and decided to leave. Ryan's chest cold had been a sharp reminder that we had no health insurance, the brakes on the Blue Elephant had begun to grind metal, and I had less than $150 left in the bank. Maybe someday I could afford nice clothes for the kids, but not now.

At K mart, I laboriously worked my way down my shopping list. For Lori: tennis shoes, a night shirt, and one special thing, a musical jewelry box. For Ryan, trousers, tennis shoes, and the big ones — a dart board and an airplane model with a .049 gas engine.

I splurged an extra five dollars on boxes and wrappings; what counted most was the spirit and festivity of Christmas.

Returning to Skyline, I found Carl spray painting the 10-speed bicycle for Ryan. "And for you, Lee ol' Buddy, how about a Christmas snort?"

He indicated the pint of blended whiskey standing uncapped on his porch. "Southern Discomfort, best going for the price."

"Merry Christmas to you, Carl," I said, as we raised our cups in a toast to the holidays; my chest burning from his hard stuff.

That night, the kids made me sit in the bathroom for nearly an hour while they wrapped presents, giggling and arguing over who got to use our single sheet of silver paper. A knock on the door rescued me. Alice Vanderburg, mother of one of Lori's school chums, Kim, had come to ask if we would like to come to a Christmas Day dinner. I accepted with thanks. Lori bounced on the bed with delight.

Ryan said he hoped there wouldn't be too many girls there. "They talk too much."

Monday, the children began their Christmas vacation. I took them to the Pacific Science Center. Three hours later, we emerged pleased with our amusement but eager to return home. I had decided not to tell them about the promising job leads for fear they might not pan out, but they must have sensed my improved spirits.

"It's beginning to feel like Christmas," Lori allowed hopefully.

"Sure is," I agreed.

At our room, they wrapped more presents and decorated the small tree we had improvised by using pine branches off a tree behind the motel. I left for my four o'clock appointment with John Sato and his two key employees.

First, Sato talked to me alone in his office. I had found him forbidding in our earlier meeting, with his dark, handsome features, narrow Asian eyes, firm jaw, and somber expression. But this afternoon, his expression of intense concern had been replaced by an easy, thoughtful smile. How were the kids? How was the job search going? What did I think of Seattle weather?

"Great" to the first two questions, and to the last: "Well, is it true that it's always raining . . ."

He chuckled. "Our Seattle tradition. Either it's raining or rain is on its way."

He asked about salary. My heart began to speed a little as I told him thirty thousand was probably my minimum, upping my expectations since meeting Warren Roth. He said he could afford to pay twenty-five thousand to start with.

I managed to receive that great news with no indication that I had less then seventy-five dollars in the bank and motel rent due.

We moved to the lobby, where his two principal assistants, Vic and Red, waited to join us for drinks at the Black Angus restaurant. Red Hampton, a freckled Irishman in his mid-forties, was the mediator of the trio. Over dinner, they were less interested in my background than in my ideas.

Seattle, growing steadily in its out-of-the-way corner of the nation, had taken shrewd advantage of urban renewal ideas worked out in other cities, the conversion of industrial complexes into shopping/activity centers (San Francisco), the gentrification of blighted downtown neighborhoods (Philadelphia), the carnivalization of tourist-intensive areas (Boston), and the control through codes of downtown high-rise curb-crowding (Manhattan).

I had observed that this very middle-class city faced a problem Atlanta had more or less solved — rising real estate prices, which eroded the residential areas supporting downtown business. As in most cities, as the suburbs spread, the shopping malls went with them, drawing business and residents out of the core and usually leaving it to rot slowly. Seattle had the geographical advantage of a system of waterways that drew the city along a north/south axis, leaving several important residential areas intact and close to the core. These would, for the most part, remain residential, but with rising property values, multi-use high rise complexes would become the highest and best use of these valuable properties. SATO Corporation could become the city's leading developer by capitalizing early on this coming trend. Even Vic seemed to warm to a few of the ideas I presented.

After dinner, John and I walked to his Mercedes to say good night. "Looks good, Lee. I'm hopeful we can work it out so you can come on board. Call me tomorrow."

Wait until I tell the kids!

I felt childish elation and ecstatic relief as I drove back to Skyline. I wedged the Blue Elephant into my slot and saw Carl with his beer, Steve with his ubiquitous can of Dr Pepper.

I waved hello but didn't go over, anxious to share the news with the children. To have relaxed among professionals in my field after six months of single parenting, to be accepted by them, perhaps soon to be working with them, felt like coming home.

The windows of Unit 15 were dark. The kids had promised to stay inside and watch television. I unlocked the door, pushed it open, stepped into dusky silence, listening. Had something scared them away, or had someone finally found us?

Mouth dry, I called in a hoarse whisper, "Lori? Ryan!"

My heartbeat was the only sound.

Then, a rustling from the bed, snickers and thrashing laughter. Their little joke! For a moment, I wanted to put them both over my knee, but the impulse passed. I had such promising news; I felt too good.

"Very funny, very funny," I said, peeling blankets off their convulsed forms, "but your old Dad has some news."

Abruptly, they stopped bouncing. Our Monopoly board sat on the corner of the bed, its cards and little green and red hotels jumbled. I picked up a hotel and put it on Ryan's favorite, Boardwalk, then put another marker on Lori's Water Works.

"It looks as though I just might have a job."

Ryan bounced up and down on his hands and knees. Lori looped an arm around my neck and kissed my cheek.

"We can go to the movies whenever we want to," Ryan announced. "And I can get a new skate board and a model airplane and . . ."

"Rich!" Lori cried. "We're going to be rich."

"Take it easy," I cautioned. "I don't have it yet."

But they were bouncing in rhythm now, chanting, "Rich, rich, rich . . ."

In the midst of my pleasure, I glanced at the Monopoly board, my gaze held by the cartoon man in black and white striped jacket and hat clutching the bars.

GO TO JAIL.

What if my children had been gone when I came home, taken by FBI agents or private detectives? Job or no job, that was still possible. Coming home to find them gone would be like not coming home at all.

SIXTEEN

HUMILITY

When you have the humility to be with people in the simplicity of what you are, not trying to hide what you are, then communion takes place.

— Vilmala Thakar,
The Eloquence of Living

Tuesday afternoon, December 21, using the parking lot pay phone, I telephoned John Sato. His hello sounded a little distant.

I asked him if he preferred to meet Wednesday or Thursday.

"Lee, we've got trouble." His voice sounded brisk.

I kept my voice steady. "Oh? What trouble?"

"We've talked it over, Lee. Vic and Red feel it is inadvisable to expand right now. I don't necessarily agree, but we're going to stick by the decision. Why don't you come in tomorrow around nine; we'll discuss their reasons."

I hung up and walked across the parking lot to our motel room. I had begun the day optimistic, calling first Warren Roth to confirm our dinner engagement at six, and then starting another watercolor before phoning Sato. Now the dingy little room reeked with my depression. My watercolor hadn't been successful either. My washes had dried dull and muddy.

Hold it. One minute Sato says they don't want me, the next he asks me to come talk. I remembered negotiating salaries, using the same last minute hesitation to coerce applicants to back down on their demands.

"It isn't over," I said as I laid out Lori's only decent dress, her Hawaiian muumuu. "I won't let it be over."

❧

Leaving behind our poop-stenched menage, we drove to the Roths' home situated on a bluff that provided a sweeping view of Puget Sound. A feeling of southern comfort pervaded the grounds as we eased down the long drive to the main entrance. A horse grazed in a fenced pasture on our left. Just beyond stood a hermitage, possibly the maid's quarters or a guest home. Turning into the front drive, we glimpsed the swimming pool, tile patio, and lawn which sloped to the bluff's edge. Westward across the Sound, the snow covered Olympic Mountains drew jagged shapes against the crimson and blue horizon.

My gnawing envy vanished under the Roth's warm welcome. Warren introduced us to his wife, their son and older daughter, as well as Miss Godfrey, housekeeper and general domestic organizer. She pinched color into Lori's cheek, ruffled Ryan's hair, and ordered them both to wash their hands before dinner.

Warren indicated our seating around the formal dining table. The stately mountain view provided its own natural mural to our luxurious setting. While we ate, Warren and Mrs. Roth moved the conversation at an easy but informative pace. As we shared stories, one leading to another, Miss Godfrey carved the leg of lamb, placing portions on each plate handed to her by Warren. Though relaxed, nothing could hide the iron hand of southern ways emanating from this ruling patriarch. Warren referred to his wife as Mrs. Roth and Miss Godfrey as Mizzzz Godfrey. I worried I had been disrespectful, by moving too quickly to using first names. Too late now. I would continue addressing him Warren.

After dinner, their fourteen year old son, Kevin, took Lori and Ryan outside to see Kevin's trail bike. Warren, Mrs. Roth, and I retired to the den to sip sherry in front of a crackling fire.

Conversation centered on my background and how the children

and I came to be in Seattle. I understood their curiosity and struggled to appear relaxed while I tiptoed through their questions. My shoulders and back ached from feigning casualness into my answers.

"It must be tough with two kids in a motel room, Lee," Warren said.

I gave my first real laugh. "Only when the dog and the cat jump up on an intense Monopoly game or decide the carpet is really a restroom."

He chuckled, swirling the sherry in his goblet before setting the glass aside to add another log to the embers. "I don't want to be intrusive, but how much are you paying there?"

I told him, hiding my embarrassment for our meager accommodations.

"Hmm, pretty stiff, considering its size." He stood, glanced at Mrs. Roth, who nodded. "Let's get some air. We want to show you something."

They led me to the guest house. As we entered, Lori and Ryan joined us. Warren told us they'd built the home for his mother, who had died before she could move in. He showed us through the two-bedroom home, furnished with his mother's antiques and old world treasures. My feet sank into the thick carpet as we toured each room.

I instructed Lori and Ryan to keep their hands away from the furnishings.

As we moved into the living room, Warren's baritone voice shifted to a solemn tone. "Mrs. Roth and I talked this over. You and the children are welcome to live here as long as you wish. Might be better for them, Lee, and Kevin would welcome some friends nearby. What do you think?"

The magnitude of his offer overwhelmed me. I didn't know how to respond and stalled by telling Lori and Ryan to sit still. "My first response is to say no, we can make it on our own. But the truth is, Warren, we don't have enough to pay next month's rent at the motel. I know we'd be happier here. If nothing else it would be better for the children."

We discussed fencing Crinkle in the dinette. I kept saying "Thank you." Mrs. Roth just laughed and said she'd been married to Warren for thirty-five years and still didn't know what he would do next.

We returned to the main house where Miss Godfrey, still working in the kitchen, learned we would be staying in the guest home. Mrs. Roth left the room and returned with two boxes filled with wrapped Christmas presents. Gifts for our Christmas.

Lori and Ryan each carried a box of presents as we walked to our car to say goodnight. Before saying goodbye, Warren pulled me aside and put a sheaf of bills into my hand.

I stared at three one hundred dollar bills. "You don't know how much I appreciate this," I told him, "but I can't take it."

He closed his hand over mine. "Listen to me, Lee. I understand pride, and I respect it. Once, during the Depression, when I was trying to get my first business started and going to school at the same time, my Uncle Dave offered me a loan. I turned him down, but he wouldn't listen. He told me he'd break my arm if I didn't take the money."

My cheeks warmed. "Warr —"

He loosened his grip on my hand. "No, I'm not going to say any damnfool thing about breaking arms. What I am going to say is that I finally accepted, and that fifty dollars made the difference, and I didn't have two kids to take care of. So, please."

I nodded, and his hand left the bills in my grip. "I'll pay you back as soon as . . ."

He waved a hand. "I know you will. And about Sato, he's tough, but that's integrity. He knows, like you and I know, the worst horses' asses and the laziest conmen all have good references. All he cares is that first, you have the goods, and second, you mean it when you say you can deliver."

He tapped my right fist, which still clutched the folded bills. "I believe in you, Lee. You're going to do just fine."

The next morning, I contemplated the possible causes of Sato's reservation. I didn't know which one weighed heaviest on his mind, but I intended to address each one: Vic or Red or both (probably Vic) were worried about expanding into new development markets; and/or my maybe salary request was too high.

One thing I knew for sure: my finances mandated I turn Sato's no to my employment into a yes.

I drove to Sato's office, rehearsing the principles of selling yourself. Listen. Speak to the question with specific benefits to the customer. Persist logically until you make the sale.

Sato welcomed me into his private office. His large desk covered with stacks of documents dwarfed his small frame. He went right to the point. "Lee, as I told you, we've decided we have too many irons in the fire to expand right now."

Listen. Address the question. First, I said I understood, considering all the projects they had going. I went on to explain how my marketing efforts would be a natural adjunct to their existing staff. In each point, I made sure to mention Vic's and Red's important role in the company, and that I knew I could work with them. I presented additional details of the marketing program I had in mind which required my particular expertise as well as their skills. In closing, I talked about my aspirations and desire to build a larger development role for them in Seattle.

He sat back, expressionless, then smiled. "From no to maybe." He checked his watch. "An hour and a half. Not bad. I'm impressed by your sales job."

"I just went straight at it," I said.

"Then we have that in common. I don't like to waste time chewing over decisions." He smiled again and held out his hand. "I'll let you know in the morning."

Thursday morning, two days before Christmas, I called. He invited me to have lunch with him, a promising sign. The kids had gone to a friend's house, so I left a note and headed downtown.

On the way to lunch, Sato pointed out some of the new downtown structures. He particularly liked one of Martin Selig's new office buildings, noting the hanging gardens and slanting undercut of the balconies.

"Perhaps a bit expensive," he said, "but worth it if we can convince the client it pays to have satisfied employees and strong community identity. We did it in Japan; now let's see if we can do it here."

The more I heard from him, the more I wanted to work for him. But he said nothing about the job, and I didn't want to interrupt the flow of conversation.

He pulled into the Black Angus restaurant parking lot. He was a personal friend of the owner, he said, and liked the special service he received.

"Being how it's Christmas," he said, "we have a right to cocktails. Martinis, dry." His dark eyes expressed a roguish humor. "I suppose you might be in some suspense, Lee?"

"Oh no . . .," I pretended a shrug of satirical indifference, while concentrating on keeping the onion in my glass from rolling.

"Well, let me relieve the suspense," he said, raising his glass. "I've decided to have you join us."

The onion rolled heavily to starboard, as my stomach flipped over with elation.

"But there is a catch."

The onion rolled in the other direction.

"To keep peace among my people, I'd like you to start at twenty-five thousand. For the first six-month trial period, at least." He paused, sipped his drink. "Vic's wife does our in-house bookkeeping. You understand?"

"Of course," I said.

"Do you accept those terms?"

I told him I did.

From his briefcase, he pulled an envelope and handed it across the table to me. "Because we had to bring the salary down and it's Christmas, this startup bonus is yours. No strings attached." His smile widened as I opened the envelope. "How do you feel, Lee?"

"Great, I said. "Thank you. I'm eager to get to work . . ." I hesitated. "I wish the kids were here right now, so I could tell them. Maybe that's the martini talking."

He shook his head, watching me with calm eyes. "No. It's good." He held up his glass. "New beginnings, Lee. Here's to your children, and to success."

I didn't bother to conceal my joy as I touched my glass to his. A merry clink and we drank. Our lunch came to a close and I slid the envelope, which had a substantial feel to it, into my pocket.

When I returned to my car, I counted my startup bonus — ten one hundred dollar bills.

All the way to the motel, I thought about telling the kids. When I pulled in, they stood on the grass with Crinkle, who they informed me in excited voices, had learned to fetch a stick.

"I've got news, too."

Screams, Ryan jumped on me for a hug. I held him high. Lori tugged at my arm. "Me too, me too."

In the room, I spilled the ten one-hundred dollar bills onto the bed. "This is our Christmas present from John Sato."

Their eyes widened.

Lori exclaimed, "We're rich, Dad, we really are."

Ryan jumped on the bed to feel the bills. "Now we can have a real Christmas. And maybe I can have a new skateboard."

Lori counted the money. Then, they counted in unison, "One, two, three, four . . ."

"Dad," Lori said, "you'll be able to buy a coffee pot."

After a while, we calmed down, but our new sense of financial security cast a glow that brightened even the stained and soiled carpet.

The next morning, Christmas arrived with its usual flourish. Dragging me from bed, Lori and Ryan pretended surprise that Santa not only had eaten their gift of cookies but had left them presents. "See Dad," Lori playing the invincible convincer, "there really is a Santa. Come on, let's open presents."

Ryan plugged in the lights, bringing a glow to his paper garland made in school and Lori's popcorn and cranberry rope. Their gleeful chatter mingled with Christmas music from the radio.

We took turns opening presents. Lori jogged in place showing off her new tennis shoes while Ryan held high his dart board. "Now I can invite Steve to throw darts with me in the parking lot." We continued until we had unwrapped all our presents. Lori lifted the top to her jewelry box. Her face glowed as she listened to the song "Raindrops Keep Falling On My Head." Upon receiving his model airplane and gas engine, Ryan put his hand to mine for a thumbs up hand shake and a hearty "Thanks, Dad." From each of them, I received socks and coffee filters. Their big present, which they'd hinted I dearly needed, was unwrapped amidst wide eyes and anticipation. Their faces beamed as I revealed their surprise. "Cooking pans," I exclaimed, 'Now we can really feast." I gave them each a hug.

Christmas at Skyline Motel had also given us gifts we'd not expected. In our simple room we'd learned the moments most treasured are those lived from the heart. We'd also been shown that one's surroundings have nothing to do with the true meaning of Christmas. The gift of love. Truly a gift we would take with us to all our Christmases to come.

Two days after Christmas, we packed to leave our dingy habitat on Aurora. We experienced a few tugging moments when we said goodbye to Carl and his family, reminders of how fortunate we were. We didn't linger; Lori and Ryan were eager to feed the horse at our new quarters.

In my rear view mirror, I saw Carl wave and behind him the rickety image of Skyline Motel. Slowly, it faded into the distance.

The next morning, nestled into what seemed a palace, I awoke to Lori's cry of delight. She tugged at Ryan to wake him. Her voice alternating between squeaking excitement and an instinctive whisper urged me to take note. Outside, heavy snow blanketed our new world. A glittering fantasy.

We dressed and hurried out into the hushed landscape.

Billowing softness covered the pasture; Roth's horse snorted the crisp morning air. Crinkle torpedoed across the deck into the field, poking her nose in the white powder, leaping up, lifting her bottom off the chill. Appearing indignant, she growled.

Ryan tossed a snowball toward the horse, then he and Lori rushed to find cardboard boxes to slide on.

The fresh snow had transformed the Roths' home into a Currier and Ives print. Any minute now, a sleigh would jingle around the drive, Squire Roth and his family bundled in furs. Our cottage under the snow-covered black walnut tree looked more stately and protective than ever. Next to it stood my new company car, a Subaru — free gas, insurance, maintenance. A future.

The children left to ask about a sled. Standing alone, a sweater thrown around me, I thought how suddenly and completely things had changed. From June heat in Atlanta, to December snow in Seattle, exactly six months, a different world.

Lori paused in her sledding to take my hand, always checking in, keeping in touch.

"Isn't it super outrageous, Dad?"

"It's hard to believe we're here, Lori."

She tilted her face to the silver sky and the few flakes drifting down.

"Dad, do you think it's snowing in Atlanta, too?"

❧

Our invitation for holiday dinner from the parents of Lori's new school friend brought the first gathering of adults I had been with since Whatzername left me fourteen months ago. After so long a time alone, we felt honored to be invited to a holiday celebration, a generous and thoughtful gesture indeed, considering how little they knew about us.

In our travels, I had instructed Lori and Ryan to express thanks for the many acts of kindness extended to us, and once more, reminded them to thank our hostess for the dinner. Indeed, we were fortunate to be welcomed guests at someone's holiday dinner. I hoped my nervousness didn't show.

Lori showed us the way as we entered into the neighborhood behind Skyline Motel. Tall pines towered over the wood houses nestled together reminiscent of my home town of Fulda. Smoke trailed from chimneys, silent signals of family and comfort within. Mrs. Vanderburg greeted us warmly, introducing us to the twelve guests already present. Congenial greetings and hearty handshakes helped reduced the anxiety I hoped to conceal.

Over the past months, I had become accustomed to avoiding people. Now I needed to reach out, do my part to make the day a success. Socializing with others my age held tremendous appeal, but my attempts at conversation sounded stilted, as I tried to cover my defensive numbness with charitable politeness. I had nothing to talk about, because little in my life could be shared.

My unease brought back memories of high school — shy, scholarly Lee Coburn, hoping nobody would notice his winged ears or detect the passions behind his quiet reserve. In my mind's eye, Shari Landers stood across the room, and I couldn't get up the nerve to ask her to dance.

After awhile, I gravitated away from the adults to the room where the kids played. As I watched them pinning tails on the rear of a paper donkey, a woman in red appeared at my side, drink in hand.

"Are you the recreation director?"

Tensing, I looked at her but saw only playful interest in her gaze. Her dark brown eyes shone with an unexpected warmth. A red ribbon in her brunette hair complimented her long dinner gown. Her poise and assurance made her that much more stunning, and intimidating. She leaned against the door jamb waiting for my response.

"No, just a father."

"Just a father?"

Something about her demeanor that came only from someone at peace with herself brought my uncertainty to the fore. Too tense with caution and wariness to relax, I stepped back, pointed to Lori and Ryan.

"Father of those two, I mean. That's Lori and this is Ryan."

"Those are my two playing with them," she said. "Thomas and the younger is Christopher." She thrust out a slender hand. "Hi, I'm Kellie Vaughan."

"Lee Landel."

We shared our ideas and experiences on raising children, a safe topic. She'd been a single parent for over a year and lived just a few houses away. She talked with animated energy, clearly an intelligent and articulate woman. I liked her. And the more I liked her the more nervous I became. She was too much, too together for me. Someday, maybe, when I had more confidence, I could be with a woman like her, but not now. We visited a while longer, and then, with welcome relief, we joined the others for dinner.

As we headed for the dining room, she cocked her head, her dangling earrings flashing attention to her striking face. Still smiling silently as if studying me, she said, "Maybe I'll see you again, Lee." Her face surrendered none of its warmth; in fact, her brown eyes seemed only to sparkle with deepened interest.

"I hope so, too," I said, telling myself I didn't mean it.

The afternoon whiled away in easy conversation. Lori and Ryan had found playmates, and I had begun to feel as if among family and friends. Their hospitality had been a gift in itself, but living day to day as we were at the Roths', I assumed we'd not be meeting again.

As the afternoon waned, guests began to leave. We expressed our appreciation for the invitation and said goodbye. Kellie stood in the center of a lively discussion near the punch bowl. I didn't understand the perplexity of my feelings. What really did I have to give her, even as a friend?

I couldn't tell whether or not she noticed us leaving, but I thought I saw her glance as we went out the door.

No, this is not the time for a woman, I continued to tell myself through that first month of 1977. I had enough on my hands caring for the children and trying to establish a home life. Although I had a job, I still did not have an established identity. No credit rating, no professional licenses, no usable driver's license. I had been carrying the Landau license in Hawaii and here, but one accident, even a small infraction, could put the Landau name and license number on the computer highway back to Atlanta and the Pilgrim Storage connection.

Once, driving on Aurora, in a hurry to get back to Lori and Ryan from an appointment, I caught myself going ten miles over the speed limit. My rear view mirror showed a police car, its lights flashing, right behind me. My throat tightened, then the car blew by me, siren screaming. That didn't mean there wouldn't be another along any minute.

With my Landel birth certificate, passport and military discharge papers in hand, I drove to the department of motor vehicles. I planned to say I had just moved here from Sydney, Australia. Because that city had an excellent public transportation system, I hadn't needed a driver's license.

With his deep drooping wrinkles and bushy eyebrows, the man behind the counter looked more like a bulldog than a civil servant. Apparently he didn't know much about Australian motoring, nor did he care. He bought the first part of my story, waved aside the rest, looked at only the birth certificate and asked for three dollars.

I passed the written and driving tests and left, sighing in relief, one step closer to being Lee Landel, free and respected member of society.

Another problem demanded attention. The Pilgrim Mini-Storage rent was overdue. I had given up hope of having the rent mailed from London. Being this late, I could no longer avoid making the dreaded contact with Atlanta. Not only was I concerned for the things still stored, but I didn't want them in the custody of anyone who might try to trace me in some misguided effort to return them.

But what telephone to use? I didn't dare use my office phone or the phone in the guest house. If Sid had been telling the truth, a connection to Pilgrim Storage could be tapped. A call on a pay phone required a pocketful of quarters and would be regularly interrupted by an operator. Then I remembered. Sato had assigned me a credit card number as part of my expense account conveniences.

To dodge the possibility of Pilgrim's line being tapped, I worked out a plan and reviewed it from every angle. On Wednesday, already a week past the due date, on a public telephone, I dialed the credit card number and the number of a secretarial service I had pulled at random from the Atlanta yellow pages.

A woman's voice answered. "Globe Secretarial Services, this is Louise speaking."

Good, Louise sounded friendly. *Lee, do your stuff.*

"Hi. Listen, I'm calling from New York for a favor. Maybe you'll think this is crazy, but I've got to catch a plane to London in five minutes, and I've been trying to get hold of Pilgrim Mini-Storage in Atlanta. You know, out on Chestnut Drive."

"Yesss . . ." She sounded puzzled but not hostile.

"All I get is the warehouse and a busy signal, and I want them to know I'll be sending the rent money right away. I wonder if you could call them for me."

"I don't see why not. What's your name?"

"Leland Landau. I used to live in Atlanta."

"Oh? How did you happen to call me?"

"I've been in your office. Maybe it was you I talked to. The manager, as I remember."

"Owner." She gave a short laugh; apparently, business wasn't all that good.

"Must have been you," I said. Then gave her the phone and space number. "Just tell them the money is on its way, okay?"

"Sure. On one condition. That you come in and see me when you're back in Atlanta."

"You bet. If I ever get off this transcontinental pogo stick. Hope you don't mind doing legal briefs."

"I love them."

And I adore you, too, Louise.

The next day, I withdrew five twenty-dollar bills from the bank, but then had an ominous thought. Was there a way of knowing where bills came from? I told the teller I was writing a short story and wanted to know about identification of bills. She sent me to one of the bank officers, whom I told I hoped to sell my story to a true-crime magazine.

He'd always wanted to do a little writing himself, he confessed. His great-grandmother had been on the wagon train of unmarried women brought out by Asa Merecer in 1878, as wives for the men of Seattle. He thought it would make a terrific tale. Yes, he was aware the story had already been done on stage and TV, but he had a different angle. His great-grandmother, refusing to get married, had had a child out of wedlock by a man she claimed ever afterward had been the great violinist Paderwerski, then on a nationwide tour of the western Pantages Theatre circuit.

Interesting. And bills, could they be traced to their place of origin? He looked at my twenties and showed me where three of them had the letter "L," indicating they had been printed in San Francisco. The other two had code letters indicating they had been made in the Midwest, and four of my singles were also from the West.

I went back to the teller, told her I felt richer with a hundred dollar bill and asked for one with a "B" designation for New York City. Perfect.

As I left, the bank officer gave me a little salute and wished me well with "your crime story."

Thursday night at home, I wrote a brief note to the manager at Pilgrim, apologizing for being late with the rent and explaining I was still on the road and expected to be traveling for some time. I enclosed my New York City hundred-dollar bill and four ones, one printed in the Midwest, two in Boston, and one in San Francisco. Addressing, sealing and stamping that envelope, I enclosed it in a larger envelope along with a note to my new Manhattan maildrop,

Downstairs Mail Service, asking them to forward it, and enclosed their fee.

The payment would arrive in Atlanta postmarked New York. At the post office, I confirmed that postage stamps, unlike bills, are the same all over the country. I stepped to the mail slot, held my letter halfway in, but couldn't let go of it.

This is too complex, something was bound to go wrong. I had to figure a simpler way to get the money to Pilgrim. I pulled the envelope out again and stuck it in my pocket. The man behind me in line shook his head.

❧

Other than the stress of paying the storage rent, we were making progress on getting settled. Both children had adjusted to their new teachers and classes. Ryan had joined the basketball league and Lori attended ballet lessons three nights a week. A friend at work had recommended an orthodontist for the children to be fitted with braces. Making a home required patience and a whole lot more than I ever dreamed.

If I couldn't resolve the mini-storage dilemma, I could at least send a letter to my parents in Escondido, telling them in general what I had done and why. But, in truth, had I really thought why? At least for now, I wanted them to know we were safe and secure, with the kids in school and me employed. I did not tell them where we lived to protect them from possible harassment by investigators. I suggested they send a copy of the letter to my sister, Randi.

I put the sealed envelope addressed to my parents in with the Pilgrim Storage envelope to be mailed to Downstair Mail Service asking them to forward both envelopes. After reviewing my mail drop plan more thoroughly, I decided to trust my plan. Our isolation provided security we had become accustomed to. Making contact with the old world, even through a mail drop, left me feeling as vulnerable as someone about to cross a river full of ravenous crocodiles.

The time had come to look for a permanent place to live. I located a four-bedroom home near Richmond Beach within the Shoreline School District. The rent seemed reasonable at $250 a month.

On Saturday, January 15, Lori, Ryan, and I went to look at the house. Built in the fifties, it had a big kitchen and breakfast area, two full baths, large windows, hardwood floors, and best of all, a fireplace for cold winter nights. A wood fence around the back yard would keep Crinkle in, and a large dogwood and tall pines shaded the house on three sides. The tree-lined drive provided a natural buffer from the street. A grass alley ran behind the house to an open play area where the kids could roam without danger from traffic. The neighborhood reminded me of my home town.

"I like the trees," Lori said. "They whisper."

"You know what I like, Dad," Ryan added, "I like having my own bedroom, so Lori can't boss me around."

"Why do you always start every sentence with 'You know what?'" Lori asked.

"I don't." Ryan said.

"Hey," I interrupted. "Maybe we'll find the Melon Kid's pirate sword somewhere around this alley."

"Aaaa," Ryan said, "that's dumb."

"No, it's not," Lori objected.

"Cool it," I said. "Come on now, are we going to take it or not?"

Lori tugged at my hand. "What about you, Dad?" Lori asked me.

"The living room. There's a place for our new grandfather clock, when we get it, and we can toast marshmallows in the fireplace."

"Then you can tell us boy stories, right?" Lori asked. "About the church bells calling the kids home at night."

"And we could play catch in the playfield, Dad." Ryan raised his voice with the air of a decision just made.

"Okay," I said. "Discussion over. All those in favor."

"Aye."

"Aye."

"Aye."

While they ran off to explore the playfield in the back, I listened to the pines. She was right, they did whisper. Suddenly my knees felt weak, I sat down on the back steps, thinking, "Back steps are a good thing, back steps are home."

On Monday, February 7, I walked Lori and Ryan to the bus, since it was their first school day from our new house. The sun filtered through the trees along the street as I waved goodbye to them.

At the office, I experienced the same coolness I had on Friday, mainly from Vic. John had left word he wanted to see me at two o'clock. No other message, not even hello. At lunchtime, he left with Vic and Red.

For that period, I sat in my car in the parking lot, too worried to eat. Had John somehow uncovered my lies?

I returned to the building in time for the meeting. Red and Vic joined me as I entered John's office. John sat behind his large desk with an open file before him. On the top lay my résumé. My stomach churned like a wasps nest.

Once we were all seated, John said something had come up, that he was unhappy about and considered it very unfortunate.

Red said, "Who's Coburn?"

I didn't answer him. John said he had decided to check my résumé and had found no verification of a Landel architect's registration, but the number belonged to Lee Coburn.

I told him I was everything the résumé claimed, except for the last name. In order to establish a new life for my children, I had changed to Landel.

John's black eyebrows moved as he spoke. He said if he had been aware in the beginning, things might have been different, but this was a breach of trust. He was too well known in the city to allow this sort of thing. In hiring me under false pretenses, he had risked the company's integrity, therefore he had no choice but to terminate me immediately. I was not to use his name as a reference, because he would not lie to anyone. He closed the file. We were excused.

As Vic left the room I thought I saw a glint of satisfaction in his eyes. Red accompanied me to my office.

"I'll take you home," he said.

I put the few things that were mine in my briefcase, then Red followed me past the secretaries and receptionist. No one looked up.

On the way home, Red said he was sorry it had happened and speculated I must have done it for serious reasons, a custody dispute or maybe financial problems. I assured him it was none of those, only my desire to start a new life for my children. They were more important to me than job security or my reputation.

"I believe that," he said.

When we arrived at my house, he helped me carry my things to the back porch. He said John had been shocked and disappointed. Hurt, really. Maybe after a couple days, I might want to phone him. He might be of a different mind and be able to help in some way. Red walked to his car, turned, and said goodbye.

The empty rooms and hardwood floors now seemed forbidding. I tried to imagine our new clock in the spot we'd chosen, but that didn't help. I didn't even know how we could keep the house.

Crinkle scratched at the back door, a scalpel drawn across my nerves. Three and a half months of job hunting, hundreds of contacts down the drain. I had sent thank you letters to the many people who had assisted me in my job search, informing them of my new position with the Sato Corporation. I had, in effect, primed the whole Seattle construction and real estate world for gossip of my downfall.

I was finished.

Our journey had ended, and so suddenly. At least a dozen people now knew my real identity. It wouldn't take long. I might even be blackmailed . . .

We had come so far, and now, without warning, the earth had fallen away from my feet, and I rode the skids again, with nothing between me and the bottom. Did Lori and Ryan and I have the strength to pull ourselves back up? Could we handle yet another run for our lives?

I went to the downstairs bedroom where we had slept until we bought the bunk beds. Ryan's clothes were still in the milk crate shelves we'd made. Lori's treasures sat on her dressing table, a box covered with pink cloth. I bumped her musical jewelry box as I dragged my sleeping bag into my empty bedroom. I lay down in the corner.

Somber light filtered through the dirty window, turning cold along the bare walls. Crinkle still scratched at the door. I crawled into my sleeping bag, pulled it over my head, and wept into the darkness.

SEVENTEEN

BEYOND THESE WALLS

Accepting where we are at a given point, rather than backing away . . . is the more wholesome attitude and choice.

— Marsha Sinetar

I read somewhere that life is about awakening, dreams, and forgiveness. I had been dreaming, there in my office at Sato's, very much the secure, confident, up-and-coming corporate executive.

There's nothing wrong with ambition, of course. It's the steam that moves the wheels of society, but when those wheels turn on you, they grind you exceedingly small. If worldly ambition is all you have, failure becomes the equivalent of death.

After a while, in that thick darkness of the sleeping bag, reason overcame my shock and self pity. I had not died. I was a father, and my children would soon burst in from school. I crawled from my protective shell and, as I washed up, searched my face for signs of the devastation I'd experienced. I found it in my eyes. The drizzle of my weary soul gazed back, pleading for attention.

Laughter sounded in the alley. Lori and Ryan swept through the back gate, book bags swinging. Crinkle noodled out to meet them, tail wagging. I sat down at the kitchen table to peel an orange.

Wham! The screen door.

Ryan skidded to a halt. "How come you're home? You get fired?"

Giddy laughter as Lori crowded in behind him.

"You're right, I did."

Ryan wrinkled his nose in disbelief, and within minutes had grabbed two oranges and was out the door to a waiting friend.

Lori brought her orange over and sat beside me. I couldn't talk about the dismissal, maybe later. My career as an attorney/architect was finished. Sato's termination had closed the door to any further professional involvement in Seattle. Not to worry her, I told Lori I had lost my job because Mr. Sato had decided against expanding his operation after all. She accepted the explanation, but probed for the feeling.

I assured her finding another job wouldn't affect our staying together. We were still safe.

She gnawed an orange peel, a habit she'd developed when absorbed in thought. She did it with her bottom teeth. I worried it would loosen them, but I didn't stop her this time.

"What are you going to do?" she asked.

"I don't know. I'm a little scared." I told her.

She kissed my cheek. "You'll find a way, Dad, you always do."

The next day, I found on the margin of my last journal entry, these words:

> *Oranges are captured sunshine,*
> *And even the bitter peel is good for you.*
> *We love you, Dad.*

❧

On Tuesday, I called Sato. I had some things I wanted to discuss with him, I said.

A long pause, then his response came on a friendly note. "What are your plans now, Lee?"

"I don't know, but I've been in hard corners before. I'll work my way out of this."

"The first thing you should do is come clean with yourself."

"I am clean in that sense," I said. "I made the decision a long time ago, and I'm too committed to turn back."

"You know, I'd really like to know what could cause someone to do what you did. Maybe I can be of some help."

And just maybe we would need his help, I thought, as I offered what I feared most. "I will tell you as much as I can short of jeopardizing the children. But it has to be in strict confidence."

"You have my word," he assured me.

A week later, we met for two hours at the Black Angus restaurant. He listened impassively as I told him of the events leading up to my decision to disappear with the children. When I finished, he nodded.

"I can see it. I can't agree with what you did, but I know other men who've been in similar situations. It's tough." He paused. "You know, if you continue to look for work in the field, I may get calls about you."

"I don't think I'll be looking in the field. I'm going to have to start from ground zero."

He studied me. "Ground zero. A dangerous place to be."

"Believe me, I know it."

"I guess you do, but you still probably want this back." He pushed a file toward me, opened it to my presentation and touched the colored photograph of me at the entrance to my law office. "I started with this."

He handed me a magnifying glass. With its help, I made out the nameplate under the law firm sign: Coburn and Ross — Attorneys at Law.

"Damn."

He nodded. "I called the Georgia Architect Registration offices, but records showed only a Lee Coburn. That's all we needed." Taking the magnifying glass, he pointed it at me. "Just don't ask me to lie, Lee, because I won't."

"As I said, I'm starting over. You won't be bothered."

He walked me to the car. We shook hands.

As I climbed in, John eyed me, "What I said about coming clean, I didn't mean just with me. With yourself, Lee."

"I know," I said. "I don't plan to be a fugitive forever, either in the practical or emotional sense."

He touched my sleeve in farewell. "You'll work it out." His dark eyes turned warm. "If you ever get in dire need, Lee, call me."

A grand gesture and an important gift. He had given me an ace card to carry in my back pocket for my last draw if I ever needed it.

❧

Lori still wore the gold and silver bracelet Dr. Reynolds had given her. Watching it gleam on her wrist, I had the fleeting fantasy of creeping into her room at night and slipping it off, them hammering it flat and mailing it to the doctor with a rude message attached.

In truth, my anger wasn't directed at him. I didn't even know the man. It was at what had happened to my life, and at Whatzername for making the break that started all this. In those difficult months after I lost the Sato job, the unreasoning rage returned often, astonishing me.

One evening, the three of us sat in the living room reading and listening to music. Barbara Streisand's "The Way We Were" came on, the song Val and I had considered "our song." I switched off the radio to avoid getting sad.

"I want to hear it," Lori said.

I snapped, "Can't you see I'm trying to concentrate on these help-wanted ads?"

She sulked. I apologized. An hour later, she started a conversation about smoking. She was glad I had given up my pipe. Dr. Reynolds smoked a pipe all the time, she said.

I sensed what was coming and took a deep breath.

"I wonder if Dr. Reynolds and Mommy are married yet," she mused.

"I would guess not," I said.

"Why?"

"Well," clearing my throat. "often when people first meet and don't know each other very well, circumstances might make them feel very close. But then afterward, the excitement wears off, and they wonder if they made a mistake. Remember the story about the cow who thought the grass was greener on the other side of the fence? He turned out to be wrong and regretted it the rest of his life."

She regarded me solemnly, this wise and innocent child who loved me. "But sometimes the grass is greener, isn't it? It can work either way, can't it?"

Trapped on the wrong side of the fence by my wishful thinking, all I could do was feel foolish. I agreed that maybe her mother and the doctor had gotten married and wished them well if they had.

But the truth was, I couldn't yet bring myself to wish Val well in anything. Relinquishing my anger meant accepting responsibility for my part in the breakup. This I was unwilling to do.

In the meantime, I had to find a new way to make a living.

Every day, I studied help-wanted ads in the newspaper, plus the papers from outlying towns. The grim truth came from between the lines:

> *Wanted-Skilled salesperson. Willing to work long hours. Encyclopedia sales, must own car, have phone.*

What about, Hungry? Desperate?

I checked through lists of real estate brokers looking for sales people. But licenses were needed and classes were required, to say nothing of references, employment records, and worst of all, fingerprints for the license. From experience, I knew it could be six months to a year to make the first commission and another year to develop a backlog of clients and build the momentum to a decent income. I didn't have a year. I didn't have a month. Within weeks I'd be out of money.

The next morning I came upon an ad in the help wanted column.

> *Retired lady needs handy man to paint house. Have room to rent in trade. I bake cookies.*

Some ads have a way of lifting you out of your gloom. Now here was something I could do, house painting.

By mid-March, we were again down to a couple hundred in the bank, and the house rent was due.

One afternoon as I let Crinkle out, I noticed someone under a red rain hat striding up the footpath to the playfield. The woman wore red-and-green-striped socks and tennis shoes. Her dark hair bounced as she walked through the dappled light under the alley trees. Was it Kellie Vaughan — the woman at the Christmas party? I nearly called out to her but stopped myself.

No. Not now. This was not the time for involvement with a woman.

A few nights later, Ryan brought home an invitation for the three of us to attend a birthday party for Thomas Vaughan.

On Saturday, another one of those damp March days, we headed up the alley to the Vaughan home. We walked three abreast, surrounded by tall evergreens.

Balloons hung on the wood fence along their drive, giving notice of the party inside. As soon as we arrived, the young partygoers collected around the games Kellie had arranged. Over the excitement, she motioned for me to join her in the kitchen. She wore loose designer pants with bright pockets and a matching green safari blouse, the sleeves rolled halfway up her tanned arms. Smiling, she extended her hand.

Her touch unnerved me. Feigning calm, I said, "Hi, nice to see you again."

"And how's the single father?" she asked.

I laughed and pretended a parental sigh. "We're all getting older by the day, but sometimes I think I'm aging faster than they."

"Me too," she said, "but it's not so bad." She indicated her youngest, Chris, who looked to be about five. "Yesterday, he put a bag of polliwogs in the freezer. A 'scientific' experiment."

"You're lucky he didn't decide to bake them in the oven."

"Oh, but he did. When he thawed them out."

It came as a relief to laugh about inconsequential domestic things. Visiting with her made me feel less alone and my life a little easier. We moved on to other topics. I asked if that had been her striding up the alley behind my place.

"Was I wearing a hat?"

"A red one."

"That wooded alley is one of my favorite places. My best bird watching is in those woods behind your house. Do you like to walk?"

I told her I walked when I had to, but had been thinking about getting into a regular exercise program once things settled down. As we talked, her eyes showed an open curiosity and candidness. I told her about our alleys in Fulda, dotted with old apple trees, big gardens, lawns, and backyard fences. We agreed that alleys were freedom-to-dream places for children.

"And some adults, like you and me," she said.

We talked about the school, the teachers, her rented house and mine.

"Ryan tells me you're an architect," she said.

The question revived my nervousness. Was I an architect, or just a man without a job? I realized I didn't know who I was.

"I'm thinking of getting into something else. Paint contracting is what I have in mind. I could start small, build it into a business . . . "

She looked perplexed. "I'm sure you can do it, if you want to. Aren't you also an attorney?"

The conversation was coming too close to home for me. I tried to cover with a brashness not at all my style. "Right. Anybody who doesn't pay their painting bills, I'll file a suit against them. Or break their knees . . . "

She studied her empty paper cup, folded between her palms. "You're not the type to break somebody's knees." She crushed her cup and poised to throw it into the paper sack in the corner. "The best part about starting a business is giving it a name. Do you have one yet?"

She arched the crushed cup into the air. It fell into the sack.

"I'm thinking of These Four Walls. What do you think?"

"I like it," she said, "but what about something with a deeper meaning, like Beyond These Walls? There's more to business than just applying the paint. Underneath, painting has to do with people's image of themselves. Also, it suggests going beyond ones inner walls to a higher wisdom. You know, like a spiritual journey."

"You're right." I said. "We really are all searching to improve our lives. Painting as well as in other ways."

She eyed me cautiously. "And you. Are you going beyond your inner walls. . .?" She paused, as though considering whether to voice her next thought. "The idea also has a bit of a jailhouse to it, doesn't it? Or are your walls not that kind?"

"Not really," I said, "but I like your suggestion for the name."

"I do, too," she said. "In fact, look around. There are walls here you're welcome to practice on."

A ruckus rose around one of the games, reminding Kellie to serve ice cream and light the candles. I helped cut the cake since no other parents had stayed. After a while, the party quieted to a close. When the kids and I finally said goodbye, I knew a friendship had been started, and maybe an important one at that.

As for the jailhouse remark, I managed to put it out of my mind. Looking back, I believe Kellie had the general outline of my past figured out that afternoon.

That evening, I experienced a new lift to my step as I headed into the kitchen to supervise dinner. Lori shooed me out, reminding me this was her night to cook. I moved restlessly about the house, tidying up, whistling out loud. Kellie stayed on my mind when I went to bed that night. My thoughts were pleasant, even warily hopeful.

❧

For a time, I considered forgetting about Beyond These Walls and fleeing to some city where no one knew us. Maybe a small town in northern Idaho where I would present myself as a laborer. If I kept a low profile, maybe no one would care enough to inquire. One thing about the poor and homeless: few wanted anything to do with them, not even the FBI.

The decision came down to whether or not I had enough energy to run. In those first days after my dismissal by Sato, I decided going through another relocation and another enrollment process would be too much strain on all of us. We would stay in the house and school district and hope to remain anonymous.

I also decided not to worry about being out of a job. I had a couple weeks to go before running out of money, and if I did I could get a job washing dishes.

By starting my own business, I wouldn't have to be concerned about people looking into my background. I still had doubts about my choice for a new business. Just to be sure, I went over the list I'd made of the things I could do on my own. Each idea: business consulting, real estate sales, or product sales, required either a capital investment or lengthy time before making a profit. I had neither.

At the bottom of the list, I'd scribbled house painting. The only painting I had ever done was to paint part of the living room when we moved in. A half-painted wall in the entry reminded us for the next five years I hadn't finished the job.

Once again, I eliminated every idea except for the last one. If I could paint our living room, though rather ineptly, I could paint someone else's. Furthermore, painting our living room had required almost no capital investment.

To learn whether painting could be my shortest path to income, I called painters' ads in the newspaper, on the pretense our house needed painting. Two painters confirmed they had jobs, but the hard part, they said, was finding enough work to stay busy.

Customers, I believed, I could find. If I could be corporate marketing director for the Sato Corporation, I could also find painting jobs — as soon as I learned how to paint.

Working from the yellow pages, I called real estate brokers with the same prefix as my number. After asking for the manager, I introduced myself. "Hi, I'm Lee Landel with Beyond These Walls. We're a unique painting company that provides quality painting at a reasonable price. If you have any houses that need painting, we're interested in providing you quotations."

I used the pronoun 'we' to sound more like a company rather than a starving painter begging for work. A few people took my name and number and said they'd call if anything came up.

I kept telling myself if I contacted enough people, I would ferret out a painting job.

Around 5:00, my last call for the day, a man seemed interested. By this time, I had my spiel well-oiled and believed I sounded like an experienced painter. When I finished my introduction, the man said he had a two room efficiency apartment that needed to be painted and cleaned. After a pause, he asked, "By the way, what's so unique about your company?"

"What's unique about our company?" I repeated, thinking fast. "Well, you see, we're a full service company. We do cleaning along with painting. That's right, we clean and paint. Beyond These Walls does it all."

"How much do you charge?"

Stalling again, I said, "That depends on the job, but we are always reasonable. And we guarantee satisfaction, or you don't pay."

"I'm blind and won't be able to inspect the work," he said. "I'll have to trust you to do a good job."

I assured him the job would be done right.

Early the next morning, I reported to his office, located in an old house in a commercial area just two miles away. A matronly woman introduced herself as Miss Matty and led me to a cluttered back office. There, she introduced me to my first customer, Mr. Buford. He instructed her to show me the apartment.

I followed Miss Matty outside to a separate entrance into an upstairs apartment. We stepped into a dimly lit two-room apartment with a sour smelling bathroom and a greasy kitchen.

"How much to paint and clean?" she asked.

Think fast. Look professional. Make an estimate.

"One hundred dollars," I said.

We returned to Mr. Buford's office where Mrs. Matty repeated my proposal.

He turned in my direction. "That sounds reasonable," he said. "When can you begin?"

"In the morning," I replied.

"Then we'll see you tomorrow morning," he said.

I had just landed my first painting job! BEYOND THESE WALLS opens for business.

Earlier that same week, I'd told Warren and Mrs. Roth about my plans to start a painting business. I explained that, after starting the Sato job, I realized my career responsibilities were in conflict with my first commitment to being an effective parent to Lori and Ryan. They were surprised at my decision but appreciated my concern for my children.

In his usual deep drawl, Warren offered, "Well, Lee, there are a few painting and repair jobs around here that need to be done. Why not give us a quote and you can do the work."

He gave me a list of what he wanted done: clean and paint the patio; clean and oil his imported hand-carved teak front double doors; paint his kitchen cabinets, and repair a hole in the hall wall. Not knowing how to do the work made it difficult to figure a price.

My price must have been reasonable, because he told me to arrange a work schedule with Mizz Godfrey.

❧

In my mind and heart, I still considered myself a practicing attorney and architect. Now, about to engage in manual labor for hire, I turned my mind to the practical.

I knew nothing about the correct paint to use or the correct tools, but each trip to the paint store yielded more information. I learned the difference between smooth and rough nap roller covers, and about using different brushes for different paints.

I worked slowly so I'd have more time to determine the correct procedure. Also, I hoped I might appear more knowledgeable if I proceeded at a methodical pace. I made it through the first day and assured Mizz Godfrey I would return later in the week to continue the work.

The next day, at the blind man's apartment, no one watched me as I attempted to paint the walls, two double hung windows and a door.

Completing Mr. Buford's apartment had taken a day longer than I had estimated. Since I had to return, I would finish the Roth's job first and get paid.

I'd left the Roth's kitchen cabinets for last. By late morning, I ran out of paint. I needed one more quart to finish. I dug into my pocket and pulled out thirty-one cents. My life savings.

Thirty-one cents and two children depending on me to keep us afloat. I rubbed the coins between my fingers. They had their own message. Give up, Lee. Your life is nothing.

I approached Mizz Godfrey, trying to act normal. She accepted my ruse of having to finish another job that day. If all went well, I would return the following morning to finish the cabinets. I stashed my equipment in the Blue Elephant, drove to the apartment, and finished the job. I asked to be paid.

Mr. Buford said, "I'd like to take a look."

Miss Matty led him from the office up the steps to the apartment. The room smelled of fresh paint. I told him I had cleaned the kitchen, including the refrigerator and oven. I went over each item completed and suggested he feel the newly polished wood paneling.

Satisfied I had done the work, he instructed Miss Matty to write me a check for one hundred dollars.

My confidence returned. I bought a quart of paint and finished the Roths' cabinets. Then back to the phone to find more work.

But finding work wasn't that simple. Calling real estate offices for several days proved to be unsuccessful. I moved to remodelers and builders listed in the yellow pages.

The first day I covered A through L with no results. The next morning, I called Modern Kitchens. When I finished my introductory spiel, my listener asked, "Are you available now?"

"Yes," I said, adding that usually I'm quite busy but just happened to be between jobs.

He said, "Take down this address. It's a house we've remodeled, and the owner needs painting done. I'll call and tell her you're coming. Do what's needed, then come see me."

I hung up, excited, but bewildered. The man's offhand manner about the work and cost of the job seemed strange, but I was too desperate to worry about formalities.

I located the house in Laurelhurst, an exclusive residential section on the shores of Lake Washington. After parking in the circular brick-paved driveway, I clanged the brass knocker on the carved wood door. I introduced myself through the intercom.

"Oh yes, we were expecting you." a woman replied.

A woman with dangling bronze earrings, wearing a sapphire and gold gown, opened the door. She smiled and motioned me in.

She led me through the house, showing me the rooms to be painted. I made a list of the work she wanted done, trying not to notice her appealing presence. As a successful architect and attorney, she might have seen me as interesting. But as a painter I felt invisible. When I finished three days later, I asked if she would check each job and accept the work for satisfactory completion.

I found Modern Kitchens, located in the Wallingford district. Inside an office in disarray, a man sat behind a rickety wood desk cluttered with files. He motioned me to sit down. Frank Hoover, the owner, a congenial man in his late fifties, had been the man who'd sent me out to the house. The remodeling business, he said, had been his life for the past twenty-five years.

I told him I had finished the assigned job and the owner had accepted the work. When he asked me how much he owed, I kept the price low, hoping he'd give me more work. He wrote a check for the full amount, then scribbled an address on a piece of paper and handed it to me.

"Go paint the bathroom and get back to me."

At the time, neither of us knew we had begun a two-year business relationship that, for my family, made the difference between eating or going hungry. I treated Frank Hoover and his customers with the care of a master artisan. He must have sensed how important his jobs were to me, because he gave me all his painting work. Painting for Frank helped me see the simplicity of who I was, and to no longer care to be who I wasn't.

Confidence as a painter did not come quickly, however. Each project presented conditions I didn't know how to handle. I seemed to be constantly worrying about finding more work, about making a mess of the job, about not earning enough money to feed us, and sometimes about whether I would get paid for the work I did. I dreaded getting up in the morning.

Dreaded, yes. Complain, no. In kidnapping Lori and Ryan, I had made a choice. Now I had to take responsibility and live with the consequences of that decision. Whining simply wasn't taking responsibility. I did, however, accept my feelings of frustration when situations seemed overwhelming.

❧

One afternoon while soliciting work on the telephone, I was invited to a contractor's office in Kirkland, a suburb on the east side of Lake Washington. The man needed a painting quote on a fourplex he was building.

At last, my first big break. A fourplex. Much larger than anything I had painted before. But how would I know how to quote it? It didn't matter. I couldn't afford not to do it.

In his office, Mr. Elliot showed me the architectural plans for the fourplex. I had drawn similar plans years before as an architect, but reading them to determine the amount of painting work was about as clear to me as reading an electronics diagram of a 747 instrument panel.

I pretended to study the drawings. After a while, Mr. Elliot asked if I preferred to take a set with me. I said, "Yes," and promised to call him with my price later that afternoon.

As I drove home, my excitement turned to anxiety. How could I quote a price on something this big when I was still guessing at estimates for small jobs?

At home, I studied the drawings rolled out on the floor. My price had to be competitive, but what was competitive?

All afternoon, I fretted. Finally, out of desperation, I picked a price; one thousand, eight hundred and seventy-five dollars. I called Mr. Elliot and gave him the quote.

"How soon can you get started?"

"In a couple of days, as soon as I finish my present job." I lied.

"Plan on doing the painting," he said. "Here are the colors you'll need."

I had finally landed my first big job! Now I had to see the building. I found it at the north end of Lake Washington in Kenmore, nestled along a small creek.

I parked under carports, which I had forgotten to include in my proposal. The units were locked, but through the windows, I could see unpainted walls everywhere.

My walk around the outside gave me more cause for concern. The creek side ran two stories high, and the gable ends were two and a half stories. Painting kitchens and bathrooms had not prepared me for painting from a ladder. Also, the siding material was unusual. It looked to be four-by-eight sheets of plywood with quarter-inch deep grooves running vertically every four inches. How would I get paint in all those grooves?

At the paint store, I learned about the semi-transparent stain Mr. Elliot had specified. Once again, I emptied my checking account to purchase equipment and the ten gallons of stain that I had estimated. That amount proved to be woefully inadequate. Thirty gallons was closer. To pay for the extra stain, I would ask for a progress payment as soon as I demonstrated my competence to Mr. Elliot.

For staining the high gable ends, I purchased a ten-foot extension pole, which lengthened to twenty feet. That way, I could apply the stain without using a ladder.

The next morning, I drove to the job and unloaded the Blue Elephant. I had deliberately come early so I could get organized without any critical watchers. It was just as well, since it took a little figuring even to remove the lid from the five gallon bucket. I assured myself once I started, everything would be fine.

When I did get the lid off, I found inside a dark liquid as thin as water. I wondered if they had forgotten to add the pigment or something. In fact, the pigment had settled to the bottom and needed to be stirred, but that was a lesson I was to learn later.

After attaching a thick nap roller to the end of the twenty-foot pole, I dipped the roller into the stain. Hand over hand, I hoisted the wobbly pole to its highest reach. Unfortunately, with the roller that high up, I had no control. I concentrated on pushing the pole up and down to spread the stain on the wall. Splashing the stain was more like it. Instead of going on evenly, it dribbled down the wall. Most of it ran down the pole onto my hands and arms.

I assured myself the stain running down the wall would not show once I stained the lower portion. I just needed to master the technique. I continued to dip the roller and hoist it as high as the pole would reach. Each time, the roller made more dark splotches and long runs down the side of the building. More stain ran down the pole into my face; I had as much brown stain on me as on the wall. Also, I noticed that this method did not get the stain into the grooves.

As I considered admitting to myself I might be in trouble, Mr. Elliot came around the corner of the building. He glanced at me, then at the dismal mess I'd made of his wall, then back at my stained face and body.

A little whimsically, he asked, "How you doing, Lee?"

"Fine, just fine," I said, dipping my roller into the stain in as casual a manner as possible. I had too much invested in this job to admit my lack of competence.

I swung the pole up to rest high on an unblotched portion of the wall, hoping that behind Mr. Elliot's Robert Redford features and steel blue eyes lay a little compassion.

After a minute or two, which to me seemed an hour, he asked, "Lee, is this the right color?"

"I think so."

"Maybe you're using the color selected for the trim," he said, with a puzzled look. "The other color I gave you is the main body color."

Oh Lord, I thought, not only do I demonstrate how little I know but I even used the wrong color. I admitted I might have interchanged the colors.

Still keeping with his pleasant, good morning cheer, he said, "Maybe the architect made a mistake. The best thing to do is stop until I check with him about these colors."

I was too embarrassed to respond.

"Pull off for now, Lee. I'll get back to you." With that, he disappeared around the corner.

I closed the bucket of stain, packed my things into the trunk, and drove home, certain I had lost the big job I needed to keep us afloat.

I'd felt like a loser standing there, and worse, must have looked like one, with the pole over my head, brown stain running all over me. I doubted if I'd ever hear from him again. *Just accept defeat, Lee, and after this stick to smaller jobs.*

Two days later, at seven in the morning, the dreaded call came from Elliot.

"Good morning," I said.

"That's easy for you to say," he chuckled.

My heart sank at his little irony. This was it. I was about to be fired again.

But he went on to say he had talked with the architect about the colors, and the architect now wanted the main building to be a solid color. "Use solid body stain color, Beige Gray. Okay, Lee?"

I wrote down the color and repeated it back to him.

"You sure you've got it, Lee?"

"I've got it."

A pause; I could swear he was chuckling again. "A nice solid color, Lee. Shame to cover up your picturesque stain work."

I cleared my throat. "Yes, well . . ."

". . . but if the architect insists on changing his mind, what can we do?"

"Yes," I said. "What can we do but proceed."

"Right." And with another chuckle, he hung up.

More lessons came as the weeks progressed. I learned the outside had to be painted with an "airless" spray machine in order to get paint in the grooves. The thought of handling a spray pump with my mechanical ineptitude worried me. Still, the job had to be done, so I rented the contraption and learned how to use it. After spraying stain on several windows, I realized the glass had to be masked and covered with visquine. Then, after I'd left the masking tape on to bake in the hot sun for a week, I had to spend two more days on a ladder to scrape the tape off with lacquer thinner and a scrub pad.

Looking back, Elliot must have known on that first dreadful morning that he had a novice for a painter, but his patience carried me through, and in the end the job was accepted. It had required double the hours and triple the paint to finish, plus more than I wanted to remember in embarrassment. After the fourplex job, he sent me on to other jobs, bigger and more challenging. Eventually, we worked together on large and often complex projects, where I supervised paint crews doing all his painting.

As time went on, Ian Elliot and his wife became cherished and longtime friends. He loved telling the story about the day he discovered me staining his fourplex with an extension pole and using the wrong stain, most of which had ended up in my face. Eventually, I came to laugh about the story also.

In time, I saw his gift. He gave to others by holding a higher vision for them. He lived in the moment and forgave in the moment, himself and others. When things didn't go the way he thought they should, he'd accept the new situation and move on with a smile. From that first day on, he saw a greater potential for me as a painter and as a human being. His unwavering belief in me gave my life meaning and aided in our surviving financially.

In the years that followed, our greeting carried an unforgettable chuckle encompassing the memory of those early days when he discovered me with my wobbly pole, drenched in stain.

"Good morning, Ian."

"That's easy for you to say."

EIGHTEEN

AWAKENING

Nothing happens out of order or
by chance, and the Great Law brings
those very conditions into your
life which you need for growth.
So accept with love all that happens.

— White Eagle, *The Quiet Mind*

A dense March fog hung over the road as I drove north on Greenwood Avenue, anxious to be home after my evening tennis lesson. I knew from our two years together since fleeing Atlanta, Lori and Ryan would begin to worry if I did not return as promised.

From my car radio came the report of another young woman's body found along the Green River. Total unsolved murders presumed committed by the Green River Killer had now risen to twenty-seven women. Nearly all had been prostitutes known to be active in the Pacific Highway South region. What were the police doing that they couldn't find who murdered twenty-seven women?

I snapped the radio off. With the stress of my job and running a household with two kids, how could I worry about another murder victim? One thing for sure, if the police stayed busy looking for a mass murderer, maybe they wouldn't have time to look for me.

As I came within two blocks of our house, smears of blue lights pulsed through the fog from all directions. I slowed to a crawl and, as the mist thinned, saw a roadblock of patrol cars. Maybe this assemblage of police didn't have anything to do with me, but I didn't want to find out. I turned off the main street. There were side roads I could take to get home.

At the next intersection, throbbing blue fog signaled another roadblock. Quickly, I spun the wheel. I would drive east to Aurora Avenue and then north to enter my driveway from Westminster Way. But as I circled north, at each intersection, blue lights tinted the mist. Had I finally been found?

I clenched the steering wheel. What could have happened? Had one of us made some slip that tipped the authorities? Had Lori and Ryan called their mother? Val could have contacted the Seattle police and told them about the kidnapping.

A waiting patrol car blocked every access to the house. What was happening to Lori and Ryan? Were they being held by the police until my unwary arrival home? Should I try calling? What were my options? For sure, I knew better than to drive into the police net.

I parked on a side street across from a little-known path that led into the woods behind our house. I felt my way through the spongy blackness, keeping to the shadows, away from the blue beacons riveting through the trees. From my vantage point under the dripping pines, I scrutinized the back of the house. Yellow light spilled from the kitchen window, but I saw no one inside. Were the police hiding in wait for me?

I climbed over the wire fence enclosing our back yard. If I stayed in the shadows of the pines while inching nearer to the front, I could survey our driveway. Most likely, a police car would be parked there, waiting.

Fear that our life together had come to a close churned in my stomach as I crept closer. The driveway held no police car. The house and yard slumbered in the misty shadows. But on the street, eerie blue lights still flashed through the fog. Patrol cars, but for whom?

I slunk to the window. Lights were on in the living room. I opened the back door and stepped in. "I'm home," I shouted. "Anybody here?"

Silence.

What was going on? I heard a shuffle. Lori and Ryan burst from the front closet. "Surprise, Surprise!" Lori ran to hug me. "We thought you'd never get home, Dad."

"What took you so long, Dad?" Ryan asked, including himself in the hugging.

"The class got out a little later than expected." My creepy jitters floated off as I held Lori and Ryan.

Lori asked if I had heard about the burglary.

"What burglary?" I asked.

She said the news reported there had been a manhunt in our area, and police had used dogs in the backwoods, hoping to track the man down. "We were scared only just a little bit, Dad."

"Oh, that's good," I said. "But nothing to do with us. Time for you kids to go to bed. I'll come up to say goodnight when you're ready."

❧

In the quiet of the downstairs, I sat for a moment, feeling relieved and safe with Lori and Ryan again. How quickly I felt devastated over the thought of losing them. Suddenly it struck me: this was how Val must have felt when she learned the children were gone. Would this haunting paranoia and fear that hung like a shadow over my life ever leave?

A few days later, I wrote in my journal.

> *My fear of discovery and potential of losing Lori and Ryan are always with me. Plus a growing awareness of Val's pain. Yet our lives move forward like a train rolling down the mountain out of control with no time to plan a different track. In this life, where nothing is trivial and our secret world threatens to surface at any moment, I live in constant fear, and something else — a growing longing to be free of our deception. Have I paid too big a price for revenge?*

❧

One evening while preparing dinner, I asked Ryan to pick up the living room. He continued playing with his friend, ignoring my instructions. I reminded him to get at it.

"I will, I will."

A familiar response that meant, "Maybe later, Dad."

When we finished dinner, Lori and Ryan cleared the table while I washed dishes. One of them picked a fight over who should wipe the table off. As I listened to their bickering, my anger at Ryan's all-too-frequent belligerence surfaced.

He finished clearing the table and ran to get his skateboard. I could feel resentment mount in me. My feelings concerned me, because I had learned how resentment can deepen and, unless expressed, become a wall of anger. I had experienced in my marriage the effects of denying my feelings. Unexpressed feelings, I knew, blocked the flow of love and communication. I wanted more for Ryan and me.

As he was about to go outside, I said, "I'd like to talk to you, Ryan."

He sat down with me in the living room, his jaw fixed in defiance. Lori joined us. I told him I had some feelings I wanted to express.

"You know how much I love you, Ryan," I began, "but that doesn't give you the license to be inconsiderate of others. You could at least make a cheerful effort to do little things required for us to live together."

Pouting, he twisted the leather lace of his baseball glove.

"You've been playing ninety miles an hour with your friends all summer, Ryan. While you've been having fun, you've forgotten what is first in being a person. What is first is to be considerate and loving to those around you and to show respect for your family members. We all must work together to live together. You spend more effort getting out of work than it would take to do it."

Tears ran down Ryan's plump cheeks. Speaking through my own tears, I said, "Ryan, I love you with your dusty face, with your messy room, your dirty knees and ragged tennis shoes. I love you no matter what. But we all must share the responsibility of living together."

As Ryan's chin drooped to his chest, he muttered, "Maybe that's true, but I don't like Lori acting as though she's my mother."

I asked for an example.

"Well, like when Lori called me at Jamie's house to have me come home one night."

"Ryan, it was ten o'clock and time for you to come home." I explained. "Her call was at my instruction; she didn't mean to be mothering."

We shared our feelings for half an hour or more. When we were finished, I stood and held them close to me.

After that, whenever any of us didn't feel right about something, one of us would call for a Family Meeting. As the years progressed, our Family Meetings contributed to our sense of belonging and trust as a family.

❧

One afternoon home from a day of painting, I was greeted with a sopping wet living room carpet and an obvious half attempt at wiping water off the furniture and fireplace mantel. Sleeping bags, blankets and pillows lay in piles on the wet floor. The kitchen appeared to be the ruins of a lost underwater city. I shouted to anyone who could hear, "What is going on here?"

From an unknown corner came Lori's quivering voice. "Oh, nothing really, just a water balloon fight with two neighbor friends."

I tried remaining calm. But when they began fighting over who would mop the floor, I yelled at them in exasperation.

"You don't have to be so loud." Lori responded. "Can't you tell us in a quiet manner. Yelling makes me feel bad."

I retorted, "Lori, it's only human to let off a little steam by raising one's voice."

They busied themselves mopping and straightening up while I showered. When I finished, Lori was dressed for her ballet class. Ryan sat reading in the newly tidied living room, his shriveling pink feet the last trace of their devilish caper.

As I passed our message chalkboard in the kitchen, I noticed a freshly scrawled note across the green surface: "I LOVE DAD. P.S. DON'T CARE IF HE DOES YELL, I STILL LOVE HIM. LORI"

Lori's spontaneous candidness reminded us of what really mattered in our family. But while every day brought new lessons about parenting, there were practical matters pertaining to our secret life that needed attention.

For instance, three risky phone calls had to be made. I dreaded making each of them. First, I had to contact the mini-storage warehouse in Atlanta to confirm my rent payment. Also, I had yet to call my parents or my sister, Randi.

Since we'd gone this long undiscovered, it was safe to assume Val still knew nothing of our whereabouts. That meant Randi and my parents also knew nothing about us, even whether we were still alive. I hoped calling would alleviate my guilt for disappearing without a word. Yet, I feared making contact might drag them into my plight, or maybe put them in legal peril.

Before making any calls, I called the telephone company. Three departments later, pretending again to be a writer working on a story, I asked the gentleman whether a long distance call to an eastern city could be traced to the caller here in Seattle.

A brief pause, then as if he were a recording:

"It is illegal for a private receiver to have tracing equipment in place, particularly if there is no forewarning of the call. Federal law prohibits intervention of private messages when neither party knows the recording is being done and prohibits intervention of private messages and/or recording of such messages. Unless . . ."

Ah yes, the big unless . . .

". . . unless the intervention is supported by a federal court order in such cases where the Federal Bureau of Investigation may be pursuing a federal case."

I decided to put off writing or phoning my parents or the mini storage, half out of mindless avoidance, half in the hope that something might somehow happen to reduce the risk to us and my parents.

❧

That same week, for the first time since coming to Seattle, a rare slip occurred. When asked to spell my name for a sales receipt, I began spelling my birth name, "C-O — " Then, catching my error, I quickly said L, and finished spelling Landel. After three years as Landel, I was surprised to hear myself using my real name.

The incident reminded me how much our birth name embodies the very fabric of who we are, the sum total of our unique life story. Taking an alias has felt like an amputation of my very being. Without a past, the benchmarks for knowing who I am have blurred. At times, I feel like a movie film unraveling off its reel into a useless heap of confusion. That rare slip into my past reminded me that forgetting my birthright is not all that easy.

❧

In September, I took Lori and Ryan to the Western Washington County Fair in Puyalup, the second largest fair in the nation.

In one of the display pavilions, we strolled into a clock shop and, just for fun, selected the grandfather clock we hoped someday to have. A few minutes later, with Lori and Ryan's coaxing, I put money down on the clock we had chosen. It came complete with moon dial and Westminster chimes that resonated like those that called me home when I was a boy.

I hadn't planned it, but purchasing the clock had become a passage of hope. The grandfather clock represented a return to that sense of history and home I feared we had lost when we sacrificed our clock in Hawaii.

A few evenings later, as we sat around the living room admiring the clock, Lori, suggested we look at our slides from Atlanta. She'd heard me agree to showing some of our slides at an upcoming potluck dinner. My stomach tightened at the thought of seeing the photos of Val and our lost former life in the collection.

"You should rehearse," Lori said.

She and Ryan raced to get the slides and set up the projector. In a few minutes, the white rectangle of light appeared on the wall beside our new clock.

First, the Hawaii slides. Lori and Ryan reminisced with enthusiasm about their island adventures. Then came Atlanta: flowering dogwoods, our trellised rose garden, the creek and the wood bridge. Lori asked about the magnolia trees and about the creek that ran behind our condo. I answered absently, dreading the family pictures just ahead. One picture in particular, I knew would trigger feelings I didn't want to face.

The slide about to appear I'd taken one September day in the country outside Atlanta. The four of us had gone target practicing with a .22-caliber rifle. In the picture, Val stood next to Lori and Ryan, her stance sensual. Her long auburn hair blended with the autumn colors and her large stylish sunglasses accented her cover girl face.

Silence filled the room as we studied the large picture beaming into the darkness. For what seemed like minutes, my heart beat with the steady tick of our new clock.

Then, wistfully out of the darkness, Ryan's voice. "Mommy's pretty, isn't she?"

"I think she is," murmured Lori.

I sensed their waiting for my response. The projector hummed; the clock ticked; the pendulum swung. Time for the truth, however difficult to admit.

"Yes, she was," I said, letting seconds pass while I longed to turn back the clock. "And she was a good wife and mother, a kind and caring person, too. I'm sure she still is." Afraid to feel more, I pressed the button for the next slide.

After Lori and Ryan went to bed, I turned out the lights again and flicked on the projector, clicking through the slides until I came to the best portrait of Val, a close-up like the larger photograph I had ground under my heel in the attic on Launch Day nearly four years before. The same auburn fall of shining hair, the same molded forehead with the two fine lines between her eyebrows, framed the same serious gaze and full lower lip.

I don't recall if I spoke aloud to the image on the wall, but later that evening in my journal, I addressed these words to her:

> *Tonight, Val, seeing your picture on the wall caught me off guard. All that anger and yet, tonight, I want to hold you in my arms, have you beside me. I long to tell you how terrified I was of my own feelings. How afraid I was to express my love for you.*

I wrote fast, almost scribbling, as emotions, long damned up, poured out.

> *No wonder you were emotionally starved for affection and closeness. Behind my walls of isolation, I lacked the courage to express my love for you or to show my affections. We cannot go back, Val, but I realize now I loved you only in my mind. I was too afraid to let go and care for such a beautiful woman. I loved you Val. Damn. I blew it. I blew it.*

Tears crawled down my cheeks as I fumbled to pack away the slides.

❧

Days later, while driving to pick up Lori from dance, I reflected more on my past relationship with Val. Looking back, I have come to see how my outer life always mirrors who I am on the inside. If I am to change my outer world, I must start by changing my inner beliefs about who I am.

Kidnapping Lori and Ryan was the outer expression of my low

self-esteem at that time. I had masked my insecurity with an overblown ego and along with it, an obsessive need to be in control. As a controller I had a fight or flight frame of reference for solving personal conflict. By healing the anger I carried within me, I've begun to change the destructive and abusive patterns which affected my life and those I've loved.

❧

One night at dinner, listening to our usual lively conversation, I realized how eating together had contributed to our relationship as a family. During meals, we have opportunities to discuss social, political, and personal ideas, and occasionally, time for just plain silliness we otherwise would not have.

That same evening Lori burst into one of her dialect characterizations just to be funny. As she carried on, I suddenly saw her as if for the first time. Her smile beamed bigger than life in a face so expressive it was a joy to watch. Here was a personality that was fresh, creative, and expressive. No wonder we call her the Pistol.

Fleeting moments like this remind me how rich an experience being a father to Lori and Ryan has been. But beneath the satisfaction of being a parent, I am haunted by the pain and sorrow of those I left behind.

The anguish I feel for those I hurt hangs like dark a cloud over my joy as a parent. At a deeper level I now see child abduction as cruel and destructive. Even when as parents we believe we are acting in the children's best interest, as I did, we are seriously affecting our children's normal growth and development. In my reading I keep finding research documenting the psychological costs to children abducted by their parents.

My own evolution has made me aware of another view previously unknown to me. Coming face to face with my dark side has helped me see that I am also a being of light. This paradox of yin and yang exists within all of us, just as it does in the entire universe. Consisting of opposite energies, the universe is either a cosmos of chaos or comprised of absolute order. Were we existing in happenstance, science has reasoned, we would have disintegrated long ago. This means we live in a universe that, by its very nature, is orderly and harmonious. Since I am one with this infinite order, from a spiritual perspective, even apparent chaos, tragedy, and suffering has within it order, harmony, and purpose. This leaves me to believe that in some way I am on a purposeful spiritual journey rather than randomly muddling through my life.

❧

Later that evening I thought more about seeing life as orderly and harmonious, even in all its apparent imperfections.

I'm inclined to judge my behavior as either right or wrong, good or bad. But by trusting this infinite order, I'm beginning to see there is divinity in everything that happens. This being true, then why not step out of judgment to look at myself and others from a higher perspective? When I do, I'm more inclined to ask myself, *What did I learn in this particular circumstance?* How might I grow or change from this experience? What part did I play in creating this event?

By looking at my own experiences with an open mind, I gain new insights for making healthier and more productive choices for my future. In this way, my past provides me hidden gems for growth. Like combing beaches for rare shells, with every find, I know I am forever changed.

Since I'm forever changing, I must remember that at any given moment I am simply the accumulated whole of my prior experiences. With each decision I make, I'm acting with the highest wisdom I have at the time. Self-forgiveness begins when I acknowledge, "I did the best I could considering where I was in my growth at the time."

Today, the wiser choice for achieving a greater role in my children's lives is painfully clear to me. Denying children access to either parent causes deep emotional scars which often require years, sometimes a lifetime to heal. No matter how loving or well-intentioned I was as an abducting parent, depriving Lori and Ryan access to their mother was a serious form of child abuse, inflicting long-term psychological effects on us all.

❧

With the onset of another school year for the kids, I was reminded to make the dreaded call to Pilgrim Storage in Atlanta.

I heard no detectable sound of a phone tap when the woman answered. After checking my file, the manager told me I had a three dollar credit. I told her I was calling from New York but living in England and would send six months' more rent.

In a large envelope addressed to the New York mail service, I placed the smaller sealed envelope addressed to the Atlanta mini-storage, containing the rent and my note. I enclosed twenty-five cents for the service of mailing the Atlanta rent envelope, thus giving it a New York City postmark.

That same day I dropped my carefully prepared ploy for obscurity into the mail slot. As it slipped from my fingers, I felt a tinge of trepidation knowing a mistake of any kind in my note, my signature, the paper, envelope — anything — might be the thread that would lead to unraveling our protective screen.

As for my parents, I would call soon, maybe on Thanksgiving.

❧

One afternoon, Ryan came home from school crying. "Can you tell me what happened, Ryan?" I asked.

He said it was hard to explain. Then, as if a cork had popped off, he blurted, "I don't like being weird, Dad."

"What makes you think you're weird, Ryan?"

"The other kids say I'm weird because I don't have a television or a mother. Also, because I ask so many questions in school."

An arrow to my heart, reminding me Ryan was just beginning to feel the deeper loss he carried silently within him. Speaking softly, I said, "Ryan, each of us has special qualities and talents that make us different from others. When others call you weird, it really means you're special and unique. See if you can appreciate how special you are. The more you do, the less you'll be bothered by what others think."

"You mean like Einstein and Edison?" He asked.

"That's right. Remember learning how they and many other great men in history were considered eccentric while they were growing up? And yet how their uniqueness helped them become great and famous men? The same is true for you, Ryan. Your uniqueness is what makes you special, even great."

He sat quietly for a brief moment before speaking. "Dad, I'm tired of having to keep my real name a secret."

"I'm tired of it also, Ryan. In fact, just last week I was asked my name for a purchase and heard myself begin spelling our real last name."

"Ryan, I know keeping your real name a secret hasn't been easy," I went on. "You've had to always be on your toes to remember. Especially knowing we might otherwise not be together. But at least living this one untruth has made us more determined to live honestly in every other way."

"That makes us special doesn't it, Dad?" he said, tossing his football for a quick catch before jumping up to leave. As the back door slammed behind him, I hoped he really understood.

That evening, exhausted from my day, needing solace and comfort, I retreated to my journal to write of my discouragement and fears.

> *I am weary of the constant struggle to keep us going. Yet I know giving in is a certain guarantee to worsen an already uphill existence. I keep trying to see good and appreciate all that we have as a family. I know I can build more for us, but tonight I am tired of continually being on edge financially, constantly scrambling to pay our bills and provide a secure and loving home. Will life ever get easier for us?*

A few weeks later, we tried mating Crinkle with a purebred dachshund male on Whidbey Island. The male was willing, but Crinkle wasn't interested. Lori said she thought the male was too pushy. Ryan said he wasn't pushy enough. When I was telling Kellie about it later at a church dinner, a woman sitting next to me offered her opinion.

"It will work out. There is a rhythm and there are seasons. Just wait and see."

After a moment, I remembered her name, Joan Wagner. I had met her and her husband, Jeff, at a potluck dinner. I had noticed Joan's earthy appeal, a certain familiar auburn fall of hair and fullness of her mouth, reminding me of Val. But her simple phrase caught my attention, and returned to my thoughts during the following weeks. The sense of rhythm and seasons, of healing and hope.

Three weeks before Christmas, while at the public library researching books on cabinet staining and lacquering, I located the latest Atlanta telephone directory. I looked through the "R"s. There it was: REYNOLDS Edwin & Val, and the address of the house on Viewcrest Drive. I also found Val's name listed under Val Coburn with the same address. Perhaps she had maintained a listing under Coburn in the hopes that someday Lori or Ryan might call her.

At least, Lori and Ryan's frequently repeated question was answered. Val and the doctor had married. I promised myself to tell them this evening.

❧

Our lives became like the changing seasons; growth occurred even when all appeared dormant. Another year had passed and Christmas came with new promise and hope. We now had small reserves in the bank and the trappings of a festive holiday season: a home, friends, gifts to exchange, love to give and receive.

On Christmas Day, we joined Kellie and her boys for our annual

Christmas gathering at the home of a mutual friend, Donna Neighbors.

Fourteen friends we regarded as our extended family had just sat down to dinner when the doorbell rang. Donna answered the door. A man about my age, slight build, reticent, stepped inside. She introduced him as Lyle, her ex-husband. I'd learned earlier they'd been divorced for nearly a year. He was there to pick up his twelve-year-old son, Jim.

Lyle waited in the foyer. Tension silenced the room as conversation around the table stumbled to a halt. Our eyes remained averted in painful embarrassment, haunted by a spirit not mentioned by Charles Dickens: the Ghost of Christmas Divorced.

Lyle's distant expression revealed how severed from our festive camaraderie he felt. He stood absently, first on one foot, then on the other; his hands fidgeted in his pockets, the pain of wanting to share family and friends with his son. Yet as he saw us, he appeared desperate to leave, to be elsewhere for whatever fleeting hours the courts had allowed him to be with his boy.

Lyle and Jim said goodbye as they hurried out the door. Conversation returned to its lively state as others quickly forgot about our intruder. But my heart had gone out the door with Lyle. I felt sad and alone for him and for every divorced father exercising his visiting rights on that sometimes loneliest day of the year, Christmas Day.

After dinner, away from the flurry of festivities I thought more about Lyle painfully waiting for his son. Underneath his passive resignation, I could feel his anger and disappointment at being excluded from the family he once cherished. His was the same pain and desperation that drove me to take Lori and Ryan.

Like so many men in our generation, Lyle and I were trained as young boys to pretend we didn't have feelings. We were taught, big boys don't cry. Be brave. After a while, we forgot how to feel. As men we'd learn how to go appear strong, macho, yet walk in a gray landscape of numbness, shut off from our feelings. Rather than grieve our losses, we grow angry instead.

Had I learned to feel and express my pain and anger as a child, I might have had the emotional openness and ability to develop a healthier relationships with my wife later in my life.

When we returned home late that afternoon, neighbors and friends stopped by, bringing presents and holiday cheer. As evening came, we relaxed in front of our own crackling fire, feeling blessed for this year's Christmas.

Crinkle sprawled in front of the fire as we sat content with our own musings, listening to the crackle of burning cedar. After a while, Lori wondered aloud how Val and the doctor were spending Christmas. I told the children what I had found in the Atlanta phone book: Val and the doctor were married and living in the house on Viewcrest Place.

Ryan studied the new model airplane resting in his lap.

"Wouldn't it be nice," Lori mused, "if we could all be together again some Christmas? You and Ryan and me and Grandma and Grandpa Sharp and Randi and . . . "

She looked toward me to finish.

"And your mother," I said.

"Like we used to be."

"I understand, Lori. But people might still be looking for us who might separate us. I promise you I will find out what has happened. And I promise that you and Ryan will go see your mother one day. We will wait until we agree that we are safe and it is time, but I give you my word it will happen."

Lori whispered, "I'm glad," and kneeled to pet Crinkle. Ryan stared into the fire.

Silently, my heart wept for days that could no longer be. Someday, I vowed, Lori and Ryan would share Christmas with their mother and stepfather. With the passing of the holidays, we returned to our active routines, which soon brought us to another season of activities.

❧

Spring dance recital and little league baseball tournaments brought us to the close of another school year. With summer just ahead, Lori and Ryan's adrenaline ran high in anticipation of their plans. Lori talked continually about sailing on tall ships like the 101-foot classic-rigged two-masted schooner on which she would be a crew member in June.

The *Adventurous*, designated as Washington State's Bicentennial tall ship, was built in 1913 as a private yacht for John Borden. After many other uses and abuses from its early days of grandeur, Youth Adventures, a nonprofit organization, restored the three-masted sailing ship to serve as a training vessel for young adults. The sailing school had become well known for teaching young sailors everything from navigation to basic seamanship on the open seas. Lori had crewed on the *Adventurous* the previous summer and this year, would sail the Pacific Ocean south to the Columbia River, up the Columbia to Portland, and back to Seattle. She would be away for nearly a month.

Two weeks after Lori's departure, Ryan left on his twelve-day, sixty-mile Ocean Trek hike with other high school students. High school science teachers served as guides and instructors. While each one experienced their own adventure, I made plans for individual time with the other.

Part of our separate time together included preparing for our annual summer Shindig. A back yard pig roast our first summer in Seattle, had become a much anticipated annual event. Our festivities came to be referred to as Landel's Western Shindig. For our fifth Shindig this summer, we'd invited eighty guests.

August came, and on the day of the Shindig, while making last minute preparations, Lori and Ryan advised me they had added another name to the guest list. Their guest was to be a surprise. Then Lori said, "Dad, we called Mom to invite her to the party."

"Oh, really?" my stomach tightened, and then I realized she was making fun.

Their joke spoke the raw truth. If they wanted, they had the ability to pick up the phone and ask the operator for Val Coburn's number in Atlanta, Georgia. I had never told them not to. We had, of course, talked about how different their life might have been had they stayed in Atlanta and lived with their mother and Dr. Reynolds. But, as Lori's little kidding made clear, with one phone call to their mother they could change their lives.

With the party soon to begin, I donned my chef's hat to baste the pig one last time before people arrived.

We had learned from previous years guests came to our Shindigs extra promptly. We weren't surprised, then, when the first couple came early, ready for entertainment and socializing.

As more guests arrived, four friends — musicians from Whidbey Island — played bluegrass music, first in the living room and later outside on the covered patio. Coals from the large grill warmed the patio as people danced to the lively folk music. While other guests sat on the straw bales that ringed the patio, enjoying the music, the one-hundred-pound pig sizzled on the grill.

When the coals died out, guests gathered to have their pictures taken with the roasted pig, garnished with fruit and flowers, looking succulent and brown with an apple in its mouth.

Lori and Ryan served as hosts and participated in the fun, and as always, the merriment of the evening brought unexpected and spontaneous tomfoolery. Door prizes were awarded for the best-dressed cowgirl and cowboy, along with most-elegant saloon lady and town outlaw. They all had come. And in the spirit of our western buffoonery, we appointed a sheriff to watch over our "ranches" during the coming year.

When the party ended, we relished reading the enthusiastic endorsements and notes of appreciation written by our guests on the butcher block paper wall in the small bedroom-turned-bar and parlor. Another great gathering. Already anticipation had begun for next year's Shindig.

In the early hours of the following morning, I awoke, startled by a dream about Val. Every few months, I dreamed of her with another man. In these dreams, Val was either trying to take Lori and Ryan, or she already had them and I was trying frantically to get them back.

This night the dream was different. Val and I met at a social gathering. I hugged her, feeling that same familiar reluctance when I'd put my arms around her when we were married. But now I could see it was my fear of rejection blocking me from wanting closeness with her.

I woke, startled by the clarity of the message. Yes, fear of revealing myself had prevented me from achieving real intimacy with my wife. In the darkness, I wondered how much this fear of rejection still limited my ability to open my heart and truly be myself with others.

As I listened to the messages in my dreams, I pondered whether our dreams are a way for us to receive guidance from a higher source than our own conscious mind. The dreams felt as if angels were whispering their loving wisdoms to me in the quiet stillness of sleep. My expanding awareness, with the help from my dreams and my own inner search, suggested I was on an important spiritual journey.

Perhaps the pain, loss, and regrets I'd created in my life were opening me to a new way of seeing and believing I didn't know existed when I was younger. Where was all this leading me? I resolved to turn the rubble of my past into a thing of worth and usefulness for myself and others.

NINETEEN

AMBASSADORS

Spiritual realization is the whole point. It is the driving force, heart's desire, and life long task of parent and child. It is the whole purpose of our being together.

— Polly Berrien Berends,
Whole Parent/Whole Child

One Sunday morning early in May 1981, I decided to risk calling my parents in Escondido.

Mother answered.

"Lee, it's you." Hearing her was like hearing the church bells across the lake in Fulda, reminding me of a time when life had seemed simple and secure. Just like the shy boy growing up, I didn't know where to begin or what to say.

Her voice trembling, she asked, "Are you all right?"

"I'm fine, and so are Lori and Ryan. We're safe, Mom." I must have sounded calm and matter-of-fact, but we'd always communicated that way: contain the emotions, avoid scary words like love, fear, and desperation.

"I'm thankful you're all right . . ." Catching her breath as she spoke. "Lewis wants to talk to you. He has serious news."

A chill shuddered through me. I was a boy again, frightened of my father, fearing I'd done something wrong. Would he tell me I had messed up again? Would he demand I return the children? Had he heard from the FBI?

Time had brought a frailness to his voice, but his familiar matter-of-fact way of speaking hadn't changed. "We've really missed you, Son. So good you called!"

"I've been wanting to, Dad, but the danger . . ."

"I know, I know. But how are you? The children. Everything." Mother stayed on the line to listen.

After telling him about our life, leaving out where we lived, I asked, "Dad, how does Randi feel about all this?"

His tone became guarded, a little sad. "We sent your second letter on to her. Well . . . you know how Randi is."

I visualized my schoolteacher sister: her prim, pursed mouth, her round face, her dimpled chin and reproving eyes. "What was her reaction?"

I pictured his short fingers covering the cough as he stalled.

"Well, as you might guess, she takes the woman's side."

"What do you mean?" I asked.

He cleared his throat again. "Well, I think it might have been Randi who . . ." he blurted out. "Lee, the FBI is looking for you. They're questioning everyone who knew you."

Suddenly, the nightmares were real. The movie had stepped off the screen, slipped up beside me to drag me into the horror.

Mr. Lee Coburn, you are under arrest . . .

I fought back the fear. "Dad, did Val put them onto me?"

"I'm not sure," he said. "I think you've been indicted on that real estate thing, along with Frank and Stan."

"The way I understand it," he said, "the grand jury handed down indictments back in '77, but they weren't pursued right away."

"Atlanta politics," I muttered.

"What's that, Lee?"

"Just a guess. I'm the only one of the three partners without any political connections, and the only one who disappeared. "

"I told the FBI we hadn't heard from you and had no idea where you could be. There were two different pairs. The last ones came back three more times. No direct threats but enough to scare us. They contacted a lot of folks in Atlanta, too, and many in Fulda.

As far as I know, Frank and Stan haven't been indicted. Looks like you're the scapegoat, Lee."

"Do you know if they questioned Randi?" I asked.

Again, a nervous clearing of his throat. "Yes."

"She doesn't know where we are, does she?" fearing to ask.

"No. We sent your letter without the envelope. But she turned the letter over to her husband's hunting buddy who's with the Bureau . . ."

"Are you certain?"

There was a long pause. "I'm afraid so, Lee."

For a moment, I couldn't speak.

"Dad, thanks for telling me," I finally said, resisting the urge to shout profanities at Randi, loud enough for her to hear me.

"It's all right, Son. We . . . your mother and I . . . we love you, you know."

I could feel the tears brimming; in the midst of one of the worst moments of my life, suddenly the cup of my heart overflowed. Never before had my father said he loved me. "Dad . . ."

"It's okay, Lee, it's okay. Don't forget to send me that power of attorney on the storage. I'll take care of it for you. Best to do things right, you know."

"Yes, Dad."

"It'll be all right, Son."

"Yes, Dad. Bye for now . . ."

"Bye, Son. Keep us posted . . ."

Hanging up, I visualized him turning to my mother, her eyes wide and imploring, "Is he all right? Will the children be all right?"

"The children will be all right, Mom," I whispered. How did I know? How would I ever know?

I had an hour alone with the news before Ryan and Lori came home from school. I took a tangerine from the kitchen and went to my makeshift office in the spare bedroom, sat down, and began methodically to peel the fruit. My mind struggled with the persistent and difficult questions: How could I have done this to us? Where was all this leading?

If the FBI came to the door this afternoon, could I at least tell myself I had done my best? Had my best produced a family with two children as happy and loved as most? Like an ointment to heal my self-doubt and guilt, I tried to assure myself; though in my heart, I knew nothing could justify what I had done.

❧

In spite of my remorse, our years together spun by like the passing of months. With little time to reflect I woke up one day to discover my children were teenagers. Lori at fifteen and Ryan at thirteen were changing faster than I could keep up. At times, they were still the innocent children I had stolen from their mother, but more often they were the confident "we can do anything" adults I hoped they would turn out to be.

Ryan still loved his rockets and his skateboard, symbols of our desperate months in Hawaii, but he was also becoming an effective competitor in football, baseball, and basketball and had begun to show an interest in girls and his appearance. We had had solemn discussions on where he should part his hair and whether he should get a shorter haircut.

Lori was always the cheery, pragmatic mother hen of our trio, but she, too, was moving out and away from us into social orbit. She had gone from complaining about boys at school to arranging slumber parties and letting me know it was time she had a brassiere.

I hadn't noticed, but trusted Lori knew better than I what stage of growth she was in. To my relief, Kellie offered to go shopping with her.

But had my children's growth also included healing the loss they suffered as young children losing their mother? Could it be that our life and the love we had created has insulated them from the true pain? They seemed to have suppressed the pain of their loss as a way to survive the tragedy. Someday they may need to grieve the tragic loss they experienced when they were young. Healing was bound to come later for each of us.

I heard the customary slam-bang of the kitchen door, the slap of books to the table, the refrigerator door opening and closing.

"Dad!" Lori, then Ryan.

I brushed the heap of tangerine peels off the desk into the wastebasket and settled back in my chair. I hadn't decided the essential question: how much should I tell them about the phone conversation with my parents?

But they would sense what I was feeling. And besides, we had always talked our concerns out, whatever they were. From those first days in Hawaii, when I had told them we weren't returning to Atlanta, we had spoken openly about matters affecting the family.

Their feet came rustling down the hall. Lori took one look at my face and drew up a chair. "What's wrong?"

Ryan leaned in the doorway, his expression also turning instantly serious. "Yeah, what's up, Dad?"

"The FBI is looking for us," I blurted.

"Oh, boy," said Ryan, fumbling for a chair. "Oh, boy."

Lori looked at me puzzled. "Is this it?" Her voice quavered then steadied. "They can't do this to us."

Ryan moved closer. "Will they take you from us, Dad? I won't let them."

"Nothing has happened yet," I told them. "It's a long way from their looking for us to their finding us. They last questioned my folks months ago. They'll have to find us first. And besides, just because they find us doesn't mean I'm going to jail. I'll look into finding a lawyer in Atlanta and find out what's up."

I managed to remain calm on the outside to avoid alarming the children. On the inside, my nerves felt as if under attack by an army of weevils. "We've come this far," I said. "I know we can keep going."

"Dad, what will we do if they take you away?" whispered Lori.

"Nothing is going to keep us apart," I said, touching Ryan on the knee. Don't forget, you are both old enough now to decide which parent you will live with."

Lori fiddled in her chair and reached for my last tangerine slice. "Are you sure?"

"I'm staying with you, Dad," Ryan declared.

"Yes," I said. "You both can decide. The point is, we have plenty of time, maybe forever." I said, hoping to reassure them. "Nothing's really changed. We only know they've been looking for us, that's all."

They each nodded in silent agreement. Lori said, "It makes you think, doesn't it? How precious every minute is."

I nodded. "So we go on living as we have. Only we'll have to continue being very careful about using names, not mentioning Atlanta and so forth."

Ryan straightened and stuck out his jaw. "We've handled it so far. When you're down six in the third quarter, stick to the basics, only play better."

"Right," I said.

"And you had better pay your parking tickets, Dad," said Lori.

I nodded. "And not get any more."

"And no more speeding."

"You know I don't speed."

"Yesterday on Aurora you were 5 miles over 35."

I gave the back of her neck a light squeeze. "With you to keep an eye on me, how can I lose?"

That red thread of fear woven through our lives sometimes tugged hard at our self-control. In these moments of alarm or uncertainty, I longed to let the taut wire binding me snap free, to ask for sympathy and support, particularly from close friends.

There were, of course, many by now who graced our lives from various corners of interest, people we knew through the church, the tennis club, folk dancing and the children's classes, and other activities. Looking back, I think some of them sensed we were a family with a hidden difference. When asked, I had told them only that I was divorced and had custody of the children.

Each of our friends, in their own way, gave us that prized gift of non-judgmental acceptance and unspoken support that people lend one another. They gave without demand, the kind of giving you don't read about in newspaper headlines and that can't be written into law, but is the heartbeat of real community. Uncertain I deserved their trust, I gave back what I could in appreciation.

Our friends came to be as much family to us as any family can be. Lori and Ryan even had their own surrogate grandparents in Ben and Dorothy Lampe, a retired couple living two blocks from our house. The friendship began during our first summer in Seattle when Ryan knocked on their door, offering to mow their lawn.

Ben asked Ryan some questions about the Richmond Beach football shirt Ryan wore nearly everywhere, even on occasion to bed. When Ryan discovered the Lampes had the sports channel on cable, a friendship began that has lasted to this day. Lori was soon included, exchanging cake recipes and sewing tips with Dorothy, while Ben took Ryan deep-sea fishing for a week and on occasion to Seattle Mariners baseball games. In the summertime, needless to say, the Lampes' lawn was a lot better kept than ours.

Every boy needs a favorite uncle or grandfather; every girl, a seasoned female advisor. Together, Ben and Dorothy Lampe gave the children that and more, with never a thought to the price of their time or love. And not once, to my knowledge, did Ben or Dorothy press Lori or Ryan about my background or their lack of a mother.

Which was not to say our friends weren't curious and didn't occasionally ask indirectly probing questions. Or to say that we didn't itch to spill our story and be done with the pretenses. In fact, it was I who came closest to letting the bird fly free, while under the spell of one of the strongest female personalities I have ever known.

Eve Robare was older than I by a measure of years she never made specific. We met at a ballroom dancing class in May of 1981 and went out for wine afterward. She was an opera singer who had married well but, like so many of us, had divorced. Though frequently away on world tours, she maintained her lovely home in fashionable Hunts Point on Lake Washington. Wise with experience, warm and entertaining, she was by nature an astutely sensitive person, immensely curious about people, their backgrounds, their motives, their secrets.

Through the next year, Eve and I spent increasing amounts of time together, dancing, vacationing, and skiing with Lori, Ryan, and Eve's son, Nathan. I became her frequent escort at gallery openings and concerts and slowly, by sheer exposure, expanded my limited appreciation for opera. She wove stories of her colorful and luminous singing career, in which she had performed in many of the great theaters of the world, into conversations, always with a softness and deference to others.

While I found her intuitive insights into people amazingly accurate and fascinating, she once referred to me as an "everyman." Unclear, I asked her if she meant by that I was commonplace.

She gave her hearty, throaty laugh, and said, "No, Lee. The straightforward and versatile yet vulnerable male is the rarest of the species. Just ask any of my women friends."

She could be straightforward, too, but she could also be oblique and persistent in her curiosity. Of course, when she asked about my marriage, I gave her the standard explanation, dismissing my story as boring. In this case, with a wry grin and a wink: "After all, Eve, divorce happens to every man."

But she remained watchful. I knew she was collecting clues when and where she could find them, and as we spent more and more time together, I found myself growing weary of having always to be on my guard against her probing wit.

April 21, 1982, brought with it another Lee Landel birthday, but this year with only modest plans for celebration. I preferred it that way, especially since it was Lee Landel's fortieth; and Lee Coburn wasn't getting any younger, either.

On the night of my birthday, Eve and I planned to have dinner at her house. I looked forward to a glass of wine with her in front of the fire, maybe listening to a little Mozart, especially since I could now distinguish Mozart from Bach.

I phoned around 6:15 to tell her I was leaving in ten minutes. She said it was raining there. Looking out my window, I saw slashes of clear sky and no rain.

As I started across the Evergreen Point floating bridge to the east side of Lake Washington, a wall of rain moved toward me. It hit like a monsoon as I reached midspan. I flicked on my wipers and followed my headlights into the downpour, driving the familiar route down Hunts Point Road, and parked in front of her house. The blowing rain, like waves of doom sweeping across her lawn, blurred my view. The only light, a small dim glow, shone from her porch. Eve almost always had a fire going in the living room, but I saw no welcome flicker in the plate glass front window.

As always, in such circumstances, I reverted to my fugitive mode, scanning the street for cars, looking for hatted men hunched and watching. There were none, but the air had an eerie feeling. I raced through the downpour, ski jacket over my head, then came up short at the top of the brick steps. I squinted at the poster tacked to the hand-carved double front doors.

"WANTED: LEE LANDEL
aka TEX."

Below, in the stark black line style of a police composite, someone had drawn two side-by-side views of my head, frontal and profile, grimly accurate and official looking.

Under the mug sketches the words: "Attempt will be made to surprise and surround suspect . . ."

No, I told myself, it was ridiculous, a joke . . . of course.

The door swung open, and instinctively, I grabbed the wrought iron rail, prepared to vault and run.

Before me, Eve, smiling broadly, held a candle, while more candles flickered behind her.

"Surprise!" shouted a chorus of voices, and their laughter rolled out the door as the house lights went on. I stood stunned and relieved.

Eve had quietly invited all my "pardners" and friends from past Shindigs to wish me happy birthday at a surprise party.

Candles went out as people jostled around me all laughing as much as I over my total surprise. Eve joined in with a birthday hug, then Kellie, then Joan; I shook hands with her husband, Jeff, and most of the others. Everyone's humor and cheer had filled the house with anticipation.

My contractor friend, Ian Elliot, handed me a glass of champagne. "Hey, Tex, how does it feel to be forty, under arrest, and still this popular?"

"Great, just great," I said. "And what a surprise, as you could tell by the look on my face."

For the party, Eve had prepared a large buffet dinner, including her own creation of a birthday cake which might well have been called a work of art. Bob Henley, our professional pianist in the group, played his repertoire of jazz and sing-along songs, adding entertainment to our spirited evening. Later, to everyone's pleasure, I opened presents and cards, each obviously given with personal thought and care.

The surprise party had been a grand gesture of caring for me, but also for all my friends as well. Eve's enthusiasm had brought us all that feeling of community, a reminder of those friendships we cherished but often took for granted.

But almost as if destined from the beginning of our friendship, I began seeing Eve less and less after that. Something told me to remain single and focus on being a father to Lori and Ryan. I'd grown to care for her and felt a deep sense of loss as we drifted apart. Slowly, the void of her absence healed, as I filled the void by concentrating on developing the business.

The last time I saw Eve was some months later at Shilshole Bay Marina.

❧

Ryan and I were at the marina seeing Lori off on her summer cruise on the *Adventurous*. This year the eighteen-member crew would sail down the Pacific Ocean, up the Columbia River to Portland and then back home. She'd be gone a month.

We were taking pictures of Lori on the 101-foot-long wood ship when Eve showed up in her gold Mercedes coupe, dressed dapper as always, bearing baskets of fruit for Lori.

The three of us stood on the dock waving to Lori as the *Adventurous* cast off under her own power. Soon the winds on Puget Sound would carry her to the Pacific.

From the taffrail, dressed in her red sailing shirt and white shorts, Lori waved back. Silently, I watched this spunky self-assured young woman sail away into another adventure. A brief adventure, I thought, but someday, she'll sail away for good as helmsman of her own life. I felt a little sadness thinking about the day when, as a young woman, Lori might wave good-bye for the last time, leaving me to wonder what my life was really about.

We returned home. Ryan went upstairs to pack for his week of ocean salmon fishing with Ben Lampe. I made sandwiches, while Eve sliced fresh fruit for our lunch. On the patio, we talked of the months since we'd last seen each other. I mentioned I'd begun the outline to the book I planned to write. Though I eluded her questions by saying the book was about single parenting, I knew Eve well enough to know she would not be satisfied leaving the matter alone.

Ever since the WANTED poster at the party, I'd expected her to press me for more details. Though her face turned intent, she kept her tone casual. "Lee, I guessed your secret early," she announced abruptly, "by certain things you said. You'd left two professions completely; and you rarely talked about your parents or complained about being a house painter . . ."

As she continued, my mind raced ahead. Eve and I had always been starkly honest with each other; but I would not violate the bond of allegiance among Lori and Ryan and myself. If Eve persisted, my answer would be flat denial. But I didn't have to decide.

She finished her concluding remarks on how she reasoned I didn't have custody of my children and that I must be living under an alias to have succeeded in not being discovered. Her voice turned softer, kinder. "You don't have to respond, Lee. Let's just say I understand."

Eve was always one to want things neatly in place. Wise and emotionally experienced, she also had the artist's inclination to bring things into focus, to give even the sadder realities a dignified shape.

"I know you did what was right for you," she said. "I respect you."

Talk turned to family news and recent events as I breathed easier. The sun had tipped behind the tall pines, putting us in cool shade. Conversation dwindled as the shadows lengthened.

We said a final good-bye that afternoon, though in spirit, she's never left me. To this day, in my solitude, I can still hear Eve Robare's clear soprano voice resonating in the theater of my heart.

❧

That night, I phoned my sister Randi in Minneapolis.

She answered, as always, like a sergeant-major manning some command post. "This is Randi Palmer, may I help you?"

"It's me, Randi, Lee."

A frosty silence, then, "Well?"

I told her I just wanted to say hello, but couldn't say where we were, only that the children were with me, and we were okay.

Another judicial silence. I pictured her pursed lips, her narrowed eyes.

"I'm glad to hear that much, at least," she finally said, "but I must say, Lee, I can't approve of what you did."

"Randi, I'm not asking you to approve. I just wanted to put this behind us. It's been nearly six years, and you are my sister, and I . . ."

"Val is my sister too," she cut in. "She is a mother, just like me. You had no right, Lee, no right at all."

"They're my kids, too. I'm the father."

"Val is their mother."

"That's true, but the law is unclear . . ."

"The law will take care of you properly, I'm sure. I don't know if Dad told you, but I felt it was my duty . . ."

"I know, the FBI," I said. "Would you like to talk to the kids?"

"There is no need for that. It's a matter of law, Nature's law, God's law."

"Well, I don't know what God thinks, to tell you the truth," I said, "but I do know the law was based on out-of-date premises, and I know my feelings and the children's. If you'd just talk to them . . ."

"Your feelings. Your revenge. I can't talk anymore. I'm too upset."

"You're upset!"

"Good-bye, Lee."

"Good-bye? Randi, look, we're brother and sister. If you won't believe me, ask the kids if they're happy . . ."

Click.

The receiver buzzed in my hand.

❧

In mid-September of 1983, I called Dad again. He said the FBI had been around for the fifth time, and again he had assured them he still had no idea where we were. I considered contacting an Atlanta attorney rather than a local counsel. Maybe somebody could make discreet inquiries about the indictments.

That fall we approached our seventh year together. Lori excelled in art and writing, and had become editor of the high school art magazine, which that year won a national award for excellence. Now at seventeen, she had worked part time for a year, saving to go to Spain with her high school Spanish class.

Ryan blazed his own trail. He became the first freshman ever to be initiated into the school's Thespian Society. He later played the lead role in the spring play, *Cheaper By The Dozen,* and in his senior year became president of the Thespian Society. He played on the school's chess team and attended most major high school functions as photographer for the school newspaper. His competence in many pursuits reflected his growing self-esteem.

From our living room, the grandfather clock ticked away moments of fulfillment, of doubt, and sometimes sorrow, measuring our days. Over my desk, the now framed and autographed WANTED poster continued its mock threat, reminding me that the rhythm could be broken at any moment.

I sought to find stability through an extended family of friends to replace the family we'd lost. I'd made friends and lost some. Eve Robare had come and gone like a shooting star, but my friendship with Kellie and others had grown to be our family. Friends like Joan Wagner from tennis was a warm, sometimes confiding friendship, but safely removed from any suggestion of intimacy. I wanted these friendships to remain just that, nothing more. Especially with married friends like Joan and her husband.

Since my divorce, I'd held to a cardinal rule never date a married woman. I did not want to be the cause of someone's marriage breaking up. Still, I found her appealing and questioned whether we could continue being just friends.

Sometimes I wondered, considering that my history included being a kidnapper, if I would ever manage to build a lasting relationship with a woman. I found it hard to imagine marrying again.

❧

Dreams of Val continued, but they appeared to be working toward some kind of resolution, perhaps a peace within myself.

In September, yet another dream.

Val and I were in a large hotel in Atlanta. We glanced at each other across the crowded lobby. She looked tired and older with grayish hair. I panicked, fearing she would report me to the police.

I rushed to get into my room and waited for her knock on my door with the authorities. None came. The dream ended.

I woke up, relieved she had not pursued me. I pondered the dream. Had she, in growing older, become less angry or vengeful? Had she resigned herself to living a life of sorrow and anguish?

I felt myself feeling Val's sorrow and, at the same time, sensed a forgiveness in the making, a resolution to all our pain — not just mine, but Val's as well.

The very next evening, I gathered the kids in front of the fireplace for a "family talk."

"We haven't talked lately about your mother, have we?"

They were immediately alert. "You mean about when we go visit her?" said Lori.

I nodded. "You'll be eighteen in a little over a year."

"And I'll be sixteen!" Ryan said.

"Right. So maybe we should begin to think about how it should be done, what it will be like."

Lori eagerly took the lead. She wondered what her mother would look like, what kind of house she and the doctor lived in. Ryan speculated as to the kind of car they drove. Lori talked about her artwork and some photographs of herself dancing she wanted to show Val. Ryan wasn't sure he wanted to go all the way to Atlanta; couldn't Val come to Seattle and watch him play baseball or ride his dune buggy?

I let them talk it out. They agreed they would miss our family. Lori added she did believe, however, that "the well-rounded person should have a satisfactory relationship with both parents."

Ryan came up with the worst case scenario. "What if we don't like her? What if she doesn't want to see us. Or the doctor is mean or a jerk or something?"

"We'll just say, 'Look, Mom, this is what I've done with me,'" Lori said. "'I'm proud of me, and I hope you are pleased, and if not, it doesn't matter, because I'm pleased with me, and that's what counts.'"

A week or so later, I was dozing on the couch and heard Ryan call Ben Lampe.

"Hi, Ben. Whatcha doin?" An easy, rambling conversation followed. "I've got some worms if you want them," I heard him say. Then an exchange of how he'd come to have a five-gallon can of fishing worms. "I'll bring the worms and help you with what you're doing, Ben." More visiting, finally, "I'll be right over." Through the conversation, Ryan's voice sang like notes of a song, animated, alive, clear, and filled with delight. "Hi Ben," that glorious sound of a fifteen-year-old boy, speaking on every word with the ring of anticipation for seeing his friend.

The back door slammed as he went to get his worms.

Lying there in the stillness, I wondered how I could preserve the joyous sound of Ryan's voice and the sweet feeling that came over me while he talked with his good friend Ben.

Some things words alone cannot describe. But I do know, for the rest of my life, when I lie quietly and listen, I will be able to hear the pure, melodic sound of Ryan growing up.

That night, Ryan's joyful spirit still with me, I thought more about my role as a parent. Many parents, particularly we single parents, find ourselves overwhelmed with the responsibility of providing for our children. But the upside is that the onerous struggle to provide emotional and physical stability for our children also brings a richness and satisfaction that is unmatched by any other experience.

I once thought being an effective parent meant balanced meals, neat beds, and earning a living. Now I see parenthood as a crash course in learning how to love and nurture the growth of another human being. Seeing and supporting my children's unique natures has helped me be less attached to whether they succeed or fail by some outside standard. The more I trust in the natural unfolding of who they really are, the less I feel a need to interfere with their process of development.

Watching Lori and Ryan grow up so rapidly has been like looking into a kaleidoscope. At every turn, one is captivated by the ever changing beauty before one's eyes. This is why being a parent is so enriching, because our children are forever growing and becoming.

To reestablish our authority as parent and our joy of parenting we must return to the lost concept of being the primary role model for our children. This means relying less on surrogate parents such as day care, teachers, television, the internet, etc., to relieve us of the important job of raising our children. Being a parent means being fully accountable for the development of our sons and daughters. In return, we receive the satisfaction for a job well done, knowing we have given the gift of all that we are to our children regardless of outcome.

Whether we're in a one parent household or two, each of us is the most qualified to raise our own children. As parents, we are blessed with a profound opportunity to contribute to lasting change in our society. By making a commitment to yourself, and then to your children's emotional and spiritual growth you become a participant in influencing our world for future generations.

No greater life mission exists than to nurture our children into the loving human beings they were born to be. Parents spend large amounts of energy striving for wealth and power and recognition. Yet they fail to see that fulfillment and greatness, for ourselves and our children, begins at home around the dinner table and in countless small shared moments of sharing and listening.

Our goal as parents is to raise happy, healthy, and productive children and to help them become all they are meant to be. In truth, they are our ambassadors of love and peace for future generations. If they do not learn values, principles, and most of all, love from us as parents, we cannot expect them to learn elsewhere. If only we can remember that peace, goodness, and prosperity for this world begins in our hearts, at home, with our children.

TWENTY

RESOLUTION

The ideal of loving all of humanity
can only follow when you have
exercised love within yourself first.

— Jacqueline T. Snyder,
Beyond Common Thought

"I hear you kidnapped your children."

You can anticipate the worst for years, try to imagine when and how it will happen and rehearse your reactions, but still it comes as a shock and all you can do is improvise.

The woman, Marjory somebody, regarded me across the coffee table with bland, violet eyes, a quizzical smile on her lips. Conversation ceased; the fire in Kellie's fireplace crackled softly; ice clinked in somebody's glass.

"Oh really?" I shrugged and looked at my drink. "An interesting idea, It's understandable how somebody might cook that one up."

"Well then . . ." the woman said. She prepared to press me harder, but Kellie cut her short. "Why not play your dulcimer for us, Lee?"

She waved her hands and Joan moved to another chair, making a diversionary flurry that got me to my feet. Now I was feeling doubly embarrassed. Building my hammered dulcimer had been easy, and taking lessons had been rewarding, but this would be my first attempt to play for others. For a moment, I wasn't sure which scared me most, the questions or my debut.

With my hands stiff and taut on the hammers, and one eye on

Kellie's encouraging smile, I played two Irish jigs and a ragtime dance piece.

I could feel their sidelong glances, and noticed the woman with the violet eyes whispering to her husband. Now that the subject of childnapping was out in the open, it was not likely to be left alone. But as I played more tunes, I began to relax about any further questioning. After all, I had faced eagle-eyed passport clerks and watchful bureaucrats of every stripe. Still, this was different, not just individual probing, but an inquiry en masse, with a host of witnesses to testify should I slip.

On the other hand, except for the new couple, the rest of the dozen people present were old friends and not likely to rush to the phone to call the FBI.

Deliberately or not, the violet-eyed woman had precipitated a crucial test of my ability to handle a group confrontation.

My short concert ended. I accepted the polite applause and a few encouraging comments. The woman spoke again. Had I changed my name? It was just so-o-o fascinating, a man running off with his children like that. How had the children reacted? What about the mother? How had I kept from being found?

Her eyes narrowed, and her mouth grew grim as she continued to surmise. "Yes, what about the mother," she repeated. "Didn't you have any feelings for the mother?"

I waited for the last of her inquiries to settle. All eyes were on me now, many anxious for me, a few as intent and potentially critical as hers.

I looked directly at her and said, "Your questions are interesting. I wish I could answer them."

Her eyes widened expectantly. The room drew in a collective breath.

"But I am not going to," I finished. "This is something I'm not yet prepared to discuss."

"But . . ." She appealed to Kellie for support.

Kellie gave a wry smile and looked over at me. "No, Marj. Best to drop it. Obviously Lee is uncomfortable with the subject." She cast a slow glance around the room. "And he is among friends. So let's change the subject."

The woman followed Kellie's glance. A few smiled, most simply stared silently at her.

"Well . . ." The woman gave a lame shrug. "It's none of my business, of course . . ."

"Of course," Kellie said.

The party resumed. Marj lapsed into disgruntled silence and less than a quarter of an hour later, gathered her husband off the couch and nodded hurried good-byes to everyone.

With her departure, the thought of childnapping became buried. Nobody else raised the subject. Quietly, except for the first flash of alarm aroused by this one stranger, I had passed an important test. Although I had made no overt admission, for the first time I had tacitly acknowledged the truth. At least, I felt certain not one of those remaining condemned me or would betray me. I was left to worry whether the woman with the violet eyes would report me.

Afterward, Joan and I walked to our cars. She had come to the party without Jeff again. When we were clear of Kellie's porch light, she kissed me. She gave that familiar nod of head, her auburn hair falling away from one shoulder.

"I liked the way you handled yourself, Landel."

I gave a shrug of mock modesty. "Oh well, the little Irish jigs are easy."

She chuckled, but I knew every nuance of her moods by now, and she had something else on her mind.

I glanced toward Kellie's house to make sure we were unobserved and moved closer to take her hand again. "There's nothing to worry about," I said. "That woman Marjory is speculating up a dead tree. She's talking nonsense."

"It isn't that," she said.

"Then what?"

She tried to pull her hand away, but I held on.

"It's Jeff, isn't it?"

She nodded, her face turning somber. "He went into one of his rages last night. He wanted to know if there was anything going on between you and me. I told him there wasn't, but I felt so awful. God, how I hate to lie!"

Being with Joan had started simply enough. The relaxed and casual friendship began four years ago — at first seeing Joan and her husband Jeff at weekly tennis games and dinner parties. After a while, Joan had begun arriving alone to play singles, more often having that weary look a woman has when her emotional life is in flux. Six months ago in August, she had left her tennis gloves at my house after a potluck dinner with mutual friends. I'd phoned to tell her about the gloves. We met for lunch and had a long discussion of life in general and marriages in particular. A week later, coffee at her house while Jeff was away on a flight inspection. As a design engineer for Boeing Aircraft, he made frequent trips out of the country.

A hug good-bye after our morning talk. We agreed to meet at my place for a game of tennis the next day.

We never made it to the club that day, and we'd been seeing each other once or twice a week ever since.

I had finally surrendered to her quiet containment I had been drawn to years before, when she'd made that remark about the seasons of life. The season of love for us, it seemed, had arrived and with it, the season of crisis in her marriage. And for me, another lesson in humility, as I listened to the hollow ring of my cardinal rule, now obsolete, that I would never involve myself with a married woman.

Everything Joan and Jeff had worked for was coming apart, as it has for so many of us. She had the feeling, she said, that her life was slipping away beneath her, like some massive rock slide she couldn't stop.

Now, standing next to her car, she pulled her hand free and turned toward me, resignation showing on her face. "I know I'm just being silly, but I'm afraid of what he might do."

"You've every reason to be afraid," I said. "And there's nothing silly about anything you're feeling. If you think about it, the reason you're leaving your marriage is because you haven't known the intimacy you deserve and want. Standing up for what you need and deserve as a woman can be scary."

She paused, looking at me over the car door, her eyes narrowed in curious reflection, as if connecting with her sadness. "Maybe I need to look at why I stayed with such an unfeeling husband all these years. And why does your gentle way give me the courage now to leave?"

She slid behind the wheel and looked up at me. "I need you, you know. See you soon."

I watched her taillights move down the street and sink into the night. Chatter came from Kellie's front door; I climbed hastily into my van and drove the few blocks to my house. In watching Joan and Jeff's marriage unravel like a pulled thread on a sweater, I had come unwittingly to a sense of déjà vu. A familiar but painful triangle of needs, desires, and emotions.

Except this time, I was the other man.

Two months later, Joan phoned me in a panic. She had told Jeff she wanted to end the marriage. He threatened that he'd see her dead before he'd let her go. He hadn't hurt her yet, but since he had become violent before, she was frightened for her life.

We arranged to meet, had dinner, talked, went to my house, and made love, bringing that fleeting calm that lingers. And indeed, the calm was brief. A week later, we met for lunch. Joan told me Jeff had refused to see a marriage counselor, refused to consent to a divorce, and refused to leave the house. He promised, if she tried to leave, he would burn the house down with both of them in it. Worse yet, he threatened to disappear with the children.

"What shall I do?" she asked me.

"First, understand when a marriage fails, the rejected partner often feels as if the earth is falling out from under them. For many of us, when we feel we're losing control, we become even more determined to stay in command. The more you claim your own power, Joan, the more desperate Jeff will likely become. Threatening you is his way of attempting to stay in control," I said.

"Why does he feel he has to be in control of everything, especially me?" she asked, her eyes flooding with tears.

I explained to her as boys we're told only sissies cry, so we learn to hide our emotions. Since we haven't learned to be sad, afraid, or to grieve, we do what we know best — we become angry, then desperate. We use anger as a substitute for all our deeper feelings because we think anger is more acceptable.

"Jeff's angry threats," I said, "are his attempts to control you and the world he fears is crumbling."

She studied me. "You've been that angry, frightened man, haven't you?"

"Yes. And now I'm a participant again, and that's what makes it so painful. Because now I see myself more clearly than before. Being with you helps me understand what my wife must have been going through when she left me."

She was right. I did understand Jeff and every man who is afraid to love another out of fear of losing himself. I felt as if I were watching an old movie, but this time I was playing Dr. Reynolds and Joan was Val.

❧

Amidst the drama of seeing a marriage end, except this time as an intimate observer, I was still a father and a fugitive. In the passing years, I had become less a participant in Lori and Ryan's lives and more an advisor; yet I cherished my parenting role with increased appreciation. Dinners out, skiing trips, socializing with family friends, all the things we had done together now occurred less frequently, and were therefore even more precious to me.

Meanwhile, Ryan continued his enthusiastic involvement in his school activities, though his grades had begun to slip a little. When I talked with him about his studies, he cocked a feisty eye at me and told me, "Keep it short, Dad. I'll give you five minutes. I know what you're going to say anyhow."

On the one hand, I was annoyed and had to insist he promise to try harder, but on the other hand, I felt secret glee at his healthy independence.

How could I complain? He was simply a product of my intention, which was to help him grow up with a self-assurance that I never had as a boy.

To encourage and build his own sense of independence, I had, in fact, chosen activities which would foster his confidence, such as the two of us building a model airplane together.

I had given him the 36-inch-wingspan Cessna Skyhawk for his birthday, along with the required gas engine. For several months, we fitted and glued, sanded and polished, and dreamed of flying. But most of all, we talked, sometimes late into the evening. When we finished our model Cessna, complete with clear cockpit windows, miniature instrument panel, and a pilot at the controls, we test ran the .025 engine, checking to see if all the remote control radio servos operated properly.

Housed within the airplane were four remote servos which received signals from the radio transmitter held by the pilot on the ground. Most radio transmitters allow the pilot to control as many as six functions on the airplane, but beginners usually start by learning the intricacies of four controls, the throttle, rudder, elevators, and ailerons. We were eager to learn how to fly our gleaming red and white Cessna.

Starting in May, we met every Saturday with other remote control hobbyists at a grass airstrip in Marymoor Park, just east of Seattle. A few Saturdays later, I watched from the sidelines as Ryan took another lesson flying the airplane. He had adapted quickly to the delicate responses of the radio controls.

I kept on eye on the airplane circling overhead, pleased to see Ryan mastering the controls. He sent the plane through two figure eights high over the grass field. Dropping elevation, he brought the plane down for a straight pass over the runway. On his next sweep around, he banked the little plane into a turn for the final approach to land, then lowered the Cessna onto the grass runway for his first safe landing.

As the plane came to a stop, applause rose from the sidelines where the regulars had watched Ryan maneuver the airplane through his first solo flight.

He walked over to join me at the sideline, his face beaming with satisfaction. In this one moment, he had grown ten feet tall and a lot bigger inside.

I said, "Great job, Ryan."

He stuck out his hand and as we shook, he said, "Well, Dad, we made it. You said we'd fly again someday and we have. Thanks. Now let's see what you can do, Dad."

I turned to retrieve the airplane, fighting the rush of tears. Suddenly, I couldn't help but be overwhelmed by the enormity of our lives all these years since Hawaii.

In that one moment, we moved beyond father and son. We'd become just a couple of barnstormers pushing our limits on the wings of time, free spirits learning to fly.

❧

While Ryan and I gloated over our learning to fly, Lori divided her enthusiasm between her first "serious" romance and her impending trip to Spain with her high school Spanish class.

Together, we'd grown through her rites of passage of becoming a young woman. Our many father and daughter talks, while not always easy, brought us closer together. Confronting our different views forged an openness and a new level of honesty between us. Our talks brought us to a place of greater acceptance and appreciation for one another. Our openness also included expressing the love we shared for each other, even when we did not agree.

My parenting role, I believed, was to trust my children, and to let them mature into sound-minded healthy young people in their own unique ways. I had observed parents imposing rigid rules that seemed unrelated to teaching the real virtues necessary for their children's lives to be constructive and life-affirming.

What mattered most, it seemed, was to teach values that would serve Lori and Ryan throughout their lives. I sought to guide Lori and Ryan into achieving a balanced, responsible, and caring approach to their lives.

As parents, we must provide consistent loving support and encouragement to create trust and positive self-esteem for our children. I hoped my steadfastness would give them both the confidence and the latitude to orchestrate their individual lives toward harmony for themselves and others. I would step in only if I sensed signs of poor judgment that jeopardized their development and safety. Until then, I would let them test their own maturing values.

Meanwhile, Lori needed a passport for her trip to Spain. She said she wanted to travel using her real name. "Please, Dad, isn't there a way we can work it out? Aren't we safe enough now so we can begin to be ourselves again in some ways?"

Were we?

Before Christmas, I'd sent a long letter to my parents through my New York mail drop. When the holidays came, Lori and Ryan asked to talk to their grandparents in Oregon. I gave in and decided to risk the call. They talked for nearly an hour, taking turns on the phone.

After the phone call, Lori and Ryan wanted to make plans to go to Eugene to see my parents. It would be their first visit in over nine years and an important first step in making a transition back to their roots. But in March, I received a letter from Dad, through the New York drop, reporting that Mother had pneumonia. The trip would have to be postponed. Also, he wrote that he'd had another visit from the FBI.

The coincidence disturbed me. Could the Christmas phone call have been tapped? It seemed extraordinary that a tap could have been maintained since my first call to Eugene. There was always the possibility that private investigators hired by Val or Dr.

Reynolds might have arranged a tap. We had been careful not to mention our whereabouts, but I had told Dad on the phone that Lori was going to Spain. A search of passports and school travel programs would quickly turn up Lori Coburn on Westminster Way in Seattle. The agents would be at my door before Lori returned from her trip.

Nonetheless, weary of our deceptive life, we applied for the passport under her real name, Lori Coburn. It was an act of optimism and a prayer for good fortune.

The night before Lori left for Spain, we gathered around the orange-frosted angel food cake I'd made for her birthday. She would be in Spain on her actual birthday, April 1.

Eighteen candles burned on the cake. The age at which we had agreed she would contact her mother. But earlier we had all decided we weren't quite ready. Ryan, especially, did not want his high school years disrupted. Once again, we'd said, "Maybe next year."

While Lori was gone, I tried not to fret about a possible trace on the Coburn name. Fortunately, painting projects kept me occupied. Economic recovery under Reagan had begun, but unemployment remained high. My ad in the paper for painters drew over one hundred responses. Less than half were from qualified tradesmen.

After the first dozen calls, I had the two men I needed, but I returned all the calls, trying each time to say the job had been filled in words that would leave them with their dignity. "I'll keep your application on file," seemed lame and empty in light of what I remembered of that feeling of uselessness that comes from being out of work. I assured each caller that new openings came about periodically and to check back. My afternoon on the phone had reminded me that even with my own worries, I was essentially a fortunate man.

True, from our desperate beginning we had found a semblance of peace and order to our lives. But the price we all paid had grown more apparent with each passing year. Our struggle to survive as a family was as much my own personal struggle to understand the travesty I set in motion by taking Lori and Ryan. No longer did I see others as right or wrong, me against them, they against me. But rather, loss, pain and struggle as providing a deeper understanding of ourselves and our purpose on earth.

Choosing a path of self-discovery released me from the anger and revenge I once knew, while drawing me nearer to the love and wisdom of the Infinite Spirit many call God. I know now the dragons spreading flames upon my life were those I carried within myself.

❧

Lori returned from Spain with a three-foot bullfight poster for Ryan, a leather wine bottle for me, a lace mantilla for Kellie, and a suede purse for herself.

Lori had grown up to become a spirited giver. She'd find reasons for giving at every turn — like sending flowers or cards with notes in them or simply being a good listener. She'd listen to me with an open heart and then accept my choices as no one else would or could. Her loving acceptance gave me the courage to keep searching personally and spiritually.

In addition to Lori's patient listening, writing in my journal helped bring insights and inspirations. After Lori's return from Spain, I found these musings I'd written in the solitude of a late evening:

> *I am feeling again the agony of divorce through Joan ending her marriage.*
>
> *Her husband, Jeff, sees her as the destroyer of a perfect marriage. His anger and self-denial prevents him from seeing the part he played in creating a marriage void of intimacy and nurturing. Reflecting on my own divorce has helped me understand that neither party is to "blame" nor "destroys" a marriage. Our outer world, particularly our closest relationships, always mirror who we are inside. Like a mirror, our own unhealed wounds from childhood are being reflected back to us in our present circumstances.*

Often we are unaware just how strongly our past experiences, particularly from childhood, affect our present life. Blaming others for our suffering, as I did with Val, prevented me from seeing where I needed to change and what I needed to heal. My anger kept me from seeing who I was at the time. Today, by using the events in my life as lessons, I'm gaining a deeper understanding of myself and others. I now see that whatever my circumstances, I can seek my highest good by using my past to transform my future.

Later on, I thought more about the ideas I'd written in my journal.

When we fear risking emotional intimacy with ourselves, finding trust and intimacy with the one we love becomes impossible. The emptiness and loneliness we experience arises from our unwillingness to face our own unhealed parts of ourselves. Too painful to face, we tuck those parts of ourselves away in some hidden corner of our psyche.

None of us, of course, chooses to disconnect from being alive. Yet to avoid being vulnerable, we close off important aspects of ourselves, and thus from everyone else. We learned as children to hide our feelings in order to keep from being hurt. Later, as adults, our control barricades us not only from ourselves, but from everyone else as well. Our self-imposed walls leave us stranded — on the outside looking in.

Fearing to let down my protective walls for Val to know me created an artificiality that numbed our relationship. Without emotional openness to create intimacy and trust, we grew to feeling an emptiness — worse still, silent rage. One way or another, a couple's repressed anger finds ways to express itself, in such forms as extramarital affairs, chronic illness, emotional or physical abuse, and depression. All place every vital relationship at risk.

❧

Watching Joan leave her marriage evoked in me a deeper compassion for Val. Joan and Val, like many women who marry men afraid of intimacy, suffered a deprivation of their emotional and physical needs. Now I see how Val became convinced she would never know affection and tenderness, least of all love, with the undeveloped man she married.

Joan's husband, as I did, tried to run from his fears by controlling everything around him. His attempts to control are the classic cover-ups for an insecure self. As Joan claimed her own life, as did Val in seeking to meet her needs, the more out of control Jeff felt. He feared, as I had, if he lost control, his world would crumble into extinction.

His attempts to regain control precipitated threats of suicide if she left. To force her into compliance, he threatened to burn the house down with her in it. Later, he threatened to kidnap the children if she divorced him. His fear of being out of control, like mine, became a desperate and potentially destructive fight to maintain his self-image. More truthfully, flight from life. When we think we are dying, we'll do almost anything to stay alive. At the time our actions seem reasonable. A madman always thinks he's sane.

By observing Jeff's behavior, I began to understand my own irrational decision to abduct Lori and Ryan.

Facing my fear of loving has been a long and arduous process. Nine years have passed since Val announced she wanted a divorce. Nine years and only now was I beginning to understand, to feel compassion for Val and what she had done with her life. That night I wrote in my journal:

> *Though you may never read these words, Val, I write them for you.*
>
> *Lately, I've been experiencing something that makes me want to speak to you. Simple as this seems, the words hold back.*
>
> *It has taken these many years for me to begin to understand the feelings you must have had during our marriage; the resentment, the bitterness, the emptiness of a joyless marriage burdening you like a heavy chain around your life.*

I understand your leaving. Your way out of the marriage, looking back, now seems natural, right for you at that time in your life. After all these years, Val, I can now feel the loneliness you must have experienced long before you left. I regret not understanding your pain sooner. I am sorry. Forgive me.

I knew, however, that the forgiveness I sought from Val had to come from within myself. Nine years of parenting, close friendships with men and women, counseling, my journal, a growing spiritual quest, had all contributed to finding my own forgiveness.

Forgiving myself helped me forgive and understand Val. She, like many women, struggled to find intimacy the only way she knew how at that time in her life.

The truth was, Val wanted something from me that I didn't know how to give — intimacy. I'd kept such a tight rein on my feelings for so long, there was no way I could let her close to me. I was afraid if she got past my defenses, I would be forced to face the emptiness I believed I would find. I see now that in order to keep a safe distance from my feelings, I had to keep a safe distance from her as well.

❧

We had come to the end of another ski season with spring perking our energy with cerulean skies and ubiquitous daffodils. But for one last time, we headed for Crystal Mountain for a final day of spring skiing. It was one of those memorable days when I saw so sharply the best of what we had, as one sometimes can in the sharp brisk air of the Northwest's snow-capped mountains.

Lori and I bundled into a chair on Lift One, up to catch Chair Two, which would take us to the top of Green Valley. From there, we could observe the eastern face of Mount Rainer. As we rose through the stately pines, Lori pointed to Ryan skiing below us. "Look, Dad, It's Ryan! He thinks he's so good."

We watched him cut across the slope, then execute a perfect jump turn. Wagging a pole in mock challenge, he tucked into a downhill posture and streaked straight down, taking the tops of the moguls as they came, literally flying. Yes, he was good, our Mercury, the scholar, athlete, actor, son, and little brother, speeding like the wind.

"Dad, let's go all the way up!" Lori clutched my arm as I was about to step off the chair.

She laughed at my hesitation. I returned a challenging squint and sat back, tilting my chin to take in the frosty, gleaming slope high above.

"Okay! But let's take it slow coming down."

Ten minutes later, we skied off the chair onto the top of the world, the thin air crackling in our lungs and a depthless bowl of sun-bright blue above. We sidestepped to the edge, stamping our skis. Lori checked her bindings, her poles, her gloves, then propped on a pole and leaned toward me, tugging her ski mask down so she could speak. "See you at the bottom, Dad."

She crouched, pushed off. I heard the scraping hiss of her edges. She skied over the lip in one clean lunge, out of sight for a moment, then hurtling down the fall line, taking the moguls as Ryan had, as they both had learned to take life — carefully, expertly, but with eager anticipation.

I set my poles, then straightened. There was no hurry now. I could watch her all the way to the bottom and know she was safe. Her life was set, she'd make it on her own. From 6,200 feet, I looked out across the vast white valley to the 14,000-foot Mount Rainer.

"All I wanted was a quiet, loving life . . ." Val had said.

All any of us ever wanted, but acquiring it was not that easy. All we could do was laugh, cry, love when we could, keep growing, and love again, never forgetting that life was forever lifting us higher.

The great mountain sat upon its centuries across the valley. No wonder the Indians had revered it as their White Goddess and prayed to it.

I crouched and pushed off, falling only three times on the way down. But no broken bones. Lori and Ryan were waiting when I entered the lodge. Lori shouted, "What took you so long?"

TWENTY ONE

GOING HOME

For me there is only the traveling
on paths that have heart . . .
And there I travel looking, looking,
breathlessly.

— Carlos Casteneda
The Teachings of Don Juan

"For my graduation present, I'd like plane tickets for Lori and me to see Mom." Ryan said.

My stomach jumped to my throat.

"Right on," Lori chimed. She was home from Washington State University for the weekend. "What better present than for us to see Mom?"

Sitting around the living room that evening in October, I'd asked Ryan what he wanted for his high school graduation present. We'd often discussed the pros and cons of ending our exile during our ten years together. But with Lori and Ryan content in their lives, the years had slipped by.

"Sure, why not," I managed, secretly fearing what this might mean. And so with little discussion, we agreed that for Ryan's graduation, he and Lori would see their mother in June.

Silently, I thought, yes, this has gone on long enough. After all these years, I owed it to Ryan to honor his wish. But in spite of my commitment, I wasn't looking forward to my life being substantially altered as I expected it would be. Nor did I look forward to the expensive and embarrassing legal snarl I believed was sure to follow. Whatever the consequences, I would make good on clearing the way for Lori and Ryan to visit their mother in June. I reminded myself to take the matter of returning to Atlanta one step at a time. Besides, Ryan's second semester would be soon enough to deal with their return.

April came and still I had done nothing. Kellie urged me to get started in case attorneys needed time to prepare a proper defense. I sent a letter to Trammel Newton, a former attorney friend in Atlanta. As an added security, I used the New York mail drop. Feeling like a trembling rabbit looking down the barrel of a hunter's gun, frozen between fear and flight, I dropped the envelope in the mail. The letter included a one-hundred dollar-retainer and stated I would call him in a week.

I proceeded through the next week feeling the dread of someone wading chin high in alligator-infested waters. This would be my first contact with Atlanta in ten years. Would Trammel refuse to talk to me? Had he already notified the authorities? Every possible scenario churned through my mind.

The morning of the phone call, I awoke with my stomach twisted into knots. Today, after ten years, we would no longer be hiding.

His secretary put me through to Trammel. To my amazement, he remembered me. "Good to hear from you, Lee," he said. "And how are the kids?"

"I'm a little nervous. And the kids . . . they're just fine, thank you." I felt reassured and relieved at his cheerful reception.

Quickly, I recapped the events leading up to my departure. He understood my concerns about the possible ramifications of the children's return.

"First, let's determine what the charges are against you, if any," he said.

He told me to call him in a week when he'd have the matter researched. I hung up, relieved to have made my first contact with Atlanta. At least now, something was being done.

❧

When Lori arrived home from college in early May, we began almost daily talks on how she and Ryan would contact their mother. A month remained. They hoped to go as soon as possible after Ryan's graduation on June 8.

I purchased two round trip tickets to Atlanta for departure on the morning of June 10. Now we had a specific day and hour. Reading Lori and Ryan Coburn on the vouchers made me feel as if I held tickets for the premier of a new drama.

And yet, strangely, Ryan acted lethargic. Instead of showing excitement or relief at graduating from high school, he gave every indication of severe depression. In the previous months, he'd done poorly in school and had several conflicts with his teachers. He trudged through the days with low energy, procrastination, and indecision.

I told Ryan I wanted us to see a counselor. I made an appointment with a therapist I'd met a few months before at a workshop. Ryan grudgingly agreed to go.

After several sessions, Dr. Marcelis said Ryan was experiencing emotional overload from too many unresolved issues in his life. His unsettled plans for college, the weight of not knowing what his future held, and most of all, the anxiety over seeing his mother had caused him to withdraw.

She suggested that as Ryan neared the time for seeing his mother, he was likely grieving for the first time the loss of his mother. She explained that people suffering tragedies often put off grieving as a way of surviving the loss. And that until they grieve, their repressed pain and sadness is commonly expressed through illness, anger, or depression.

The sadness Ryan had repressed, she explained, was beginning to surface as he contemplated seeing his mother after all these years. "He may also be getting in touch with the anger he has for you for taking him from his mother," she said. "Understandably, he's suppressed his anger fearing that to express it, he might lose your love. He may also be in fear of what he will say when his mother asks why he and Lori didn't call all those years."

Learning all this, I assured Ryan he had a right to his feelings and that I would continue to love him even if he did unleash his anger at me. The counseling brought to my attention the need to be patient with Ryan and to give him an abundance of love and acceptance during this crucial turning point in his life. Most of all, I needed to trust Ryan's growth and know that, given enough time and support, he would heal in his own way.

While I tried to lend support to Ryan, I found myself wandering through my own dark valleys. In spite of my vigilance to achieve security and peace of mind, painful reminders of my negative beliefs kept coming like piercing arrows. As I struggled to change my beliefs, more arrows found their mark. Piercing blows like the ending of my engagement to the woman I planned on marrying: another from business losses reducing me to counting coins from my change jar to survive.

My difficulties, I suspected were showing me the need to resolve my inner turmoil, and to begin making different choices — most of all, to take responsibility for the beliefs that were directing my life.

Feeling as if my life was in disarray, I called my friend, Dana Marcelis hoping to gain some insight. She invited me to come over.

We'd stayed in touch after our counseling with Ryan. Over time, we'd become good friends. We'd talk for hours at her home nestled on the edge of a small lake in the middle of the city. It was there she greeted me with her usual radiance, which, as always, made me and anyone else who came near feel changed by her presence. She led me into her living room. I sat on the couch, from which I could watch the birds in the aviary just beyond a small lagoon.

She set a tea tray on the magazine table between us before relaxing into her favorite wicker chair. Stillness settled around us as we sipped our tea in silence.

"So, how have things been going for you?" she began.

"The truth is, I'm angry, but I don't know what about. And I'm depressed," I said. "I thought life was supposed to get easier the older you got."

Dana sat in silence for a moment and then spoke. "Since nothing happens out of chance, Lee, consider looking at your anger and these struggles as if they were voices telling you something you might need to look at."

"You mean like looking at myself instead of blaming everyone else?" I asked.

"That's my point. We're often unaware how unhealed parts of ourselves are reflected back to us in the events of our lives." she said. "Peace comes by accepting where we are in the present moment. Once we accept our feelings and know that whatever we're feeling is okay, we can express our anger."

"Truth is, I'm still holding on to feelings of resentment over things that happened long ago," I said. "Even painful feelings I remember as a child."

"It's these unexpressed feelings that pollute our very being and can literally make us sick," she said.

"That's what worries me."

"You can let go of these feelings if you want. Holding on to things that happened years ago drains you of your life force energy, Lee."

"Then why have I clung to these unwanted feelings when they're doing me no good?" I asked.

"People hold on to resentments because they either don't know how to express the feelings, or they're afraid to face the deeper pain beneath the anger or grief. Like keeping an old pair of shoes, we feel safe holding on to our feelings. By staying angry or bitter, we avoid the deeper feelings of our losses, but also the joy of love in our hearts."

"So where do I begin if I truly want peace and harmony and love in my life?" I asked, ready to turn my life around.

"You begin with forgiveness. This means *you* choosing to forgive those you feel have hurt you."

"How can I forgive when I'm still angry? Deep down, I believe I'm still angry at my parents. And maybe at Val, also." I said.

"Forgiving doesn't mean you have to stop being angry. If you're sincere in your heart about forgiving those who have hurt you, your anger and bitterness will in time fade. You may never be fully free of anger, but you can still forgive. Forgiveness allows you to move on with your life. By forgiving and accepting the present moment you begin to see all events as blessings in your life."

"Is it really that simple?" I asked.

"Simple, but not easy," she said.

"Why's that?"

"To forgive means feeling our anger and grief. We must mourn our losses. In this mourning we feel our sadness and pain," she said. "Forgiving is a process that requires time and a willingness to move on. It means remembering that those who hurt us also believed they had been victims. They, like us, have good and bad sides to them."

"I really hadn't considered everyone being the same as me," I mused.

"The truth is we are one with all things, just that we have to go deeper to see that everyone is our brother and sister."

"Okay, on rare occasions I have experienced a connectedness with everyone around me. But then what?" I asked.

She continued. "Forgiving means being willing to be vulnerable and open to peace in your life. In doing so you'll discover you've opened to the Divine within yourself and the Infinite Power of the universe."

Her words gave me a feeling of hope. "Tell me more," I urged.

"Our life, Lee, always mirrors the truth we hold within ourselves. I suggest looking at this dark period in your life as a encouragement to making peace with your past, and as a way of opening you to your sacred self."

She sipped her tea as I sat silent for a moment, contemplating her ideas.

"You're saying the difficulties I'm experiencing are part of my spiritual journey?" I finally asked.

She nodded. "Often, it's in our darkest hours that we're being shown the need to change our perception. Life is neither bad nor good, it just is. We can choose to see events as random and therefore live as victims. Or we can seek the divinity in all things and know there are blessings in even our most troubling times. In truth, everything that happens to you, Lee, is part of your spiritual journey. It's your perception that you need to change, not the world around you."

"You mean, like taking responsibility for my actions and my thoughts, rather than blaming others for what's going on in my life?"

"Exactly," she said. "Hardship takes you to the edge of your sacred self where you begin living from your heart. In the dark night of your soul you are closest to the light within you and to the Great Spirit to which we are all a part. Your experiences are here to teach you surrender and humility. Consider, if even for a moment, looking upon these struggles as opportunities to grow in compassion and love for yourself and others."

I reflected on my earlier life when, in the heat of anger, I'd decided to become a runaway father. How differently our lives would have been had I changed my perception during those months after Val and I separated. Rather than seeing myself as a victim, I could have taken responsibility for my part in the breakdown of our marriage. Dana was right. I could have asked myself, "How are these events asking me to grow?" At that time the roar of my anger silenced the whisper that urged me to grow and change in ways more constructive. I see now why she says to be grateful for everything that happens and to listen to what is being shown us by the events of our lives.

"Think of it this way, Lee. Your thoughts are like the wind. The same wind blows the boat against the rocks as sails it into peaceful harbors. With each thought you are directing the wind and thus the harbor which you will experience. You can choose a calm harbor of peace, harmony, and love, or be marooned on the rocks of anger, revenge, and despair. It's your choice."

I pondered her ideas for a moment. "Okay, maybe if I had believed in peace and harmony for everyone when I got divorced, I wouldn't have followed Sid Silano's advice to take Lori and Ryan."

"Rest assured, Lee, Spirit never punishes or condemns. But by opening to the love of the life force many call God, you can let go of the past and old patterns through the thoughts you hold. Don't forget, you're at the helm, directing the wind of peace and goodness into your life."

Dana rose to take the tray into the kitchen. The idea that by changing my beliefs and becoming open to the existence of an Infinite Wisdom greater than myself was exciting. Why not, I thought, begin believing harmony, peace, and love are my birthright, and hold the same for everyone else?

Standing at the patio door I watched a goose feed off the bottom of the lagoon. It's feet and white, feathered tail were turned unabashedly to the sky. I wondered if, like our feathered friends, we humans sometimes have to be turned upside down before realizing we are all spiritual beings on a journey of awakening to our true natures.

Dana returned to the living room to stand beside me. "Be comforted in knowing the spiritual journey is the one trip we're all taking together. It's often during times of our greatest despair that we open to our greatest good and also are nudged to surrender to the wisdom of a higher power."

Her voice had turned passionate. "Remember, Lee, spirituality is the sacred center from which all life comes. It's what the soul is up to while we attend to daily living. It's commitment in our hearts, minds, and actions to letting the divine operate in our lives."

We continued our exchange. Dana moved closer, her eyes met mine. "I leave you with this thought," she said. "We're all healers simply by seeking our own spiritual truth. And we're each emissaries of peace and love to the degree we have committed to resolving our own inner wars."

We moved into the soft light of her foyer. Evening had crept in over the now still lagoon. The geese nestled quiet for the night, while city lights had begun to sparkle against the indigo twilight. We hugged good-bye.

Lori and Ryan continued to disagree on how they should contact their mother. They worried over explaining why they hadn't contacted her before. Would she be angry? Would she want to see them?

The uncertainty put us all under continual stress. Lori's erratic emotions showed in her behavior; at times calm and confident, other times depressed and anxious. Ryan remained listless. My uneasiness continued even after my second conversation with Trammel. He informed me the old real estate charges against me had been "administratively closed." But Val could still sue me for depriving her of the children all these years.

On Wednesday, a week before their scheduled flight, Lori and Ryan still had not contacted their mother. That same afternoon, Lori suddenly announced, "I've had enough. I'm sick of the whole thing. Let's just call Mom and get it over with."

After months of discussion on how to contact Val, the simplicity of phoning appealed to us all. Once we had agreed, Lori and Ryan couldn't wait to call. They agreed to phone her at six o'clock Eastern Time when Val would likely be home from work. Ryan asked to speak to her first. Lori and I huddled close to the phone.

Ryan first called Dr. Reynolds' answering service and asked for Val Reynolds' home number.

Then without a word to Lori or me, he dialed her number. "Is Val Reynolds there?"

"This is she."

"Hi, Mom, this is Ryan."

Lori and I exchanged nervous glances.

"You're alive!"

"Yes, Mom, we're alive and doing fine. I'm calling from

Seattle." After a few more exchanges, he seemed lost for what to say. "I'll let you talk to Lori."

Lori spoke calmly, her voice clear with enthusiasm. No hesitation from her; their conversation brimmed full. From the couch, Ryan and I listened as Lori told Val we had lived in Seattle for ten years.

"We're happy, Mom. Dad has taken good care of us. He's fine. Grandpa and Grandma Coburn? They're fine too."

Lori's relaxed responses suggested she was speaking to a gentle person at the other end. Lori told us later Val's mild southern accent radiated a sensitive and caring woman. Lori told Val as much as she could about their life in Seattle in the short time they talked.

Then came the big question. Lori asked if it would be all right for them to come to Atlanta. The gleam in her eyes as she looked over at Ryan told us Val said yes. Lori told her. "We have plane reservations for Tuesday, June 10. We fly to Atlanta on Delta flight 176, arriving two o'clock in the afternoon. We're looking forward to seeing you, Mom."

At the end of the conversation, Val asked if she could have our telephone number. Lori looked at me, "Just a minute, I'll ask Dad."

"May as well," I told her, shuddering at the thought of our protective walls crumbling in just minutes.

Lori gave her our number. She told us later Val had asked, "Is it safe for you?" as if concerned about everyone's well being.

"Good-bye Mom. I love you."

Lori looked at Ryan and me. Seconds passed. New fresh joy flooded over us. Lori clapped her hands and cheered. Ryan sank into the couch, looking giddy with relief. I unfixed myself from the rocker, elated to have come so far, yet anxious for us all. They both said their mother sounded gentle and loving. I feared her politeness might be surface; beneath could be a torrent of unreleased anger. Still, we couldn't stop talking about their visit.

On Sunday, June 8, we attended Ryan's graduation ceremony. A grand day full of proud parents, including me. I beamed with pride to have brought my son this far. The moment rode high with hugs, handshakes, and picture taking.

With Ryan's graduation over, we turned our attention to preparing for their departure. Lori and I purchased gifts indigenous to the Northwest: a gift package of smoked salmon, two bottles of Saint Michele gold medal wines, a box of locally made Dilettante chocolates, and a jar of Yakima Valley jam. They wanted to arrive bearing gifts, but as Lori said, "Ryan and I are the gifts that really matter."

The night before they left, Lori and Ryan announced they were taking me to dinner to celebrate my birthday since they would be in Atlanta on the exact day. "Besides," they said, "tonight marks the end of an era. We've had a decade of making a family with only one parent. We don't want to be 'We Three' any longer." Yet we couldn't help feeling sad that we had come to an end of a chapter in our lives.

We cherished the memories of our journey, but now Lori and Ryan could fill the empty corner of their hearts. They would no longer have to pretend they didn't miss their mother.

At one of our favorite restaurants, the Acapulco on Shilshole Bay, we were seated next to a window. Dusk shimmered across Puget Sound, meeting us at the water's edge as the sun sank behind the Olympic Mountains. Sailboats slid by like passing dreams. We were within hours of a moment we'd known for years would come. The certainty of their seeing their mother gave us a feeling of satisfaction and relief from the harrowing months of planning and anticipation.

While waiting for our order, Lori and Ryan presented me with a birthday card. Inside were two tickets for the George Winston concert at the Seattle Opera House, and a note signed, "Love from Sassafras and The Melon Kid."

I thanked them. I wanted to say how much I appreciated their loving me "no matter what" all these years since "Launch Day" ten years ago. But I feared they might think I was overly sentimental. I remained quiet, savoring one of the most memorable moments of my life.

We hurried home for them to begin packing. Midnight came and Lori and Ryan were still at it. At this rate, I thought, how are they going to be ready to leave? Before I went to bed, I told them to be up and ready to drive to the airport at 6:45. The plane departed at 8:05. I wanted us to be at the check-in counter at 7:15.

I awoke at five, relieved to see their bags packed and sitting in the living room. I called upstairs to wake them. They came downstairs half asleep but exited about finally meeting their mother.

Lori's bags and carry-on items were packed. She assured me she'd be ready to leave at 6:45. Ryan had more packing to do, a shower to take, and he still hadn't dried his blue jeans. I pushed him to get moving. Shades of our ten years, Ryan lagging, me nagging. Infuriating. Marvelous.

Lori coaxed him to hurry. She shouted. Nothing helped. We'd still be all right if we left at seven. At twenty after seven, we left for the airport. I'd forgotten to get gas, another echo of the crazy, wonderful years.

On the freeway, morning rush hour traffic deterred us. I felt sure they'd miss their flight. Miraculously, traffic opened up. We reached the airport as Lori finished her makeup.

At the departing lane, I paid the porter to ticket their bags for the flight. We checked the monitor for their flight gate, walked hurriedly, then ran. A decade earlier, I had run for the plane to escape Atlanta. Now we ran for the plane to return to Atlanta. We found our gate. Passengers had already boarded. We had five minutes to confirm our tickets with the agent and say good-bye.

At the counter, we anxiously waited for the agent to stamp and approve their tickets for boarding. He looked up from the tickets, his face expressionless, "No available seats remain on this flight, sir. You will have to reschedule."

Good God! What did he mean there were no available seats? I had made these reservations over a month ago.

He stared with stubborn blankness. "Due to an equipment failure, we're using a smaller airplane."

I didn't care about his equipment failure. In a voice I hoped he would interpret as trouble if he didn't arrange a quick remedy, I said, "I want my children on the next flight for Atlanta."

I must have rattled his pen, because he said to wait while he checked other departures. He studied the computer while his fingers diddled the keys. Silence. I feigned breathing flames to keep the pressure on.

In less than a minute, he announced, "I have a United flight departing for Atlanta via Chicago in ten minutes. First class seats will be reserved at no additional charge. Shall I confirm, sir?"

"Yes," I said, thanking him for keeping us on schedule.

He directed us to the United boarding area.

We walked to gate 22, laughing about the change of plans. Then laughed more when Lori imitated the gruff voice I'd used to intimidate the agent. Ryan said he was glad they were flying first class, because he'd heard that in first class you can eat all you want.

"Not only that," I said, "you deserve to fly first class to see your mother."

At a snack counter, we ordered orange juice while we waited for their flight to board. In a few minutes, they would be on their way.

Many times, I'd thought about this moment. Keep it light, Lee, I told myself. No time for sadness now. Relish the joy. Lori and Ryan quipped and hammed about for a little fun. I welcomed the humor. We didn't want to be sad, though inside we knew we were.

The previous evening, we had mourned the loss of our family, the loosening of our bond. For them to be with their mother, I had to let go of them, and they had to stretch the closeness we'd known to include her.

Through tears, Lori had said, "I don't know if I can adjust to having two homes."

But she would. We would. And now, their antics and banter helped us avoid this last sad good-bye. They had done a double roll and were enjoying the anticipation of seeing their Mom, the thrill of going home.

When the announcement directing passengers to board came, they moved into the line of travelers. Ryan stood proud and handsome, his face radiant; he looked confident and pleased with himself. Lori seemed more poised and grown up than ever.

I wanted to hug them good-bye, but their making fun had set the tone. Their spirits rode high, and I could see they had already leaped ahead to Atlanta.

What could I say? I raised my voice for them to hear. "Well, how does it feel to be going home?" But they didn't hear me. They waved good-bye. They were gone.

TWENTY TWO

REUNION

Love is the great healing power of life. To extend love is to truly empower. There is nothing that shared love cannot heal.

— Alan Cohen
Joy is my compass

I watched Lori and Ryan disappear through the double doors leading to the boarding ramp.

Our bond of love, always so solid, now seemed to stretch taut. Would their traveling to Atlanta sever the ties I'd long focused my life around? Would their seeing their mother be an end to their loving me? Would they become swept up in Val's hatred and vengeance for me and turn against me? Was it now my turn to feel the agony of being cut off, forgotten?

In meeting their mother, they would also meet Val's pain. In doing so, they might find a depth of love for her that proved greater than their love for me. And once united, perhaps they might choose to stay with her. Maybe I had invested too much of my life raising Lori and Ryan. Had being a father been the source of my identity? I was soon to find out.

I returned to my car feeling throbs of anguish rise to my chest. Anonymous faces floated past me, hollow voices announced arrivals and departures. I left the airport thankful for the activities I had planned. Time spent with friends would help fill the void created by Lori and Ryan's absence. Many had shared in my vision for a peaceful reunion, but in spite of their support, I felt frightened and emotionally scattered. My stomach quivered like fish in shallow water.

All afternoon at a painting job, I dreaded returning to our empty house. Rich memories of Lori and Ryan would be my only solace. Going home to those silent walls meant I would have to look inside now and find my own self. It meant taking responsibility for finding purpose and fulfillment in my life, knowing that my role as a father was no longer crucial. It meant knowing that though I had forgiven myself, I would always in my heart feel the pain I had brought to Val.

As I entered the house, months of anticipation and planning gave way to a tomb-like stillness. Through dirty windows, lazy afternoon sunlight reached in across the living room floor. Crinkle lay dozing on the carpet, unconcerned she no longer napped in the warm rays. But as always, the rhythmic tick of the clock's pendulum welcomed me home with predictable promise.

Wanting to understand my feelings, I sat down to write in my journal.

> *I long for what will no longer be, the closeness the three of us shared, the purpose they provided me, as if parenting had been a beacon keeping me on course, but also blinding me from looking at myself. Now I must look deeper to discover who I really am.*
>
> *Looking back, though tragic, the road now appears purposeful, as if it was on this path I would finally begin to wake up to see myself. The inner man I am today has come out of all which has gone before. Ironic as it seems, some part of me says thank you for the harsh difficulties I brought upon myself. For without them, I would not have learned that I, and all of us, are in essence, one family on a shared path toward harmony and love.*

❧

A couple evenings later, I was about to leave for a bike ride when the phone rang. It was Lori and Ryan calling from Riverview. I had suggested they wait to call when they were settled and had more time.

"Great to hear from you. Is everything all right?" I kept my voice light.

"We're fine, Dad," Ryan said. "Lori's on the other line."

"Did your mother recognize you at the airport?"

Lori answered. "She recognized us as soon as we entered the baggage claim. Mom is really beautiful, Dad. There's an elegance and grace about her. I tried to be strong and not cry when we hugged, but I didn't do very well. Hugging Mom felt like home."

"Not for me," Ryan said. "At first, she seemed like a well-dressed stranger. I couldn't feel a connection. It was like a play and we were the actors."

"Dad, Dr. Reynolds was with Mom." Lori's velvet words flowed to me across the distance. "I gave him a hug. Ryan shook his hand. We didn't know what to say, or where to begin. We talked about our flight on the way out to the car. During our ride to the country club for dinner, Mom just kept staring at us."

Ryan spoke up, "It gave me the strangest feeling, Dad. She kept looking at us as though if she looked away, we might disappear again."

"Mom said my mannerisms and laughter were like she remembered when I was ten," Lori said, her voice brimming with energy. "But Ryan had changed. He's more like you, now, she said. And she was surprised how well mannered we were. I can tell Mom really loves Dr. Reynolds. They told us to call him Edwin. When she looks at him, her expression softens and the shadows leave her face."

They continued taking turns telling me of their first hours with their mother. Their voices rang with anticipation but also concern for how their visit would turn out.

Knowing our telephone call was getting long, Lori hurried in to tell me more. "Dad, Mom's been receiving bouquets of flowers from people congratulating her on our coming back. She let us see the cards she received. They all must have shared Mom's pain at your stealing us away."

Ryan broke in, "We'll call you again when we have time and more news." Together they chimed, "Good-bye, I love you."

I hung up feeling pleased that Lori and Ryan's courteous manners and quiet composure had been noted by their mother. But even more, after a decade of increasingly feeling remorse for Val's pain and sorrow, I felt an overwhelming rush of relief that at last she could be a mother to her children. Though I missed them, I wanted even more for them to know their mother and to begin healing the trauma of their past.

When they returned home a few weeks later, they shared with me more details of their visit to Atlanta. Filled with my own questions, I wanted to understand how well Lori and Ryan had traversed this extraordinary emotional bridge back to their mother.

Their first evening back, we gathered on the patio for a summer barbecue. We relaxed over talk of their travels as the late afternoon sunlight cast long shadows across the yard. Above us, two squirrels chased each other through the cedar trees, dropping pinecones to the ground. Not long into our conversation, I asked the question we all had struggled to find an answer to. "Did your mother ask why you waited so long to call her?"

Lori spoke first. "It was the first thing she asked us. I told her we had often talked about calling her. Just that we were afraid of the turmoil we'd cause if we did."

Ryan slid his lawn chair over to be closer. "I tried explaining to Mom we really had missed her all those years, but that we also knew how much you loved us. I tried to tell her in a nice way that we were happy and calling just wasn't that easy, even though we wanted to see her."

"Dad," Lori said, "I'm not sure she understood when I told her

I wanted her to be proud of me when we met. But maybe they couldn't understand with their still being so angry with you."

"Mom and Edwin kept making you out as a really bad person," Lori went on. "After a while, I told Mom we didn't want to hear anymore about how bad she thought you were."

"Besides," Ryan said, "I asked her if she thought you were such a rotten person, how come we turned out so good? I explained to her that trying to make you look bad didn't hurt you, it was hurting us." He leaned over to feed Crinkle the last of his hamburger. "After that, they stopped trying to convince us you hadn't been a good father to us."

"But just imagine the horror and grief your mother must have felt losing you two," I said. "No doubt your return brought back all that anger and pain."

While Ryan served us double chocolate cake for dessert, our visiting continued.

"Guess what, Dad?" Lori exclaimed. "Mom still had my canopy bed and musical jewelry box. She'd stored it in the attic all those years. She said she would put the bed in my room if I came to live with her and Edwin." Lori's tone became soft. "Dad," her heart welling into her voice, "I want you to know I plan to go back to Atlanta. I need more time there. Maybe I'll even go to college there and live at Riverview."

"I'm happy for you, Lori," I said, taking a deep breath.

"Mom invited Ryan and me to come live with her. We're both thinking we'd like to do that."

"I'll miss you both." I said. "You've been the focus of my life. For a long time I've struggled with how to unravel what I'd done. I'm thankful you'll be back with your mother."

We talked for another half hour about their returning to Atlanta. Without knowing when or how, we'd come to a sense of conclusion, of peaceful understanding among us.

During the three years that followed, their dreams of reuniting with their mother shattered, one by one, into disillusionment.

Lori dropped out of college in her third year to live with her mother. An urgency had come over her she could not explain. She said waiting to finish her junior year of college would be too late. Halfway through, she packed and moved to Atlanta.

That following summer, Ryan joined Lori in Atlanta as a camp counselor. He, too, planned to live at the Riverview house and attend college in the fall. But adjusting to a new environment and different priorities made reconnecting with his mother difficult. Also, Val's and Edwin's continued anger at me was being unconsciously directed at Ryan. Their schedule for healing the past conflicted with Ryan and Lori's peaceful vision of life with Mom.

At summer's end, Ryan returned to Seattle disillusioned and depressed. He lamented to me, "I feel like I don't have a mother."

At eight, Ryan's small boat had capsized when he was taken from his mother. Now at twenty-one, without the bond he dreamed would be there with his mother, he felt lost, adrift at sea. His pain became mine. I urged him to stay in touch with his mother, keep an open heart, and be patient. "With enough time, Ryan, a new and close relationship will grow between you two." He listened, eyes dark, shoulders burdened by the weight of feeling he'd lost his mother again.

Mid-autumn that same year, I began having long conversations with Lori in Atlanta, mostly listening, trying to help her understand the depression she found herself in. She had already told her mother and Edwin she planned to return to Washington State University starting in January. But by October, her dark moods made her wonder if she could stay through the holidays. After more phone calls and much soul searching, she decided she could not, and flew back to Seattle in time for Thanksgiving.

❧

A few weeks after Lori returned to Seattle, I was in the kitchen about to leave for work when Crinkle let loose with loud barking. The hair on her back bristled. She'd heard gravel crunching in the driveway.

Crinkle always let us know when strangers had entered the property.

Indeed, a stranger had come up the driveway. I looked out at a silver, late-model mini-van with mud flaps on the rear fenders. I'd never seen the van or the lean, well-dressed man walking toward my front door.

Before me stood a man, maybe mid-thirties, wearing a sport jacket, a tie, and a blue denim shirt.

"Hi, I'm Glen Mueller. I know you don't know me." He spoke quickly, his voice urgent. "Word has it you kidnapped your kids. My ex got custody of my six-year-old daughter. She's taking Marie back to Santa Fe to be near her family. I don't have money to hire a lawyer to stop her, so I've about decided to take off with Marie. Will you help me?" His eyes had turned hard with anger.

"Why don't you come in for a cup of coffee?" I asked.

He joined me in the kitchen.

I sympathized with his anguish over feeling discarded as a father. I remembered feeling irrelevant myself and needing someone to talk to who understood my desperation and anger. I'd turned to Sid Silano. He understood my anger, but unfortunately he knew only rage and revenge. I had a different vision for this man.

We carried our coffee into the living room. He perched himself at one end of the couch. I sat in my well-worn chair.

"I know how you feel, Glen," I said. "I wanted a bigger part in my kids' growing up, too. But there's a downside to taking your daughter. For starters, you'll constantly be looking over your shoulder. Fear and paranoia will be a way of life. And if you do get her into a school, the secrecy and lies she'll have to live with may cause her to withdraw or become reclusive.

"The truth is, Glen, parental abduction is an extreme form of domestic violence. Taking Marie from her mother will have a traumatic effect on her that will take her years to heal," I said.

"Going on the run doesn't sound very easy," he said. He then began sharing how angry he felt, how much he loved his daughter, and how badly he wanted to be a father to her.

"But think about your daughter. To justify why you're not going back, you may even have to tell Marie that her mother has died or doesn't love her anymore," I explained.

"Anything would be worth it, if it meant I could be a dad to her," he said, his tone defiant.

"Glen, I understand your anger. I was that angry myself," I told him. "Disappearing with Marie feels right, because you want to get back at the person you believe has caused you all this grief."

"Right on!" he said.

"I know how much being a dad means to you," I said. "But trust me, Glen, in taking Marie, everyone becomes a victim, including you."

"Hey, I'll love her. That's all she needs," he asserted.

"It's not that simple. The day you skip, you'll begin panicking at every flashing blue light and late night phone call. And when they do catch you, you're finished as her dad."

His face turned grim. "They'd keep me from my daughter?"

"Maybe occasional supervised visits. But basically, you're finished as a father to your daughter, Glen."

"A little harsh, isn't it?"

"Not really. A lot of abducted kids come back abused both physically and emotionally, often malnourished or severely neglected. It happens. Even in the best cases, the emotional toll on the family is devastating."

"I just didn't think about the future that much, I guess." Frowning, he rubbed his chin.

I ran through the alternatives for being an effective dad to Marie, that in the long run were more supportive and ultimately more caring of his daughter and himself.

Instead of acting on his desire for revenge, I suggested he get involved with other parents who have become successful single parents. "Learn how they do it," I said. "By improving your life you'll have a better chance of being awarded joint custody of Marie. Plus she'll have the love and care of her mother. Let's face it,

Glen, the best parent for your daughter is both parents." I reminded him he had many more constructive choices for being a good dad to his daughter.

"I hadn't really looked at it this way before," he said thoughtfully.

We talked about the benefits of joint custody and how the laws were changing in favor of shared parenting by both parents. How dads were now being seen as important and as necessary in parenting their children as their mothers.

"Don't forget, Glen," I said, "Marie loves and needs two parents. She deserves you both. The greatest gift you can give her is to be the best dad you can be, which starts with honoring her right to a loving relationship with her mother."

I assured Glen that shared parenting was not only fair to the growing numbers of men who assert their parenting instincts, but was best for the women as well. Mothers could continue as involved parents, while also having the opportunity to pursue careers and education.

"I didn't know all this about joint custody," he said, leaning forward as if eager to know more.

"The other good thing about shared custody," I said, "is it eliminates the desperation of being left out as an active parent to your child. Plus, it saves the children from being a pawn between feuding parents."

Our morning had grown late. But before he left, I wanted him to have one more thing to take with him.

I'd found this gem written by Circuit Court Judge Edward Sosnick, in the state of Michigan, founder of the S.M.I.L.E. (Start Making It Livable for Everyone) Program. Written for divorcing parents, attorneys, mediators, and caregivers, this Children's Bill of Rights is edited here for brevity.

> *CHILDREN'S BILL OF RIGHTS*
>
> 1. *The right to be treated as important human beings, with feelings and desires, and not as objects to be fought over.*

2. *The right to a continuing loving relationship with both parents.*
3. *The right to express love and affection for each parent without fear of disapproval by the other parent.*
4. *The right to know that their parents' divorce is not their fault and that they will still be able to live with both parents.*
5. *The right to honest answers to questions about the changing family relationships.*
6. *The right to know and appreciate what is good in each parent without one parent degrading the other.*
7. *The right to support from both parents for the time spent with the other parent without threatening to withhold time as punishment.*
8. *The right to regular and consistent contact with both parents and to be protected from parental disputes or disagreements.*
9. *The right to be a child and participate in his or her own destiny.*
10. *The right to decide for themselves whether there is a power in the universe greater than themselves.*

I handed Glen a copy of the Bill of Rights, suggesting he read it the next time he thought about becoming a runaway father.

He thanked me for my advice. "I'm glad I came. No one else would have understood how I felt," he said.

"Anytime, Glen. I wish I'd had someone to talk to when I was in your shoes. Be sure to let me know how things turn out," I said.

"Sure will. But how do I get in touch with you?" he asked.

"Here's my card with the address to my website, RUNAWAY FATHER. Check it out. You'll find useful information and a forum where you can talk with other parents exchanging ideas for being involved with their kids.*

* See Appendix for RUNAWAY FATHER website address & information.

"Thanks, I'll be sure to look you up," he said, putting the card in his wallet.

We walked out to his car. Sparse winter sun had warmed the morning air.

"Take it from me, Glen," I said. "When your kids are grown as mine are, you won't want to look back knowing you kept your daughter from being loved and cared for by her mother. Trust me, it will haunt you the rest of your life."

He gripped my hand. Silence held us. "Thank you." He climbed into his van and drove away.

❧

My morning visitor reminded me how much I had changed, and my children as well. Ryan had taken a few tumbles of his own, and Lori, too, had been through her stormy seas of confusion and attempts to stabilize her life. In 1990, at twenty-three, Lori earned her degree in psychology from WSU and met a man she adored. After graduation, she traveled to Atlanta to share her success with her mother.

It was from Atlanta that she called to tell me she was getting married. Steve was an instructor for one of her psychology courses. From the start, she knew this was the man she wanted to marry. He had followed her to Atlanta and proposed to her there.

"We plan to get married in a country church north of Seattle, where Steve grew up," she said, calling from Atlanta. "We've set the date for Thanksgiving weekend."

"But that's only three months away," I protested. "Why the rush?"

"Because this feels right," she said. Her voice had the power of a woman who had claimed her independence.

That evening over dinner at our favorite Chinese restaurant, I told Ryan that Lori and Steve had decided to get married. "How come she didn't ask us for our opinion?" he complained.

True, over the years we had become accustomed to checking in with each other about things. I explained to Ryan we had outgrown the family unit. "We've all become adults, Ryan. She's old enough to make decisions on her own without consulting you or me."

"But we haven't even met him," he grumbled.

Driving home that night, I realized the thinly veiled chip on Ryan's shoulder revealed a deeper anger he carried within him. His unreleased anger burdened him like a sack of rocks he didn't know he could drop. I couldn't turn the clock back, but I only hoped the peace and forgiveness I'd achieved for myself could some day help him lessen the load he carried.

❧

Lori's wedding night arrived all too soon. My father and I were the first to arrive at the old country church. We waited in the arbor as evening light painted the white church steeple in crimson hues.

Val and Dr. Reynolds had flown in from Atlanta to attend the wedding. My feelings vacillated between anticipation and dread. I hoped our meeting would, in some way, be the beginning of healing old wounds.

Dad and I watched up the road for Steve and Lori, who were bringing Val and Edwin. On the near horizon, the sawtoothed edge of tall pines turned rich ebony against the autumn moon rising into a painted orange sky. Across the harbor, distant lights blinked on while small boats slid through the growing darkness. Soon, Steve's car wound its way down the winding lane leading to the church.

His car came to rest. My heart came to a stop. Dad stepped closer.

Watching Val walk toward us suddenly made our fifteen years apart seem like days. Dr. Reynold's calm, methodical walk suggested a surgeon's steady presence. With both hands, he shook mine firmly as he said hello. His eyes showed caution, yet a willingness to make peace.

I turned to Val. Her cover girl eyes and smooth complexion were as I remembered. Her rich, auburn hair folded softly around her face. For an instance, we stood face to face, loving each other as we had many years before. The feeling came as a surprise. I saw the same caring in her eyes. She moved toward me as if she were about to hug me. Instead, we shook hands, holding longer than expected. I heard hesitation in her voice when she spoke my name; her eyes expressed warmth and softness which told me all was well. At least for then.

Inside the historic church, candlelight reflecting off the stained glass windows cast a warm glow over the small sanctuary. Planked floors hollowed by the soles of countless parishioners creaked as friends and family filtered to their pews. The sanctuary, filled with memories of sacred vows taken over the past century, exuded a rich and joyful expectation.

As guests entered, musicians played Celtic folk songs on harp and hammered dulcimers. The music seemed to call forth the many blessings from ceremonies of long ago. We were given to feel this lasting sacredness would also bless Lori and Steve as they took their vows to begin a new life together.

Candles burned. Music melted hearts. People waited in anticipation. None more than I. Happy. Sad. Nervous, as I gave my daughter away to the man of her dreams.

Watching Lori and Steve exchange vows, I thought of when Val and I had last cared deeply for each other. Another sacred time, but I did not understand then how sacred. Now, years later, we shared this joyful celebration and union of our daughter. Had we come to mend our past? Perhaps silently. Maybe unconsciously. It didn't matter. I felt in my heart a step toward forgiveness of each other had begun.

After the ceremony, family members stayed for wedding photos while guests filed to the reception room. Best wishes, hugs, handshakes, and kisses were showered on Lori and Steve immediately after the wedding, while the photographer arranged for family pictures.

Before we had time to react, the photographer grouped Edwin, Val and me, along with Ryan and my dad, behind Lori and Steve for a family wedding portrait. Perhaps our standing next to one another in celebration of our daughter's wedding was yet another step toward forgiveness and acceptance of each other.

All evening, I'd been edgy knowing I had something important I wanted to say to Val. I did not expect to see her again until Ryan's wedding, which was likely years away.

For a few moments, I watched her collecting champagne glasses in one corner of the room. I had not seen her alone all evening. My temples throbbed at the thought of speaking to her. Time was running out. I hurried across the room to where she stood. She turned to me, startled.

I blurted, "There's something I need to say to you. I know I can't take back what happened, but I want you to know, I am sorry for the pain I caused you."

Her eyes flooded with tears. I wanted to hold her, take back every hurt I'd caused her.

"Thank you," she said softly.

The moment had come and gone like the flicker of a firefly flashing in the summer night. A sudden glow. Then darkness. But for one brief healing moment, I had opened my heart to the woman, who, after all these years still held a piece of me.

Soon after, Dad came to tell me he was ready to go.

Driving home, I couldn't stop thinking of Val. I had long grieved the devastation I'd made of my life by my chosen course of action. But these later years, the sadness I carried was Val's. I'd forgiven her for her part in the drama of our divorce and had accepted that her path might not include forgiving me.

After all these years, my words of apology seemed so small. Yet, saying "I'm sorry" helped me know I had forgiven myself. And her.

❧

The next morning, I awoke from a dream with a start. For a moment, I listened to the rain outside, feeling peaceful and sure that everything would always turn out right. I lingered with the pleasant feelings, wanting to understand the dream's message.

In the dream, I was a trapeze performer in a three-ring circus. I had never swung on a trapeze before, yet thousands watched breathlessly for my death-defying aerobatics to begin. Standing on the highest perch, my moist hands gripped the bar. Petrified, I pleaded not to jump, but an unseen force pushed me to leap. I stepped off, swinging fast. At the highest point, I let go. Falling, I rolled three somersaults. In perfect time, my partner's hands reached out to clasp mine. Together, we swung to safety. I had let go. I had surrendered. The exultation of reaching the other side rushed over me. I stood serene, awash in light, as applause filled the big top.

The dream had come like a voice urging me to acknowledge the God spirit within me. The dream told me that when we take that leap of faith and trust Divine Presence in our lives, we gain a new life. Yes, we can let go of our need to control and trust that a hand will always reach out to carry us, no matter the crisis we face. Part of me had always known this, but I had feared surrendering to this Power greater than myself.

Looking back on the difficult years helped me see that our lives are about moving from darkness into the light. My journey helped me understand that all experience is about our spiritual life. The events and people in our lives — the twisted, often tragic turns we choose along the way — are reflections of our spiritual maturity at any given moment. Our awakening comes out of our gradual giving up control to allow Spirit into our lives.

We cannot change what we've done, but we can learn from our past to make new and healthier choices for our future. Disallowing my children access to their mother opened me into my inner turmoil and my disharmony with my Highest Self and the God Spirit within me.

In my dream, I struggled against letting go of the trapeze bar. But Spirit had come to nudge me one more time. Yes, I could jump into the unknown, knowing the hand of God would always carry me to safety.

I've learned there's no divorcing spirituality from our lives. It's as integral as breathing itself. Many of us believe we are human beings becoming spiritual, when in truth, we are spiritual beings learning to live the human experience.

These years have shown me life is not about whether someone will do what I want him or her to do, but rather, whether am I going to resolve my own inner turmoil? Am I going to commit to raising my own level of consciousness? This is what healing ourselves and our lives is all about. Whenever I'm judging another, I can be sure I'm out of balance with myself and with Spirit.

Sadly, we are showing evidence of our becoming a nation without guiding principles of moral and spiritual values. Too many of us allow anger to rule our lives, thus preventing us from seeking our deeper truths and higher good. Only by accepting responsibility for our actions will we be able to make lasting changes within ourselves and our world. By looking for the greater good unfolding in our lives, we can begin to transform the pain of our past into an expression of peace for ourselves and the world around us.

❧

Life has a way of moving us forward faster than we think. Like sleeping on a train, we wake up surprised to find the landscape outside looking very different. After Lori's wedding, our trains steamed ahead, leaving me amazed at how rapidly the scenery around us had changed.

Lori and Steve returned to Idaho. Steve continued his career as assistant professor at the university, while Lori earned her master's degree in clinical psychology. The train must have been racing through the night because one morning, I woke to learn I had a granddaughter. Two years later, a grandson arrived.

Ryan's train also kept speeding forward. He completed his fine arts degree in sculpture at the University of Washington and then added a B.A. degree before applying to schools for his master's degree in fine arts. He and I worked at releasing past judgments, and as we've come to greater acceptance of each other, our relationship has grown supportive and harmonious.

My train also continued making new turns along the way. My sister released old judgments of me. I now receive occasional newsy letters from her signed "Love, Randi." On another long curve, I looked back and saw a boxcar with Sid Silano's name on it disconnect and drop away. I became released from him and the bitterness I once found comfort in. Another car fell away — that old indictment in Georgia was officially closed. As my life rolled on, I also knew no matter how far I traveled, I would always carry in some small berth within me my sorrow and loss of my mother. Fortunately for us all, we had reunited with both my parents before her departure.

❧

One evening in 1994, weary from the day, I settled into my favorite chair needing to put order to my thoughts when the phone rang.

It was Lori calling from Idaho to confirm her graduation plans. Her voice carried its usual excitement. "Dad, guess what — just two more weeks and I'll have my master's degree. I'm still counting on you and Ryan coming to help celebrate. Besides, the kids want to see their granddad."

"We wouldn't miss it for anything, Lori," I assured her.

"Dad," her voice turning soft, "I know we're all busy and not as close as we used to be, but I want you to know how much I appreciate you. Even more now that you're Grandpa to Janelle and Steven."

"Thanks, Lori," I said. "Watching you raise your children makes me realize how important being an involved parent has been. I now see how who I was as a parent ends up being passed on to a whole new generation."

"You're right about that, Dad. Hey, tell Ryan I love him. You too. See you soon."

I hung up. The house had grown quiet as the sky deepened behind tall pines, leaving pink- and azure-tinted clouds to collect for another sunset across Puget Sound. Through still dirty windows, a remaining spear of sunlight angled in across the living room floor, casting an amber glow into the room.

Out of the stillness came whispers of times past. Sounds of a hundred little moments, of Lori and Ryan growing up. The screen door slamming shut. Ryan on the phone, "Hi Ben, what are you doing?" "Dad, you want to play catch?" "Sure." Lori's husky voice. How I cherished her laugh. I could hear her clamor down the stairs in a hurry to get to dance. "Let's go, Dad, I'm late for ballet." Pure, clean energy that electrified anyone who came near.

How I love them. They have moved on with their lives in such a short time, but they'll never move out of my heart.

As the three of us journey toward deeper understanding of ourselves, we will always travel together in spirit. Apart and together, Lori and Ryan will forever be the rhythm in my life. Though we've moved into our separate ways, nothing will really change, only expand to include their mother.

Tonight, the house brings a special calm. Outside, dusk relinquishes its light as evening turns to darkness. On the patio, a family of quail scratch for food at my bird feeder.

My spiritual mentor was right when she said there is nothing that is not Spirit. She reminded me during my lowest times that my life's purpose is spiritual evolution. "Everything that happens to you, Lee, is for healing your soul and moving you closer to your own inner essence," she said.

Yes, I've learned that by listening to my Higher Self, I can let God be my guide. I can trust I will always be given the perfect circumstances for my growth.

Looking back, living through the many dark nights of my soul has brought feelings of gratitude for the changes which have occurred within me. I entered this earth experience forgetting I'm pure light. Now I realize my worst crises, my darkest shadows, were opportunities to heal my soul.

As my hair grows thin and I find myself more suited to romping with my grandchildren than cooking dinners for my own children, my heart fills. I pray that through your own experiences, you discover the Great Spirit within you and the unique light that is yours. May you live well knowing your life is in Divine Order, even in your darkest hour. I am reminded of the thirteenth-century Sufi poet, Rumi, who wrote of our shared humanity:

Out beyond ideas of
wrongdoing and rightdoing,
there is a field.
I'll meet you there.

With love and peace. Goodnight.

Missing Children's Organizations

Listed here are just a few of the many excellent missing children's organizations in the United States and Canada:

National Center for Missing & Exploited Children
2101 Wilson Blvd., Suite 550
Arlington, VA 22201-3077
Tel: 703-235-3900
Call Toll Free 1-800-843-5678
Fax: 703-235-4067

Children's Rights Council
220 I (Eye) Street N.E., Suite 140
Washington, D.C. 20002-4362
Tel: 202-547-6227

Vanished Children's Alliance
2095 Park Avenue
San Jose, CA 95126
Tel: 408-296-1113
Fax: 408-296-1117

North American Missing Children Association, Inc.
202 Brownlow Avenue. Bldg. F, Unit L
Dartmouth, Nova Scotia B3B 1T5
Tel. 1-800-260-0753
Fax 902-468-2803

P.A.R.E.N.T.
Parents Advocating for Recovery through Education by Networking Together
308 General Gage Rd.
Virginia Beach, VA 23462
Tel/Fax: 757-497-0042

Child Quest International
1625 The Alameda, Suite 400
San Jose, CA 95126
Tel: 408-287-HOPE
Fax: 408-287-4676

Missing Children Society of Canada
3501 23rd St. N.E., Suite 219
Calgary, Alberta T2E 6V8
Tel: 403-291-0705
1-800-291-9728
Fax: 403-291-9728

Missing Children's Network of Canada
231 St-Jacques, Suite 406
Montreal, Quebec H2Y 1M6
Tel: 514-843-4333
Fax 514-843-8211

Child Find of America, Inc.
243 Main Street
PO Box 277
New Paltz, NY 12561-0277
Tel: 914-255-1848
Fax: 914-255-5706

About the Author

Lee Coburn has traveled a dramatic journey of personal and spiritual growth. His careers as an architect, attorney, businessman, national public speaker and writer give him the qualifications to assist those who are facing child custody crises in their own lives. His years of psychological and spiritual growth have transformed him from an anguished husband and father to an outspoken advocate of healing for parents, and children. He is the author of *Glimmerings of Love*. Lee is available for lectures and seminars and makes every effort to accommodate all requests. A variety of speaking formats and topic focuses are available. Lee also provides legal consultation and mediation services in divorce and custody issues. He lives in Seattle, Washington.

For more information, please write to:
Red Fox Publishing
677 120th Avenue N.E.
Bellevue, Washington 98005

The author is interested in receiving any comments you may have regarding your experience in reading this book. Please write to the above address or email to: Lee@lcoburn.com

How to Order

Additional books may be purchased by visiting the Runaway Father Website at: http://www.lcoburn.com You may contact the publisher, either by email; RedFox@lcoburn.com or by Fax 1-425-455-4629. To obtain additional copies of this book by mail, you may photocopy this order form and write to us directly.

____
Name

____
Address

____
City State Zip

Requested_____ x $18.95/copy = books' cost ____________
Postage & Handling $2.00 for first copy ____________
$1.00 for each additional ____________
Total Cost ____________

Make check payable to Red Fox Publishing.

Mail the order and payment to:
Red Fox Publishing
677 120th Avenue N.E.
Bellevue, Washington 98005

Delivery will take 7-14 days.